MW01690476

Not Your Ordinary Fishing Stories!

By Jim Pepper

JIM PEPPER'S NOT YOUR ORDINARY FISHING STORIES

Published by The Old Weather Bureau Publishing Company,
Abilene, Texas

To order Additional copies by e-mail: duckcampusa@moment.net

Library of Congress Control Number: 2010931297

ISBN: 978-0-692-01067-9

First Printing, August 2010

Printed in the United States of America

Dedication Page

This book is dedicated to all fisherpersons everywhere. And to unborn generations of fisherpersons who will follow; "may their legacy include the joys of fishing." And to my Dad; who helped teach me the love of fishing; Jesse Pepper (deceased 2000). And to my original fishing partner, my older brother, First Sergeant Ben Pepper, USMC Retired. And to my three sons, Chris, Ladd, and John James; "who I've had the privilege of introducing to fishing ... teaching them what I could along the way." And to my two grandsons, Weston and Nolan, who are "already out there fishin!" And to the sport of fishing; which for our family, for four generations,
spanning nearly a century, has profoundly helped build warm relationships.

Nearly sixty years after my dad kept his promise...
my son **Chris** teaches his son **Weston** to fish. (2009)

About the Author

Author **Jim Pepper** fishin on one of his good days. (2006)

Jim Pepper was born a Baby Boomer in 1947 and grew up in northwest Missouri in a tiny town; "There were only fifty-one in my graduating class... I would have been Valedictorian... except for my grades. I'm proud of being a surviving son of a genuine American Tobacco Farmer... currently an endangered species."

Jim attended the University of Missouri in Columbia, where he studied journalism; but ended up with a degree in economics. "I changed my major to get away from long-haired ... non-showering ... pot-smoking liberal-minded and clueless-about-reality students ... who filled nearly every journalism class."

After graduation from MU, Jim joined the Marines; where he rose to the rank of captain. Proud to have survived and to have been decorated for his service, Jim enjoys pointing out that he is a 'Crazy Viet Nam Vet' and claims his highest achievement in the Marines was being handpicked by Ollie North to attend Army Ranger School; "Where me and my five Marine buddies... all SIX of us... graduated in the top ten of 280 Rangers! That's more than half the top ten... for you hanging chads folks from Flor-i-DUH!"

After Viet Nam, Jim returned to Missouri where he grew "a lot" of burley tobacco; concurrently helping build for First Wife Jen-Jen and himself three successful businesses. "We owned everything from a tobacco warehouse

... with one hundred employees ... to a bait stand ... with one employee ... ME! In 1974 a business partner and I built a world-class, private, hunting and shooting preserve; one of the fishing stories featured in this book takes place on that Missouri hunting preserve."

In 1983 Jim and his family moved to Texas where he became an RV park and real estate developer, and later a business broker; a twenty-eight year career from which he recently retired; "Now I'm really busy... with grandkids and writing."

Of himself, Jim says; "I've fished and hunted all my life. I first joined Ducks Unlimited at age fourteen. Thanks to my Dad, Brother Ben and the Marine Corps ... I'm an expert shot with a pistol ... rifle ... shotgun and about a dozen other weapons we used in the Marines. I have hand carved and painted four dozen duck decoys ... own a collection of nearly one thousand decoys ... and caught my FIRST fish using a safety pin for a hook and a bobber made from a whiskey-bottle cork. I live life to its fullest. I leave few bullets unfired ... few stones unturned ... few dollars unspent ... and nothing worth mentioning untried. A lot of what God has allowed me to witness ... and do ... is worth sharing ... and most of it's not too embarrassing.

I've had two books published. Currently I'm writing a series of books entitled 'Not Your Ordinary______________' ? My books are collections of non-fiction short stories ... with dozens of pictures thrown in to validate places and faces. After my fishing book ... the next two (books) are about bad-ass snakes ... absurd business transactions ... or idiot brokers I've randomly killed ... captured ... conquered ... or closed along life's meandering trail. You'll need to read my books to find out what action applied to which subject? I'm the father of three SONS... three aging Labs... and married to one very smart and tolerant wife. I believe there's a minimum of ONE book in every person I meet. I've merely managed to sit down and squeeze out a few of mine. Try writing one yourself. You'll enjoy it. It's one of the most rewarding things I've ever done. Well... With my clothes on!"

Preface

When we first do something new, even something we really want to do, we're usually not very good at it. But trepidation doesn't much apply to fishing! Nope! Any man, woman, or child capable of picking up a rod and reel can fish. Catch fish as if he or she had been an aficionado all their life; at any juncture in their life; at any age; all of it accomplishable within a wide variety of socio-economic settings. From the frozen tundra of far off Alaska, to tropical vistas of Hawaii, to the sun drenched shores of peninsular Florida, to the whispery sea breezes of the Pacific Northwest, to the sultry Third Coast here in Texas; we live in a nation supremely blessed with places to fish. "If we aren't officially a nation of fisherpersons ... we should be .. .its in our blood ... part of our heritage ... born in our hearts."

We fish when we're sad; fish when we're happy; busy; distracted; free of worry or consumed with it. We're a nation of pleasure seekers, and no outdoor sport holds wider appeal or is available to a broader range of Americans than fishing. Equipment requirements are minimal; a cane pole, a few feet of cotton line, a couple of hooks, a red and white bobber, and a little bait; "Anyone can be a fisherman."

Venues abound. Cost is whatever you decide. Goals are what you say. Details as you make them. Going is up to you. "Whether it's catchin a few bluegill for Momma's old iron skillet ... or hangin on your wall a picture of the brightest smile your child ever flashed ... or creating a lifetime memory shared with a long lost friend ... the joys of fishin are limited only by our imagination."

Fishing is an interpretation of our soul. This book is about the experience of fishing; "**NOT** another 'How To Fish' book." Ninety percent of the pleasure of being a fisherperson is in the pursuit of, not in the consumption of, the fish we try so hard to catch. It is the act of seeking fish we so much enjoy; the time spent together we so much enjoy. This is a collection of true short stories, wherein I attempt to convey a sense of the pleasures of the "fishing experience".

Son **John James** and author **Jim Pepper** fishin on JJ's birthday, Lake Buchanan, Texas. (2000)

TABLE of CONTENTS

Other Books by Jim Pepper

Not Your Ordinary Hunting Stories

Distributed by:

Duck
Camp
USA®

Chapter One

Promise Kept

When I was born, my parents were living on a small tobacco farm located about thirty miles north of Kansas City; out in rural Platte County midway between KC and St. Joe, Missouri. Our family moved to town in 1952, a few months after this story occurred. April 11th, 1952 was my fifth birthday; I will always remember that birthday; after reading this story, I hope you'll remember it too. Not that April 11th was my birthday; remember this story and the lesson it teaches. If you do, and if you apply that lesson to your life and your relationships, especially with children, you will greatly profit. "Of that I am certain." Here's the story.

As far back as summer 1950, that would have made me three at the time, I recall our Dad coming home and dumping gunny sacks full of catfish on the grass in our backyard; yelling for our Mom to bring out the cleaning stuff; a sharp butcher knife for cutting, pliers for skinning, a dishpan for washing, and lotsa newspapers for covering the chopping block. Sure to produce a quick smile on his handsome face, no other pastime provided our Dad greater satisfaction than bringing home freshly caught or killed critter dinners. Necessity, as well as pleasure, stoked his enthusiasm? His family benefited in the process; regularly dining on fresh squirrel, rabbit, catfish, and carp. Occasionally there were delicacies like bass, pheasant, or quail; but those were treats not staples. We also ate a lot of fried pork, chicken, and beef; "Back then ever body ate homegrown meat."

When Dad arrived home and dumped his trophies in the backyard; Brother Ben and I would jump in and help clean whatever fish, fowl, or game Dad caught or killed. Ben was five years older than me and useful; I remained a 'too young to help' pain in the butt. Not required to skin, gut, clip, or cut; I had plenty of time for inspecting the next victim waiting on our Dad's chopping block; "final stop" for millions of God's creatures. The positive fuss and special paraphernalia made an impression on my skull full of mush. Result; I became a fisherman before I could tell you what the term meant.

Before actually participating, I tagged along on fishin trips with Brother

Ben and Dad. One to a neighbor's pond, where Dad and Ben caught bullheads until our gunny sack lay bulging on the weedy shore; another to a neighbor's pond, where Dad caught a bucket full of bluegill. "I don't know why Dad used a gunny sack for catfish...and a bucket for bluegill?" At age four I didn't know a catfish from a carp; but realized it was important when my Dad, Ben and I sacked the critters and dragged them home to Mom. There was a third trip to the flooding Platte River, where Dad caught big carp and buffalo with his dip net. A sack full of what Dad called "rough fish"! And a fourth trip; when I was allowed to tag along to Dad's favorite fishin hole; "The Chute".

The Chute was a geological phenomenon common to the engineered Missouri River; a permanent oxbow lake created by damning the Mighty Mo's vacated original river channel. A long, skinny lake formed during the 1940s when The Army Corps of Engineers cut a shorter path overland, permanently rerouting the river's main channel; then damned off both ends of the cutoff channel. Closed in at both ends by monstrous earthen dams, the 'U-shaped' Chute was the bypassed river channel. In the process of cutting overland and rerouting the river, The Corps of Engineers also created a large island; the massive area inside the 'U'. The body of water known as "The Chute" and the manmade island referred to as "Chute Island" were owned by one of my Dad's lifelong friends; a friend who saw fit to allow our family unrestricted fishing privileges on The Chute and mushroom hunting privileges on Chute Island. Morel mushrooms grew in profusion in ancient hardwood forest covering Chute Island. Two dozen species of freshwater fish indigenous to the Missouri River thrived in The Chute's three mile long, perpetually murky, lake waters. Flocks of migrating ducks and geese, a healthy population of native whitetail deer, coveys of bobwhite quail, flocks of pheasant, and a host of varmints such as raccoons and coyotes thrived in, on, or near Chute Island's primal virgin timber or fed in the island's perfectly level grain fields. "The whole damned place was a sportsman's paradise...perfect stomping ground for 1950s outdoorsmen forced to get by on tight family budgets...for men like my Dad."

Because I HAD previously been fishin with Brother Ben and my Dad, and HAD enjoyed the livin shit outta goin; and because I HAD repeatedly been made aware of the importance of catchin fish to feed our family; and because I HAD seen the joy written on our Dad's face when he dumped sacks full of fresh fish in our backyard for cleaning; "I wanted to go fishin...TOO!" Go today, tomorrow, next week, next month, next year; any time, every time! When Dad mentioned going fishin, I begged to go. "Would you expect less from a five year old blessed with an active mind?"

Because I begged; because he was a Good Dad; because HE enjoyed it as much as anyone; because it was simple and inexpensive; AND because it usually resulted in productive family entertainment; I discovered that, more often than not, Dad willingly obliged my whining and took Ben and me fishin. "IF?" IF time and money allowed; both onerous, overriding factors. Dad never seemed to have much of either. Scarcity of money or time meant fishin was limited to local venues. Back then local venues were ponds, lakes, or muddy rivers; "the total sum of our 1950s choices." Good choices mind you; where our family seemed to always catch a nice mess of fish. "Dee-luscious!"

[Footnote: A nice mess of fish was an indeterminate amount; an amount based on satisfying the wants, needs, and desires of the recipient; a highly variable amount of fish, fowl, vegetables, mushrooms, or other procured food product given or received by...the mess; with mess defined by giver or receiver without question. As in; "Here...Enjoy this nice mess of fresh garden greens." OR! "Thanks...I will...And here's a nice mess of fresh catfish to take home to The Misses." OR! "I caught a sack chock full...why don't you grab yer self a nice mess?" That could mean grabbing ten to twelve fish if the mess was intended to feed our hungry family of six; three to four fish if the mess was feeding an elderly couple. Either way, a nice mess was simply "a mess"; no one ever bothered explaining or defining its meaning; everyone just knew.]

Traveling through the minefield of life from childhood to maturity; "a dangerous road most of us are forced to travel"; one threshold indicator of having achieved a modicum of success is demonstrating the ability to understand the abstract. Grasp the concept that; "we are repeatedly presented with options...given choices...from which we must make selections"; "must choose one thing over another...based on minor details"; "as we seek the best path forward." Such was the case concerning April 11th, 1952; "my fifth birthday." As a wee lad of five I was offered conflicting choices; either option would have been fine; two equally pleasant choices regarding what our Dad was willing to do for me,

Fishing with grandsons **Chris and Ladd**, my dad caught the biggest Bass of his life! (1983)

do with me, on my upcoming fifth birthday. It was a family tradition; "Allow the person celebrating his or her birthday to choose the day's dinner menu and recreational activity de jour." Our sisters had their ideas, Ben and I had ours; and believe me, the twain shall never meet. "Always fightin two mean sisters for a place at the table was one reason I grew up a misogynistic...chauvinistic sexist."

"SO!" What were the two conflicting choices offered up by our Dad? One; enjoy an all-day fishing trip at The Chute. Or two; enjoy an all-day mushroom hunt on Chute Island. And why would my Dad lay those two particular tuff choices on a young lad regarding how to celebrate the lad's fifth birthday? "Morel mushrooms...That's why!"

In Missouri, morel mushroom season usually begins in April; often within a few days either side my birthday. Days off for our Dad were few and far between; therefore precious. Dad worked two fulltime jobs and part-time at a third; "For months at a time!" There were few days leftover for recreational activities; such a low priority during the 1950s, the concept had yet to be articulated; "I assure you of THAT!" Only the very wealthy or very lazy had time for prescheduled recreational activities. Since our Dad was the antithesis of wealthy OR lazy, he, like most post-WW II Dads, was forced to grab a stray day off here and there; as weather and work allowed. Realizing Dad's days off WERE scarce; given two options, the details of which were carefully spelled out in Dad's oral presentation, I immediately opted for the all-day fishing trip to The Chute. "End of debate...I thought."

I've been intuitive for as long as I can remember. The instant I said "FISHIN", I realized our Dad was disappointed. I wasn't sure why, but it was clear Dad wished I had chosen "MUSHROOM HUNTIN"! I didn't. I picked fishin. But that changed. Dad went silent and let my first choice simmer for a day or two; allowed excitement to build; then came home the day before my birthday and called me aside for what I remember as our first "man-to-man chat". Dad wanted to talk about a compromise. He didn't call it that, but that's what it was; an alternative; a substitute. Dad had gotten word of great news! Wildwoods morel mushrooms were popping up all over the place, especially out on thousand-acre Chute Island; where Dad and our family, for as many springs as I could remember, had enjoyed hunting the tender vittles. Dad wanted to switch entertainment de jour to number two; switch TO mushroom hunting. Dad persuaded me, convinced me, we could go fishin any ole time; but that mushroom hunting was a temporary choice. Taking his time, Dad pointed out that mushroom season lasted about two weeks; and would then be gone for an entire year. My Dad's thinking sounded reasonable. Wanting to do 'something out of the ordinary' on my birthday, I readily agreed.

"However! What I really wanted to do was BOTH! I wanted to go fishing…TOO!"

Without having the foggiest notion of what I was doing, I suggested a 'negotiated compromise'. Forty years later, my second wife, Nurse-Wife Peg, a student of modern "birth order" theories, pointed out that as Third Born of four siblings I was the peacemaker, the negotiator, the consensus builder. And while Nurse-Wife Peg may have been decades down the road in my future, she was 100% correct about my 1952, five year old's outlook on life. I negotiated. Ben wanted to go fishing too; but was too timid to say so. My lively, lovely sisters could not have given a shit less, either way, what I chose to do on my birthday. "BUT…You can bet your sweet ass none of us four Pepper kids would have thought of uttering words like shit OR ass! How things DO change!"

Negotiations, emotions, choices, compromises, and 1952 dirty language aside; I wanted to please my Dad, by going mushroom hunting; but wanted to please myself, by going fishin. The fact that it was MY birthday and that I was supposed to be allowed a freewill personal choice seemed to have little, if anything, to do with the overall decision making process. A blind hog finding an acorn, I proffered a counter to my Dad's genuine point about mushroom hunting being a temporarily available choice. Emphasizing that fishin was still my first choice; I suggested that I would be perfectly willing to go mushroom hunting instead of fishin; IF Dad promised to take me FISHIN the following Saturday.

Since both options were pleasant choices to my Dad, and since wet spring weather and current circumstances allowed him a smidgeon of free time, Dad quickly agreed to my suggestion. Dad stuck out his big, hard hand and shook my little, soft hand; squeezed my hand in an affectionate way, simply saying; "DEAL!"

Then, as an afterthought, Dad added an important point. "Jimmy…Since you've been so BIG (mature) about this…and gone along with what the majority of our family wants to do…I'm gonna make it up to you. I promise I'll do whatever I have to…will see to it…that we go fishin NEXT Saturday…PROMISE!"

I smiled the smile of a victor. I absolutely KNEW my Dad ALWAYS kept his promises. Really! I had heard hundreds of grownups say that about my Dad; I knew that a promise from my Dad was pure, 14K gold. I KNEW I could count on him taking me fishin; NEXT Saturday April 18th, 1952!

But! On my birthday, April 11th, we all went mushroom hunting; the whole Fam Damily! Mom packed a huge basket of fried chicken and baked goodies; filled a rusty metal thermos with strong, sweet ice tea; and all members of our happy little family headed to Chute Island; "where we found a boatload of fresh morel mushrooms." My fifth birthday turned into a genuine family outing; way more than it would have had Ben, Dad, and I had merely gone fishin. The women folk in our family hardly ever went fishin, almost never; fishin was strictly up to men folk. Looking back, I realize the "family outing" aspect of our day had something important to do with why Dad SO vigorously argued in favor of mushroom hunting, versus fishin; something important like the right to sleep in Mom's bed? "But...Who knows about stuff like that at age five? Not me."

"But...What about my Dad's bigger promise...to take me fishin...TOO?"

The following Friday, April 17th, Missouri weather turned bad. A late spring Northerner blew in and temperatures plummeted into the 40s; thirty mile an hour winds roared. By suppertime frost was nippin Mom's emerging potato and green bean vines. "Mom always grew a garden." At our always bustling family supper table; always attended by every member of the entire clan, plus our live-in hired hand; Dad got right down to THE big question, saying in effect; "Jimmy...We need to talk about our fishin trip...planned for in the mornin." Even at age five I had been around long enough to realize things weren't always simple; that this was a real doozie of a situation for my committed Dad. He had repeated himself a dozen times that week. "Yes Jimmy...We're goin fishin...I PROMISED! Come Saturday...Hell or high water...we ARE goin fishin. No matter WHAT!" During the twenty-four hours prior to Friday night's suppertime family confab, I noticed my Dad had begun adding; "No matter WHAT!"

I believed my Dad. So too did every adult Dad and I encountered that week. But the subject seemed to pop up everywhere Dad and I went. I wondered why people kept asking. Wasn't the answer obvious? Did the hometown folks know something I didn't? The question kept coming up; at the grocery store, the hardware store, the fillin station, the drug store, the feed mill, even during Dad's pitch games at his place of business.

[Footnote: "pitch" is a simple, six cards per hand card game, played by four to eight players; a game that involves bidding and scoring per hand, and cumulative scoring per game, and usually includes small friendly wagering; typically twenty-five cents per game for my Dad and his friends. Dad loved playing pitch and played his entire life.]

OBTW! "Ever where Dad went...Jimmy was sure to go." For the first six years of my life, I followed our Dad like a shadow. Our Mom worried; thought maybe I was touched with an undiagnosed 1950s weirdness causing me to feel compelled to go absolutely everywhere Dad went; including his place of business. Weather permitting, I even followed Dad out in his fields. I never DID anything, nothing really; just tagged along. Rode barefoot on the fender of Dad's 8-N Ford tractor, by the hour; followed him up and down every row of his tobacco and corn crops; raced to the passenger seat of our family sedan ever time Dad headed in to town. "No matter what!"

But ever where Dad and I went THAT week, the subject of our upcoming fishin trip seemed to be on people's minds; "Jesse...Heard yer takin Jimmy fishin fer his birthday...Sounds like the weather might be turnin a bit nasty...Seen the forecast?"

"Of course Dad had...Seen the [frickin] forecast!" Ever mornin at six! By the time us kids were rousted out for breakfast...rain or shine...Dad would be sittin at Mom's kitchen table...listenin to KFEQ radio broadcast out of St. Joe...farm news... commodity prices mostly...and...WEATHER! Farmers lived and died by the weather. Ask any farmer if he has seen the forecast...and if he says NO...he ain't no farmer! That simple! The forecast for Saturday April 18th, 1952 could not have been worse! 'Cold...Below freezing temperatures...Heavy snow'. Yes...SNOW! The forecast was...'several inches (of snow) by morning'."

Three to four times during my lifetime it has indeed snowed in Missouri ON my birthday! One year, 1973, my first year back from Viet Nam, it snowed eleven inches ON my birthday; twelve newborn spring calves out of my herd of twenty-four, died in near blizzard conditions. "Died dead"; while I lay flat on my back in a hospital bed in Leavenworth, Kansas recovering from a severe relapse of chronic malaria; a serious tropical disease contracted weeks earlier in Viet Nam. "Ironic Huh?"

But! Back to April, 1952; I went to bed the eve of my "negotiated for" but also "postponed" birthday fishin trip not knowing what morning would bring? I could hear the howling north wind whistling through large cracks in the tired siding of our non insulated old farmhouse. I snuggled deeper in my featherbed mattress and worried.

At six, Saturday morning, April 18th, 1952, I ran downstairs to Mom's warm kitchen. I almost fainted. The wall directly over Mom's kitchen sink was taken up by a large window made up of a dozen small panes. Staring in young boy disbelief, the only thing I could see was white. "White!" "White!" "Pane after pane of...WHITE!" It had snowed TONS during the night! It was still dark outside and no one could get a panoramic view; but Dad confirmed that it was still snowing.

"BUT!" Dad quickly added; "Don't worry Jimmy...We're still goin fishin...I told you we would go...No matter WHAT!" I was thrilled. I had been counting on going for the better part of two weeks; ever since making the "peace-preserving" family compromise with my Dad for THIS Saturday to be the day my Dad, Brother Ben, and I devoted to fishin. The thrilling prospect of getting outside in what amounted to a winter wonderland, and having a genuine go at fishin in accumulating snow, was nothing less than lagniappe to Ben and me. Standing there mouth agape at the snow, I recalled fishin in the rain, but snow would be different; "Even for our Dad!"

Mom remained silent. She knew we were going; no matter what. After all, Mom had been married to Dad for twelve years. Mom knew the tenacity of Dad's word; the hardness of his head. Mom may have been worrying about me or Ben backing out; one or both of us being intimidated by the snow and wanting to not go, thereby disappointing our Dad? If so, Mom never said a word; but did seem preoccupied about something? It never occurred to me Mom might be pondering the ludicrousness, the sheer madness, of Dad keeping his promise; no matter what. And! It never occurred to me that Dad would do anything OTHER THAN take us boys fishin; no matter what.

Dad had morning chores to do, including milking our gentle old milk cow. For Brother Ben there were a few odd jobs too; but by eight, we were off. "Things really WAS different back then!" Further complicating a burgeoning situation; adding adventure to Mother Nature's freakish whiteness; at the last minute, just before departing, Dad informed Ben and me that Dad's good friend and hunting buddy, 'Frog' Wright, had been invited along and would meet us in town; five miles south on a gravel road.

On his way into town, Frog's dilapidated Chevy pickup slid in a deep ditch. Frog had to roust out a nearby octogenarian neighbor to have the errant truck pulled from three foot deep snow clogging the soggy bar ditch; making good use of the kind and older neighbor's always near-at-hand, always dependable to start, Super-H Farmall tractor. That convoluted rescue effort occurring BEFORE Frog showed up in town, a smidgeon late, to go fishin with us. The eight-decades Older Neighbor, the man with the handy Super-H Farmall tractor and heavy log chain; "a large tractor for its day"; was yet another of my Dad's good friends. As a direct result of becoming involved, as absurd as it may seem by todays far more socially disconnected and culturally diverse standards, the aging but firm-bodied neighbor decided that he TOO would join our snowbound fishin odyssey. Now a company of five Conqueror Weather Beaters; on our intrepid way to The Chute; to catch a gunny sack full of catfish; during a freakish April snow storm; on a child's postponed fifth birthday excursion. "A strange feat we remarkably accomplished!"

Arriving at The Chute, the five of us were pleased to see the sun peeking out and the wind ceasing to blow. Three days earlier Dad had dug a large can chock full of fresh juicy fishin worms; gathered by the spade full from our continuously fermenting hog lot. Back then fishin worms were always kept in a three pound Folgers coffee can; always a three pound can; always Folgers. "Don't ask me why...that's just the way Dad and ever other fisherman...in our hometown...did it." Ben and I were given a little help baitin up; our tender fingers frozen stiff within minutes of arriving. By the time Dad and Friend Frog and Older Neighbor baited up and cast their lines in the steaming water, Ben and I were shivering; our scruffy, once-upon-a-time brown colored, leather soled and bootless street shoes, already hopelessly soaking wet. Whatever semblance of waterproof footwear Ben and I had been sporting all winter were either hopelessly outgrown or worn to ragged tatters; shirts, shoes, blue jeans, five buckle rubber boots, and other cold weather apparel items were bought but once a year! "No matter what!" I clearly remember having wet feet and cold hands...and that NO fish were biting! But things were about to change.[1]

Dad and Friend Frog decided we should build a fire. "What a brilliant idea! And if you don't think so...just ask Jack London!" But who would have thought of it? Who would have been prepared to do it? Not to mention; who in today's wussified America would even know how...in seven inches of fresh wet snow? "Yes! Officially seven inches of wet snow...that would melt away in two days."

Brother Ben and I were recruited to gather firewood; anything we could tug or lug back to our fishin site. Dad, Frog and Ancient Neighbor got busy scraping away the wet snow and kindling a flame. "Don't ask particulars...I don't recall any...Don't know that I even considered starting a fire in wet snow a challenge...not at the time?" Within minutes, maybe ten, we had a three foot high roaring FIRE! Firewood was no problem; the flooding Might Mo had deposited dead trees and large limbs in huge piles everywhere any of us looked. The wood was essentially dry; "wet only on its surface from snow." Tossed aboard our roaring blaze, the driftwood caught and burned nicely. "We had ourselves a useful and toasty bonfire...and ever thing changed for the better!"

I swear to God; we had no more than warmed our numb fingers, me and Brother Ben, when one of Ben's two fishin poles was nearly jerked

---

[1]Footnote: The Chute's relatively shallow water, previously warmed by more typical warm spring weather, was many degrees warmer than the cold air immediately above it; all things, including the definition of warm, being relative. When the wind quit, before the frigid air was warmed by the emerging sun, the brownish water of The Chute began emitting puffy clouds of steam; "like a pot of boiling rice carried out in the cold."

into the muddy waters of The Chute. A minute or two later Ben landed a two pound channel cat and our self-inflicted "cold day in Hell" took a definite turn for the better. "One cat in the bag!" Pretty soon ever body's poles started going off! Ben and I always fished with two poles. No one ever said "fishing rod", we always said "fishing pole". By noon our slimy gunny sack was bulging; everyone was smiling. Beaming as only successful fishermen beam, everyone agreed to head home. Dad, Ben, and I cleaned fish for two hours. Mom stunk up the house; "even though…as just pointed out…our old farm house was well ventilated on windy days"; frying up our fresh catch of the day, a nice mess of channel cat, carp, and one freshwater drum.

During the next few days a legend was born. Ever where Dad and I went, the legend was sure to follow.

Months went by; years went by; decades came and went. In June, 2000 my Dad died at age 82. At his funeral and during his wake, I retold, for the millionth time, this simple story; a quaint story that grew into a legend; about a farmer, his son's birthday, and a promise kept. Later on in MY life it was easy and natural to adopt my Dad's "promise keeping" attitude and his "stick-to-the-plan" philosophy; use both while rearing my three sons. In 1981, thirty years after my snowy birthday and our "promise kept" fishin trip, MY two sons and I suffered through one of life's worst traumas. The Boys bio-mom; EX Wife Jen-Jen; ran off with her kinky, well endowed high school sweetheart. But! With a lot of help, from a lot of Fine Folks, I managed to keep heart and soul stitched together. By strictly adhering to a valuable lesson I learned on April 18th, 1952. "Keep your promises…No matter what!"

At my dad's eulogy, I told the story. (note morel mushroom grave marker extreme lower right) (2001)

Chapter Two

Bait... Boys... and Granddad's Cow Pond

In 1952 our Dad sold his farm and relocated our family. Moved us into an extreme fixer-upper; a relic of a house built in 1836. A two story brick house built by slaves before the Civil War, using brick kilned 'just up the creek'. An historical and colorful old house lost by its original owner in a poker game, to Stage Coach King, Doc Holladay. Owned for years by Weston's only doctor, a few patients were known to have died in his treatment room; "our Mom's front parlor!" A solid old house bought by our Dad from an impoverished widow at a tax foreclosure auction in 1951; "for twenty-five hundred dollars ($2500)!" Restored and continuously occupied by our family since 1952; current home of our ninety year old Mom. The home in which older Brother Ben and I; "along with two mean as hell sisters"; grew up. A warm and full house where we four kids enjoyed an 'Eisenhower era' childhood; major portions of which, for Ben and me, were taken up workin, fishin, and doin things related to fishin. Fun boy things; "like catchin wild critters and sellin them as fish bait."

Ben and I were refugees; part of America's post-war mass migration away from the farm. But! Ben and I; "and our mean sisters"; took root, blossomed, and grew up as townies. Adapting overnight to our urban environment, Ben and I took advantage of our townie opportunities. Enjoying our metro-ization, Ben and I adapted; quickly organized a few 'money maker' projects performing a myriad of boyhood chores. Stuff like mowing yards for a thousand friendly widows, running the wheels off a hundred bikes delivering a paper route, moving a million household items for ten thousand little-ole-lady patrons, AND selling thousands of metric tons of fish bait. "I never exaggerate."

And of it all, selling fish bait was our most interesting entrepreneurial enterprise; a profitable gambit that immersed us up to our skinny, brown necks in the magic realm of 'The Great Outdoors'. Focused our unfocused minds; "previously filled with runny... boyhood mush"; on good stuff, like hunting, fishing, gathering bait, catching frogs, killing turtles; "to ward off the danger of being eaten alive by the prehistoric creatures"; avoiding snakes; "to save our skinny asses from certain death"; and sidestepping scores of dangerous critters, thereby negating the requirement of EVER explaining to our parents exactly what we were up to. Generally frolicking in, what was for two country boys, an awesome way to fill real summers. Overlapping, multiple faceted, "Father Knows Best", outdoor experiences; that helped shape our townie lifestyle into something Ben and I could endure. "Ever boy should be so lucky!"

"A colossal blessing in disguise"; a small tract of land came WITH our parent's newly-acquired, derelict, old house; sizable acreage, located on the far edge of town; landward of heavily forested river bluffs surrounding our hometown of one thousand hardy souls. Fortuitously; "for Brother Ben and me"; a large, spring-fed creek flowed through and bisected our family's deep-woods urban estate. That big and clean creek; "and two more just like it"; wound-round-through-and-across the city limits of Weston, contributing mightily to Brother Ben and me "enjoyin the livin shit outta our early-1950s townie life experience". Looking back; our childhood revolved around gathering and selling fish bait, fishin trips to Granddad Notley's farm pond, and working with our Dad on our homestead located within the city limits. "And since this book is about fishin… I'll tell you about fishin…and fish bait."

Following in his footsteps and keeping in mind 'training' we received as boys, while fondly honoring our Dad's memory, Brother Ben and I have worked long and hard at fishin. From when I can remember 'til now, Ben and I have fished without ceasing. Fished every environment encountered along life's way; including Viet Nam, Thailand, and Japan; not to mention ponds, lakes, rivers, bayous, bays, and streams from California to Carolina, from Canada to Mexico! Mention fishin and I say; "Me and Ben BTDT!" And in the end, our abiding love of fishin had a common denominator. "Bait!"

No matter where we fished, no matter how we fished, no matter what species we were seeking; no matter what monetary price or personal sacrifice Ben and I were asked to pay; "including time spent defending our country half-a-world away"; if Bro Ben and I were out there fishin, we required bait. "Yes…Bait!"

Simple, glorious, sometimes plentiful, sometimes difficult to come by, "Bait." Sometimes expensive, sometimes free; sweet and attractive to fish; funky and foul to man; some live, some dead, some frozen, some concocted and rotting in a rusty can; "Bait!" In my feeble and fish-befuddled mind; "Tryin to catch fish without bait…is like tryin to have sex without a partner. It's possible…it can be done…but who would wantta try? Either example would take way too much effort! You'd get tired...or go hungry tryin."

In Weston during the 1950s, bait was two, maybe three things; or a variation of three things. First; "bait was worms." With the help of our Dad, Brother Ben and I were digging fat, juicy, earthworms out of fresh, steaming hog shit several years before I was old enough to attend school; "While our family still lived back on the family farm." We used big, red Folgers coffee cans for worm buckets. And after our family settled in good at Montage; "a flowery name our Mom hung on our extreme fixer-upper antique house"; Ben and I started growin our own; "Night crawlers that is!"

Giant night crawlers that escaped The Big House, "That's right!" One summer after working his shift at the Federal Prison over in Leavenworth, Kansas; "ten miles due west across the Mighty Missouri River"; our Dad came home with a three pound Folgers coffee can brim full of genuine night crawlers. Outside the towering brick walls of Leavenworth's Big House, where my Dad had been walking his midnight-to-dawn yard watch every morning since early spring, night crawlers were filthy thick on the lush, pristine lawn manicured by federal prison inmates. Our Dad began his worm heist modestly; but soon escalated his effort. Carried home and planted within the confines of our huge backyard, thousands of giant night crawlers for the purpose of eventually establishing our own offspring colony.

Not nearly as easy a task as one might imagine, the oversized fishin worms

First Seargent Brother Ben, USMC retired, kisses the first striper bass he ever caught, as **Nephew Ladd** looks on in "awe". (1990)

had to be planted. Carefully planted; three feet straight down, in clean, roomy holes. Holes dug by hand with a posthole digger; with the hole refilled a few inches every day. Gingerly planted; in well-drained, stone free soil that was shaded throughout the day during Missouri's hot summers. Eighteen inch night crawlers, that could not be crushed or allowed to dehydrate before releasing them into the wild; where, hopefully, the giant worms would quickly acclimate to their new environment and thrive. Iron-headed at most things he attempted, it took our Dad several tries, but within a year or two Ben and I had more premium night crawlers at our call than we could rightfully say grace over. One random spring day in 1957; "I was in the fourth grade"; Ben and I accidentally sold a few behemoth worms to an old, crotchety, retired railroad man. Thereafter Ben and I were in the bait business! Word spreads fast in small towns; ours was a perfect Norman Rockwell tiny town.

With a little coaching from our Dad, Ben and I quickly realized; "If we're gonna be sellin fishin worms...we might as well be sellin minnows TOO!" So! Minnows are the second bait 'honored' in my short story.

With a large, clean creek flowing through our property mere feet beyond our family tobacco patch; "just over a steep dirt bank"; Ben and I were practically standing in minnow money up to our barefoot knees. Millions of minnows thrived there in that clear creek, waiting to be trapped, seined, or caught by hook and line; waiting to be gathered en masse and sold. "Minnows!" Just saying "minnow" makes me think of fishin trips and childhood; "Both made whole for me by the inclusion of frisky minnows."

During our 'early years', Bro Ben and I used glass minnow traps; the kind with inverted, cone-shaped holes molded into otherwise typical one gallon glass jugs. That odd configuration: "known to date back five thousand years"; allowed minnows to swim INTO the trap, while mysteriously making their escape OUT next to impossible? We baited our gallon jug minnow traps with stale Butternut bread; "the most popular brand of bread for miles around"; or a few of Mom's hard, two-day-old, homemade, lard biscuits.

Ben and I grew our business by adding traps; new fangled, cylinder shaped, wire traps that some marketing guru decided should replace glass traps. "Piss on that modern innovation!" Later on, in order to keep our thriving bait stand supplied with greater numbers of fresh minnows, Ben and I were forced to add a seine to our equipment list; "We was on to somethin BIG!" By our third summer, we were having difficulty keeping up with rapidly expanding demand.

During our first summer of operation, Ben and I stored our inventory of minnows in a ramshackle collection of scrubbed-out, five gallon lard cans; strategically stashed behind our house in knee-deep water in the creek. We poked a million holes in the metal lard cans using a hammer and nail. Our used lard cans in the creek method was simple, inexpensive, and worked; until a toad strangling rain swept in late one night and carried away our entire storage facility and stock of minnows; "nearly putting an end to our season!" After that disaster we were forced to upgrade; by adding a huge water tank. An old, leaky, horse trough Ben and I dragged down-creek after discovering it half-buried in sand. Our neighbor, Mr. Webb, outfitted the water tank with a small electric water pump salvaged from a decrepit but still working Sears & Roebuck washing machine; "also located up-creek"; dug from silt at the edge of a huge community dump located in the creek hollow. "Our pump circulated cool creek water and our minnows thrived."

Not long after establishing our thriving night crawler and minnow trade, Bro Ben and I soon got into crawdads. When our string of wire basket minnow traps were baited with spoiled raw bacon or chunks of beef tallow we began catching large numbers of crawfish. We had used stale bread or biscuits in our glass jug traps for years; but bread disintegrated too rapidly in the wire traps; forcing us to explore alternative bait...to catch...BAIT! "Rest assured. Ben and I NEVER called the crustaceans crawfish or crayfish. Ever body in our hometown called the little freshwater critters crawdads!"

By summer, bait-sized crawdads would begin entering our minnow traps; larger crawdads could be seined anytime after hot weather hit, usually late May. And! The best feature about selling crawdads? Bro Ben and I were the only reliable source for miles around! Every crawdad we caught could be sold to desperate bass fishermen. Back then; no one I knew gave thought to the notion of having a crawfish boil or eating crawdads. "Although...I WILL admit our Louisiana-born Mom talked fondly of eating the little mud-dwelling critters...that Ben and I considered BAIT!"

Most summers crickets and grasshoppers were catchable in numbers sufficient to be advertised 'For Sale'. However; both insects were considered a bonus. Consistent supply was our problem. A modest number of crickets could be hand-gathered while mowing our big yard or that of a neighbor. A predictable haul of crickets could be caught overturning recently baled alfalfa hay early in the morning following heavy rain. Sellable grasshoppers could be caught in open fields anytime Ben and I had energy and inclination to chase the scratchy pests. Grasshopper species varied depending on the time of year; big gray ones in spring, the biggest green ones in late fall. Gathering and selling grasshoppers was based on demand; "We insisted on a minimum order of four dozen!"

Another live bait that consistently 'Sold Out' anytime Bro Ben and I caught a good supply: tobacco worms; fat, green-striped, thumb-sized, horn-tailed, caterpillars, the larva stage of the tobacco moth. Typically present in large numbers during mid-to-late summer, on up through harvest, ending in early October. Large, juicy tobacco worms fetched a premium price when available. Common summer visitors to vegetable gardens throughout the US, tobacco worms are more commonly known as 'tomato horn worms' in NON-tobacco producing areas. In tobacco growing communities; "places where familiarity with the big worms has NOT bred contempt for the worms almost scary horned appearance"; monster-sized tobacco worms are considered topnotch catfish bait. Tobacco worms were our little bait stand's favorite choice as catfish bait for a dozen local trotline fishermen; men who used our 'backer worms on heavy lines, fished all summer, in a half-dozen swift-flowing nearby rivers. Full grown tobacco worms are cloaked in enough tough hide to absorb a lot of catfish chewing before disintegrating and requiring replacement. Brother Ben and I caught tobacco worms by the gallon bucket full; hand-plucking the pestilent chewing beasts off badly infested tobacco fields or gathering them by the hand full during harvest, directly from dirt floors of harvest barns. During extreme infestations, while nervously waiting for the area's LONE crop duster plane fly over and to eradicate the pests from their fields, a few farmers would call our Dad. Give Ben and me a heads up; offer us the chance to glean easy pickin big worms from the suffering farmer's field in advance of the death dealing biplane. Large, fresh, full-grown tobacco worms sold for a nickel apiece in our '24-7' bait stand.

"For you folks from Flor-a-DUH...that's a buck for twenty (worms)...big money for barefoot boys helpin neighbors by handpickin...then hand deliverin...buckets of ruthless pests to trotline fishermen. During two particularly horrible summers...during prolonged rainy spells when the area's one unreliable 1950s crop duster plane was grounded...desperate farmers resorted to paying Ben and me one penny apiece (bounty) for every tobacco worm we counted OFF the threatened tobacco field. Other worm pickers used the pests for bait too. Still others...their souls twisted by hatred for the ruinous worms...ran over the big juicy worms with tractors...smashing tons of valuable fish bait to pulp on gravel roads. Another few...the wiser few...carried the chomping live larva to our bait stand in messy buckets...pails smeared inches deep with fresh worm shit. That's right! Brother Ben and I purchased worms during the worst infestations... for resale. But most were gathered by us...and sold TWICE! Once as bounty paid by desperate farmers...once as fresh bait paid by desperate fishermen...maybe not the BEST racket I ever had...but a good one."

Regularly catching BIG messes of healthy bullfrogs was a natural byproduct of Ben and I chasing up and down the freshwater creeks flowing through Weston. Wading barefoot up and down MILES of heavily shaded creek banks during hot summer days, routinely brought us boys eye-to-eye with monster bullfrogs; many of them whoppers! A ten foot cane pole with a couple of feet of stout fishin line tied on; a small treble hook tied tight to the line; add a two-inch square of bright red clothe for bait; and Bro Ben and I could catch all the bullfrogs we could carry. We never used a .22 rifle to shoot the townie bullfrogs. "We couldn't!" We were always within the city limits; actually, many times we were right downtown. Occasionally we did capture bullfrogs with a large dip net; but the red flag and treble hook method was our best bet for daytime bullfrog hunting; "Bro Ben and I were NEVER allowed near the snake infested creeks during the night." Bullfrogs cannot resist jumping for red bait dangled within their feeding sphere. It worked every time; "Try it if you can locate a pond full of bullfrogs." Occasionally Ben and I also caught a few leopard frogs. If leopard frogs weren't too big we could sell them to bass fishermen as bait; "Fifty cents a pop!"

Did I mention snakes? Imagine how many harmless, and in rare cases, NOT so harmless, snakes Brother Ben and I may have walked over in our years of harvesting bait up and down Weston's creeks? Plenty; that's how many. We never once saw a rattler, but we DID face off with a couple of pissed off cotton mouths and a dozen or so fat bellied copperheads. Our protection? "Try to avoid stepping where we couldn't see."

During our short reign as Bait Kings, Ben and I caught sundry forms of creek dwelling wildlife; including turtles, salamanders, and dragon-looking boogery things that someone identified as mud puppies. One day we encountered a snapping turtle sooooo enormous we were afraid to tackle it alone, so we raced home for our Dad. Dad listened to our breathlessly told story; "one brother beginning a sentence…the other finishing it"; then patiently gathered his requisite turtle dispatching equipment and carried it a mile down the creek and shot the monstrous snapper between its beady turtle eyes. It took hours to accomplish, but our Dad cleaned the stinking turtle and our Mom made a family sized pot of turtle stew. "Back then…with six hungry mouths sitting around staring at whatever Mom fixed…ever thang on our dinner table was family sized…but that stew WAS a loooooong country mile from being among the best I've ever eaten. However! NO ONE in our family would have dared say so…not to OUR overly sensitive Mom!"

The funky old turtle was big around as a Saturday night washtub. And coated head-to-toe-and-all-about its legs and nasty neck with inch-long, spotted leeches. The lurid looking leeches were repulsive, but their presence on the unfortunate turtle's slimy hide never once, not even for a minute, deterred us boys from working the creeks for bait; from searching high and low for precious minnows. Much later; later like in 1981; MY preschool-aged sons and Nurse-Wife Peg and I discovered that big leeches were favored bait up in Minnesota and Canada fishing for smallmouth bass; "Too bad I didn't know all that 'slick leaches as bait' shit years sooner...Huh?"

Eventually Brother Ben and I began seeking and getting permission to hike out to our Granddad Notley's farm pond; "When I was in second grade." That would have made me eight and Ben around thirteen. Both of us owned old bikes but preferred to walk because then we could carry more gear. It was exactly one mile from our house in town to our Granddad Notley's farm pond, but seemed much farther to young boys on hot summer days. One fine day Ben and I attired in blue jean cutoffs ONLY; otherwise barefoot, shirtless, burr-headed, and brown as Chilean coffee beans; fished all day and caught over one HUNDRED small bullheads. After usin up ever fishin worm in our can, we chased down a few cow pasture grasshoppers as emergency bait. Neither Ben nor I could carry fifty pounds of live, dripping-wet, bullheads; every last plump catfish jam packed onto one, tiny, metal stringer. So! Ben and I improvised. We ran up the hill to Granddad's farmstead and acquired ourselves two, four-foot long tobacco sticks, from the tobacco barn where the sticks were stored, and made ourselves two parallel carrying poles, with our overstuffed fish stringer draped over and tied to the poles. With Ben in front and me in back, two carrying poles resting on our bare, brown shoulders, Ben and I carried our precious load just as we had seen jungle porters carry Clark Gable's hunting gear during an African safari movie we had just seen at an afternoon matinee the previous Saturday. "It worked!"

However! Bro Ben and I nearly caused a dozen car wrecks as curious passing motorists slowed down to gawk, laugh, or offer us a ride. Or, in most cases, do all three. Ben and I declined all offers from friendly neighbors and casual acquaintances; we instead walked all the way home. NOT because we were afraid to accept a ride from a stranger. Nope! Because after a point it became a matter of boyhood pride; "And we were getting SO much attention...we hated to see it end."

Brother Ben and I began fishin with Granddad Notley when we were VERY young. Dad would haul us out to Granddad's farm pond for a relaxed evening of family fishin. Granddad would join us as soon as Dad and us grandsons showed up with fresh bait; AND younger ears to lend to Granddad's old fishin stories; several of which old stories dated back to the turn of the century; "Granddad's turn of the century...1900...not 2000!" Granddad loved joining our family fishin visits. We in turn enjoyed fishin in Granddad's small farm pond; "in spite of hearing early-1900s fishin stories ten thousand times!" It really wasn't much of a pond, built in a small pasture to accommodate Granddads few old milk cows. And for all the many years our family fished in it, we caught only one species of fish; bullheads! "With ONE notable exception!"

When I was in first grade our Dad was Cub Scout Den Dad for Ben's Cub Scout pack. One evening after work Dad arranged to take his Cub Scout pack out to Granddad Notley's pond to go fishin. I was too young to be a Cub Scout, but after hours of unbearable begging I was granted permission to tagalong. I didn't own a fishin pole of any size, shape, or description. As part of their scout training the older Cub Scouts were required to provide their own poles, hooks, and fishin stuff. However! Being typical townies, not one single boy in that particular Cub Scout pack owned anything resembling a legitimate tackle box or useful fishin gear; just sundry fishin stuff, fairly meager stuff at that. Anyway; feeling sorry for me, Dad finally agreed that I could go. He also agreed to help me rig up an all-natural cane pole; a fresh cut willow from the thicket down on our creek. Dad outfitted me with items he had on hand; rigged me up to fish without buying one single store boughten item; "NOT EVEN A HOOK!" And even though I was allowed to participate as a too young guest fisherman of the Cub Scout pack, I have long since concluded our Dad was mostly humoring my budding ambition.

Our Dad cut and I drug to the house, a five-foot willow sapling; then he peeled off every scrap of bark and robbed a little black cotton line off his open-faced old bait casting reel; "The only kind of fishin reel I had personally ever seen." With no adult helping, I carved a workable bobber out of a whiskey bottle stopper cork. Dad tied on a small steel hex nut for a sinker and I was outfitted. But alas, I had no hook.

Mom came through in spades. Taking down her five hundred year old sewing basket she scrounged up a large safety pin. A little Yankee ingenuity and elbow grease, using Dad's needle-nose, tackle box pliers, and Mom was able to fashion a not too bad looking hook from her worn out safety pin. "Don't ask me why Dad didn't go out and buy me a stinkin hook...or give me one? Part of my scout trainin I guess?"

Dad led our predominately townie procession as his Cub Scout pack hiked the long mile out to Granddad's cow pond; "I tagged along...keeping up better than townies five years older than me!" When we arrived, Dad's Cub Scouts set about cumulatively catching a respectable stringer of bullheads; not a challenge except for the fact several Cub Scouts had never in their townie lives been fishin. Meantime I appeared pitiful. I had one homemade, twisted hook; a short bit of frayed, black cotton, line; an irregular shaped, waterlogged bobber, which refused to float upright unless the line was held 'just so'; all of it tied to a slick, white, willow pole, which was a tad too long for my size.

Dad's Cub Scout pack of neophyte fishermen brought along a big can of fishin worms fresh dug from our neighbor's hog pen in downtown Weston. "I was plenty skilled at baitin my own hook. Not a problem...I had seen it done a million times. And! Contrary to Nurse-Wife Peg's opinion some fifty years later...I WAS reasonably able to tend to my own needs...especially for a six year old. Maybe no one else did...but I firmly believed I had a real shot at catchin myself a fish!"

But I had nearly given up when my sagging, homemade bobber disappeared with a remarkably loud plumph! A swift tug on my frayed, black line that brought me back from boyish dreams to fishin reality; so powerful a tug it nearly jerked the slick willow pole from my sweaty hands. Up I tugged; and UP came a huge bluegill. Not only the biggest bluegill I had EVER seen, but as far as anyone knows, the ONLY bluegill EVER caught out of Granddad Notley's cow pond! No one need tell ME I had accomplished a Great Thing. But! Every one of Dad's older Cub Scouts, green-faced with palpable and undeniable boyhood envy, DID tell me! Dad grinned all the way home as our entourage of misfits and mavericks hiked back to town. Forty years later, when I; "on a dream come true day for ME"; reciprocated by taking our Dad striper bass fishin with Jerry Moore, a top-notched guide on Lake Buchanan, one of Texas' premier striper lakes. Dad was still talking about and told Guide Jerry the story about; "That giant bluegill Jimmy caught on his little homemade willow pole." I heard our Dad tell that soft-hearted story more times than wild birds shit black seeds; WAY more times than I've told the simple story about my Dad taking ME fishin in April in the snow...on my fifth birthday.

Brother Ben with two dandy redfish taken in Aransas Bay, TX. (2007)

Chapter Three

Big Lake... Big Problem

I grew up in a tiny tobacco farming community in northwest Missouri. During those years, mostly years I was in grammar school, our family of four siblings and two biological parents made annual summer pilgrimages to Louisiana. "It may sound odd... but back during the 1950s a vast majority of America's kids endured childhood with their biological parents...four kids in one family was typical." Every year, for several years running, our family of six drove hundreds of miles due south on narrow, winding, two-lane highways; down through Missouri and Arkansas' Ozark Mountains; across the rural flatlands of northern Louisiana; to vacation. "Why did we do that?"

Why did our family pack ourselves in one overcrowded sedan; "a four door Ford with ZERO air conditioning"; and risk our lives making such an arduous journey? Because of our Mom; that's why. Mom was Queen Bee in our family hive; commanded and demanded respect and attention. And. Our Mom was a native born Louisianan.

Still tough as a nail, our Mom turned ninety the year this book was published. In July 2009 she drove herself to Kansas City's airport so she could fly down to Texas, alone; "just to see her newborn Great Grandson...Nolan." At ninety our Mom was still feisty; still sober as a midwife at a triple birthing; still sitting in stern judgment of her four adult children and our spouses. And. Still extremely proud to have been born in and to have grown up in America's original Sportsman's Paradise; a swampy piece of earth originally thought of as...the center piece of the Louisiana Purchase...Louisiana! It was simple. Everything was simple back then. Our family made all those tuff 1950s summer visits to Louisiana because our Mom was a native daughter of Louisiana; a war bride and refugee from one of the backest backwater parishes of Louisiana. During the 1950s Mom still had six older brothers and one older sister subsisting in those dark wetland Parrishes!

Our Mom's entire family resided in Louisiana; as did uncountable hoards of our early-bred, often-bred, over-bred, and occasionally in-bred Louisiana cousins. Considered Damned Yankees by our toothless counterparts, we outcast Missouri Cousins would make our way south every summer simply to see and be loved on by our Maternal Grandparents. Drove there and back, primarily to see and get better acquainted with our dozens of cousins and Aunts and Uncles; risked life and limb on narrow winding roadways, and motel littered byways, to play simple kid games with hundreds of hungry Louisiana Cousins. It was ritual cast in stone. It was fond memories made.

And from a prolific litter of surviving family tales describing our travels and travails, my fondest tale of all, the longest-toothed memory stuck in MY mind, the adventure greatest to ME, occurred one particular day when Brother Ben and our Cousin Joe and I accompanied Mom's youngest brother Jack; "Bro Ben's and my Louisiana Uncle Jack"; and our Dad on an all day fishing trip. A day ever body went fishin. All five of us Gone Fishin on a mysterious dark lake surrounded by a tall forest of stately cypress trees shrouded in thick blankets of low hanging Spanish moss. A huge lake clogged here and there with odd-appearing cypress knees protruding above the water's surface from the roots of centuries old giant cypress trees. Bayou D'Arbonne Lake; located about an hour northwest of our Uncle Jack's Monroe, Louisiana home.

Two dads, three sons, one in-lawed family; Gone Fishin for the day. And while all five members of our two-family fishing party were already comfortably acquainted, the five of us already warm and fuzzy in our familial relationships; our two attending Dads repeatedly pointed out to our patiently listening Moms that the entire day was meant to be a special day. A day intended to benefit three cousins; a day thoughtfully set aside so three cousins could go fishin with our Dads and "remember it". And although contrived, to the point of being transparent, our Dads accomplished their mission. "Yes indeed! As intended... our day out there fishin proved memorable alright! But then... so did sinking of the Titanic... prove memorable."

Fishin, especially fishing in Backwater, Louisiana with our LA Cousins during the 1950s was in a word... simple. Back then, no one I personally knew, no one I had ever spent the day fishing with; had much extra money. Fishermen we knew had zero access to grand and glorious fishing venues routinely enjoyed throughout Louisiana or Texas today. But! Our combined 1950s Missouri-Louisiana families DID do a lot of fishin. However! Ours was strictly freshwater fishing; mostly local, mostly fishing with members of our family, mostly done on the cheap, and nearly always ending with over whelming success for the fishermen. "Scruffy... poverty stricken... MO-LA... barebacked skinny cousin fishin at its best... AFTER us boys had been taught the fine art of fishin by our empty-pocketed but always loving Dads. OBTW. Girls didn't much fish during the 1950s and '60s. Mostly boys wanting to become men…taught by men…wishing they were again boys?"

Big Cousin Joe, Big Brother Ben and I didn't own rods and reels; not even cheap or used ones. Nope! We were instead outfitted with nine-foot cane poles bought at a local fillin station; where our Dads stopped for cold beer and Super Colas ™ while in route to a large public lake. Our shiny, new, cane poles each adorned with heavy, black, cotton line; one red and white bobber, big as a quarter; one split shot, the size of a pea; and one long-shanked single hook, the size of your pinky nail. That was it.

Young son **Ladd** grimaces as he holds up a large Missouri bluegill... what our **Uncle Jack** called Louisiana Brim. (1981)

Our Dads had a few spare hooks, an extra bobber or two, a few extra split shot, and a smattering of odds and ends embellishingly referred to as artificial baits; most of it stored in plastic boxes in rusty tackle boxes. "The oddest things in our Dads tackle boxes? Red worms…white grubs…green grasshoppers…made of rubber that weren't actually lures and didn't remotely resemble modern Dow Chemical compounded plastic lures available today in every bait shop in America. But…odd things were about all there WAS back then…back during the 1950s. Oh yes! About all there WAS…except for our Dad's mandatory hook remover…or a rusty pair of needle nose pliers.

Initial excitement associated with that day's five-person, bi-family, out there fishin expedition, had begun weeks earlier with incredible family news; "Our Uncle Jack had acquired a brand new fishin boat!" Uncle Jack and Cousin Joe had used Uncle Jack's new boat only ONE time prior to us Yankee Cousins arriving down in Louisiana from up north in Missouri. Excitement that special family outing morning was palpable; most of it focused on Uncle Jack's glistening new fishin boat. Mom told us four Pepper Kids that our Louisiana Uncle Jack timed buying his expensive new fishin boat to coincide with our family's annual pilgrimage to Louisiana. Our Mom bragged to us four kids about how our Uncle Jack bought the boat just so he could take his Yankee In-Laws out for some real Louisiana fishin. Just so we cousins could go along with our Dads and do some real fishin in Uncle Jack's secret honey holes, hidden away among flooded cypress trees in the far reaches of the backest and sluggiest byways of Bayou D'Arbonne Lake.

Even though Brother Ben and I had previously enjoyed a few highly structured family boating adventures, neither of us had ever before actually...fished while sitting in a real fishin boat. No one in our immediate family, other than our Dad, had ever actually fished from a real fishin boat. Notice! I was careful to NOT use the term bass boat. Bass boat means something entirely different; especially bass boat as embodied by the fabricated behemoths of today, capable of tearing across lakes near the speed of sound.

Our Uncle Jack's boat was a small family style fishin boat. Nice but modest. Neat lines. Well constructed of riveted aluminum. Sturdy. Uncle Jack's fishin boat provided a reasonable amount of space for two fishermen; "into which our combined two families stuffed five." Uncle Jack's fishin boat was functional. Practical. Came equipped with a modest sized motor; "I have no idea how many horsepower or what brand...That sort of thing didn't matter so much back then."

By far the most significant thing about Uncle Jack's fishin boat was that it and its big outboard motor were brand spanking new; "Shiny new." Setting atop its two-wheel trailer, the three-part fishin rig cost our Louisiana Uncle Jack a LOT of jack, money! "That much I clearly recall...for reasons that will soon be crystal clear."

So! In the real world, where Brother Ben and I were forced to spend the majority of our youth, neither of us had EVER actually...fished from a real fishin boat. And when we finally did, as were the intentions of Uncle Jack and our Dad, the experience was, figuratively AND literally, part of a big deal lifetime memory for two barefoot MO youths. "Whose primary legacy up to that point in life had been a wooden handled hoe... bravely manned in one of our Dad's steamy tobacco patches in far off Missouri!"

After a brief stop at a fillin station; "a fancy one...with clean gravel covering its entire driveway...as opposed to dirt or mud"; to buy fresh white gas for the boat's motor; "twenty cents a gallon gas...into which Uncle Jack poured a pint tin of dark gooey oil"; we were off to the lake. Finally; after Uncle Jack also bought three new cane poles and a six pack of soft drinks for us three cousins; and two six packs of cold Schlitz for himself and our Dad. Finally; our fully outfitted and well provided for two-family fishin party of five headed north in Uncle Jack's Chevy pickup. Finally; bound for a big lake, the name of which we Missourians had been hearing since arriving in the pine forested Parrishes of northeast Louisiana; "Hearing about...but as Yankees...unable to pronounce."

Our Dad and Uncle Jack rode in the front seat of the pickup; "Naturally!" While us three shirtless cousins; "attired in badly faded blue jean shorts…ONLY"; rode three-boys-abreast STANDING, barefoot in back, on the hot wooden bed of Uncle Jack's pickup. What we boys would have said or done if some Do Gooder had strolled up and suggested we boys use sun screen, I have NO f—ing idea? Peering forward over the shiny top of Uncle Jack's truck, slapping at butterflies and grasshoppers frightened our direction as the vehicle tore down a narrow, blacktop highway towing the new boat and trailer at fifty-five miles an hour, our three-boys-wide spectator gallery had not one care in the world. Crisp, new, five dollar bills wouldn't have been good enough to wipe our happy boy asses. All three of us, three suntanned naked boys, had brand new nine foot cane poles secured in the bottom of Uncle Jack's new boat. Shiny cane poles tucked safely there, along with our Dad's rods and reels. All of it carefully stowed in the clean new boat; along with three kinds of natural bait, one wicker picnic basket filled to the brim with fried chicken and fresh snacks, prepared by our fussbudget Aunt Pinky, and a smattering of sundry other fishin items. "Sundry other fishin items that did NOT include a set of oars…or paddles…or floatation devices…or life jacket…for any of us!"

When we arrived at the public boat ramp, really not much more than a sloping gravel road disappearing into blackish colored but clean water, Uncle Jack and our Dad busied themselves launching the shiny new boat. We three cousins were sternly warned; "Do NOT wander off!" Near the boat ramp a weedy, tree-lined slough led out of sight around a blind bend in the lake; we boys took off like three flushed cottontails, following the slough. The three of us, Cousin Joe leading, had gone mere yards from the public boat launch when I stopped; froze dead in my barefoot tracks. Some sort of prehistoric critter, one that I had never before seen nor had any knowledge of, darted across the footpath directly in front of Cousin Joe. Cousin Joe, studiously gazing across the narrow lake channel, was unaware of our trio's near encounter with a terrifying beast. Alerted to the presence of the creature by Bro Ben's and my girly-boy high pitched screams, Cousin Joe laughed. Appearing unperturbed, he gave the silent, waddling, mute beast little more than a passing glance. Out of fear or astonishment, Bro Ben and I remained frozen in place. Ben and I had just seen, up close and personal, our first armadillo! The very first in our entire Damned Yankee lives!

The ungodly beast, like none I had ever before seen, seemed waist high on me; "I was seven…goin on ten." I had never known such animals existed. The resulting joke on Bro Ben and I was great. Our brotherly humiliation continued unabated well beyond time allotted by our Dads for launching Uncle

Jack's new boat. "My first encounter with new Louisiana wildlife was a big deal…to me. NOW I had another creature to fear besides black swamp panthers!"

Tamping down our skin tingling fear, Bro Ben and I, along with hee-hawing Cousin Joe, were summoned by our Dads. Called back to Uncle Jack's launched boat; summoned…as in; "BOYS…Get the HELL over here…and leave that filthy armadillo alone…those damned things smell like a goat's ass…and carry leprosy!"

Safely aboard Uncle Jack's small, snug boat, set for a fun day of Louisiana fishin, the five of us motored out into a wide channel and headed towards a deep cove Uncle Jack had that very morning proclaimed; "a sure bet for being loaded with big brim the size of a man's hand."

Turned out Uncle Jack was correct about the big brim. Once on site and fishin, we cousins could barely return our baited hooks to the water before our red and white bobbers disappeared beneath the blackish lake. Uncle Jack explained that the odd color of the lake water was the result of sunlight reflecting off tree sap and organic minerals deposited in the water by thick forests of cypress trees lining the lake's picturesque shore. Here and there our smoothly cruising but heavily laden fishin boat encountered large patches of floating, bulbous vegetation sporting pinkish-white flowers sprouting from a leafy sea of green. In many places the bright green, succulent vegetation entirely covered the lake's smooth surface; in randomly shaped house-sized patches. Uncle Jack cussed the lush plant. Saying it was a newly introduced weed that was threatening his favorite honey holes; a rogue species; currently wreaking havoc on Louisiana's freshwater fishin habitat. And, although Uncle Jack WAS an educated man, he didn't call his favorite fisheries habitat, nor did he use the stilted term fisheries. "Hell! I was a senior in college before I heard ANYONE use such fancy-ass ecological or environmental terminology."

While we cousins were busy catching fish, unhooking fish, placing fish on our stringers, and re-baiting our bare hooks; our Dad's were busy attempting to catch a few largemouth bass. Both our Dads were casting live minnows, affixed to single hooks, up into two-foot-high cypress knee clusters. If our interfamily fishing party's results had been a contest decided by numbers, we three boys would have prevailed; our Dad's had yet to land a single fish. While we three boys remained red HOT!

For bait, we cousins were using black and yellow striped catalpa worms; a garden variety, grub-sized, worm found in huge numbers on catalpa trees throughout The South during most summers. Our Dad's also brought aboard the new fishin boat, one hundred fishin worms dug the night before from Uncle Jack's. For their bait, our Dads were alternating between common creek minnows and small goldfish. During the 1950s, using large goldfish as bass or channel cat bait was a new rage. The only goldfish I had ever seen were in fish tanks in Katz Drug Store in North Kansas City in the pet department. Uncle Jack laughed when he realized Brother Ben and I thought goldfish were rare. "Ben and I weren't stupid...goldfish WERE rare...on a tobacco farm up in Missouri!"

However! As neophytes, we cousins were NOT allowed to use goldfish or precious minnows for bait. Our Dad's coveted baitfish were said to be too complicated for boys to properly place on a hook; too expensive to be wasted by ornery boys thrashing the water; skills required for properly fishing with minnows far too complex for boys to master. "But it didn't matter"; we cousins contented ourselves pulling in brim, one after another, jerked from the lake's tannin water; overgrown here, there, and yon, by common lake moss or dreaded bulbous hydrilla (derticillata). "Actually...It was quite a spectacular plant Uncle Jack insisted on cussing...All day long?"

As we three boys steadily added to our haul, fish by fish, our boatload of brim increasingly became a chore to hoist aboard. For three exuberant cousins our day had turned into...a fisherboy's dream come true. No one, least of all our adult supervisors, EVER mentioned one word about bag limits or size restrictions? And before our big day out there fishin ended, we self-integrating, North-South melding, Mason-Dixon Line crossing Cousins, eventually caught something approaching one hundred Louisiana brim; "A handsome species of fish...which according to our Dad's finely tuned identification skills were really nothing more exotic than gigantic farm pond Missouri bluegill."

After we three boys had two stringers packed double full; metal stringers with large metal clips that required opening and closing after each additional brim was strung up; with two brim hooked on each of the stringer's dozen clips; our Uncle Jack suggested we weigh anchor and move to a different location. Suggested we boat farther back into more isolated waters to one of the lake's long, narrow creek channels. Where, according to our Uncle Jack; "The really BIG bass are sure to be lurking."

Evidently where we were currently fishing was where really ELUSIVE bass were sure to be lurking? Our Dads had nada to show for drowning two dozen minnows and mutilating a dozen fat goldfish. Didn't matter; our dual-family quintet's numerous boat rides from minnow drownin location to minnow drownin location proved to be a feature attraction for Bro Ben and me. Ben and I remained in a constant state of awe, our boy mouths fully agape. Zipping by our boy vista in a blurry, panoramic haze; gigantic sequoia-like cypress trees, hung thick in dark shrouds of Spanish moss; acres of floating hydrilla and giant water hyacinth, laden down by a million chirping frogs; Paleozoic era, armor plated armadillos, scurrying to and fro on a vine tangled shore; large, white feathered, long billed, water birds, identified by our Uncle Jack as cattle egrets or pied billed ibises, perching in every tree; and oddly staged and arranged families of turtles scurrying for cover off every log our fleet boat passed. "Our Mom was right...Louisiana WAS a wonderland...a TRUE sportsman's paradise!"

"And!" There was yet another varmint lurking out there; an even greater critter about which we Missouri Cousins had repeatedly been told; about which we cousins had repeatedly been warned. An indigenous critter far more menacing and more feared than the occasional random snake. Snakes were common. Snakes were ubiquitous. Snakes could be seen anytime we took precious boy time to look. Big and little, long and short, fat and skinny, bright and dull; a wide variety of different sizes and colors of snakes could readily be observed, nonchalantly swimming in and out of different fishin holes. Slumbering snakes were intentionally run over by Uncle Jack.

But what of that greater critter, the exceptional critter about which we boys had recently and often been warned; the much ballyhooed and talked about, but as yet unseen, greater critter? First Amphibian in the hearts of Louisianans? First Critter among Louisiana's many families of wild critters? The state of Louisiana's undisputed Critter Champion? "I'm talkin about gators! Uncle Jack and our Dad kept mentioning gators... but be damned and run home naked if Bro Ben and I actually got a glimpse of one? And you can bet the last curly hair on your sweet fat ass we were tryin! But! None gators is how many gators we Missouri boys had seen."

I was so anxious to renew my personal assault on the lake's brim population, it seemed like years before Uncle Jack finally cut the motor and everyone resumed fishing. There were a few other fishin boats coming and going on the lake, but none in our immediate area; the lake wasn't close to crowded. More accurately, I would say the lake was barely inhabited. Crossed hither and yon by men in other boats; just a few, speeding to and fro, waving as they passed, occasionally stopping to chat with gregarious Uncle Jack. "Seemed Uncle Jack knew everyone on the bayou...and everyone knew him?"

More brim died on we cousin's third and fourth stringers. Number four was our final stringer; loaded down, two brim per snapped metal hook, for a grand total of nearly one hundred. Nervously glancing at our bulging stringers dangling from the side of his fish burdened boat, Uncle Jack declared need for yet another move; "Suffering badly from poor results...he and Dad...for all their intense manly effort...had caught no bass!"

Announcing his intentions in a gruff voice, Uncle Jack ceased fishing, raised the anchor, and heaved ho on his boat's new starter rope. The new motor started, chugged to smoky life, and we were off seeking another hot honey hole. So our two, adult, male guardians, our Good Daddies, could try bass fishin in another spot; "Why did old fashioned 1950s outboard motors smoke so badly…even when brand new?"

Good fishermen, knowledgeable fishermen, men like Uncle Jack, always tried another spot. Fact; one of the best fishin guides I ever hired, lived and died by what he called…the five minute rule. "No fish of the correct size or species (caught) within five minutes…and that particular professional guide…[his name is Walter…and Walter still fishes fulltime out of Port O'Conner TX]….pulled up anchor and moved! That's right! If no one had any luck, or caught any decent fish, after allowing five minutes of concentrated fishing by proficient client fishermen, time very carefully measured by Guide Walter's clock; Walter moved! No luck? Walter moved! No luck? Walter moved again; and again; and again; until fish of the proper size and species were located and landed by his clients. Sooner or later, usually sooner, Walter found fish!

Uncle Jack's intentions were equally as well-founded and intense as Guide Walter's. So; off across the placid lake we went; Good Uncle Jack our Captain! His new boat moving at full throttle; moving in a direct line towards an area of deeper, more open water; "It was a good day for catchin big brim…one of the best days EVER for sackin fat brim…Until…Suddenly…It wasn't!"

A good day until our boat was suddenly racked by a loud, jolting thud! One of the best days EVER until a crunching calamity of noise signaled our boat's horrid underwater impact with an unknown object. A good day, a best day until something solid, something rock hard, something hidden beneath the water, seemed to reach up and grab our small low-flying boat; threatening to shred asunder, into small and separate shreds, our over crowded boat. A terrible screeching, a loud and memorable noise; "A tearing of metal I easily recall fifty years hence."

We three boys, we three cousins, were jolted into a daze and propelled forward. Every loose item in our small, family-laden boat seemed airborne. Uncle Jack had hit a snag! Had hit a submerged cypress stump so solid and so immovable it might just as well have been the sunken keel of the Great Ship Titanic. Our heavy but small fishin boat careened sideways; slip-sliding. At first impact no one on board realized exactly what had happened. Likely as not standing UP at the precise time of impact; doing exactly what we had been told a dozen times to NOT be doing; we boy cousins were tossed forward into a jumbled boy heap. None of us went overboard, more luck and good fortune than boating skill; "But…overboard could easily have happened."

I recall righting myself and yelling. Wanting; no demanding, an explanation! I instinctively realized something serious, perhaps even something dangerous, had just taken place. As a child of seven I wondered silently in my still ringing head; "What the HELL just happened to us...to our family out here fishin in Uncle Jack's new fishin boat?" "Not that us boys were EVER allowed to say...HELL."

Uncle Jack's exquisitely beautiful; and until that horrible moment of sudden impact, valuable boat; was gashed; breeched and ruptured; by a tearing, sheering force yet to be defined. "AND...Worse?" Uncle Jack's twice-used, and therefore essentially new, outboard motor was MISSING! GONE! Where seconds before Uncle Jack's new motor had been powering us forward like a leaf in the wind, there now remained a gaping irregular hole; rent in the tiny aluminum boat's stern.

Racing across the lake at or near full throttle, our boat had hit a huge, rock-solid, stone-hard, totally submerged, cypress stump. The force of impact had decapitated our outboard! "Or should I say...in-capitated?" It doesn't matter; Uncle Jack's brand new, precious motor was G-O-N-E! I can't remember every last one of Uncle Jack's and our Dad's exclamatory, shock-provoked cuss words; and I certainly had zero insight into how terrible Uncle Jack felt; but I WAS old enough and savvy enough to realize; "We was in some deep shit...even before I was allowed to say shit."

However! Our Dad WAS allowed to say shit, and often did. So; our Dad said shit, several times that day. Fact was; our Dad seemed to spring a leak from which that particular word flowed in rapid staccato bursts. When it came to cussing, Uncle Jack was no downstream piker; he matched our astonished Dad word for word, explicative deleted per explicative deleted! Boys become men in subtle phases. Boys become men by living life as boys, but then experiencing, at just the correct moment, turning point events that bring boys to the threshold of becoming men; by being around, by witnessing, by emulating things men do; by learning from men what men say and what men do; by taking in and absorbing what men, who boys KNOW to be men, do or say. These days ever body calls that process "role modeling"; back in 1954, we simply called it being a good Dad. Our fun fishin situation had suddenly become ominous, and we boys realized it. On THAT day, in our dual-family, suddenly missing motor situation, two men, who also happened to be THE two men we cousins most loved and most admired; two men who were, by shocking events, suddenly propelled close enough to the edge to temporarily be a tad out of their usually better-controlled, adult, male minds; two men who were undoubtedly at their fatherly wit's end; suddenly began practicing role modeling for their three astonished sons by freely expressing every manly opinion they could conjure up; expressing themselves in language so gruesome it landed just this side of blue black.

"But...Other than repeatedly yelling a bizarre litany of manly things at the top of their manly lungs...what else was there to do? Other than shouting disconnected sordid things like feces...or something weird having to do with unnatural intercourse with members of one's own family...including having intercourse with one's own mother...or being born without a dad...or doing strange disfiguring and debilitating things with one's male anatomy...and a smattering of FAR worse stuff I wasn't certain actually existed...or can't recall...not in enough detail to restate here on the record...all of it... every word of it...delivered in Mad Dad voices loud enough for the entire Louisiana Purchase to hear. What ELSE could our Dads do?"

Our Uncle Jack was an educated man; an experienced civil engineer. Our Dad was an educated man; salutatorian of his high school class and college graduate. But! Educated or not; experienced at life or not; both men were so stunned that both were, for the moment, uncharacteristically out of their adult minds; temporarily incapable of coherent speech beyond astonishingly brutal swearing. "So there we was!" Two highly intelligent Dads; highly respected Dads; appearing to us astounded cousins as if they, our Dads, had become clueless, blithering maniacs. Neither All American Adult Male Role Model; "neither"; seemed capable of articulating, much less solving, our genuine delima.

Which was; "Our small boat...containing five shocked occupants...was suddenly in peril...had been placed in jeopardy...by a well hidden underwater cypress stump."

And. To paraphrase an old cliché; "Our family fishin party was up a lake without a paddle." Remember me mentioning, in passing, the innocuous factoid that our small boat contained neither life jackets, nor paddles, nor oars? "Well...as things turned out...that WAS important!"

We were stranded, a long way from home; three to four miles from the boat ramp, in a remote stretch of a swampy, deep woods, Louisiana lake. There were other boats out and about, but none within easy haling distance. Uncle Jack and our Dad sort of huddled up to converse privately, "among themselves." Then Uncle Jack bluntly announced that our boat's motor was lost and that he, Uncle Jack, intended to go overboard and try diving down into the lake's murky depths to retrieve it. By the time Uncle Jack got around to articulating his intentions of getting in the water, it was already apparent; "Uncle Jack was going for a swim...in the big dark lake." And when we three wild-eyed boy cousins finally realized exactly what's up, all Hell broke loose. "Why?"

All morning long our Dad and Uncle Jack had repeatedly told us boys to keep our hands and feet out of the lake; to NOT dangle our boy appendages in the water; "as three young boys out there fishin all day in a small boat are not only inclined to do...are compelled to do!" We cousins had also been repeatedly warned to be extra careful about NOT slipping or falling overboard. "Why?" Because the lake was permanent home to large Louisiana alligators! Yes! Alligators! Big ones! Or, so we three boy cousins had repeatedly been warned!

By the time Uncle Jack had stripped down to his boxers, his son, our cousin Joe, was hysterical; begging his Dad, our Uncle Jack, to NOT go diving in search of the amputated motor. And when Cousin Joe became upset and began crying, older Brother Ben and younger cousin I were sure to follow. No amount of persuading could deter or tamp down our childhood terror. Sheer boy terror brought on by boyhood imaginations, all three of us having logged hundreds of hours witnessing Charles Weissmuller narrowly escaping sudden death. "That's right!" We cousins unanimously believed Uncle Jack's life was about to abruptly END! "For those of you fortunate enough to have been born after 1960...that would be Charles Weissmuller...aka: Tarzan of The Jungle!"

Personally; I was terribly afraid for Uncle Jack! I had seen every Tarzan matinee that had ever been made; three times! I knew what alligators could do to Great White Hunters! I had seen alligators in action; "which were actually African crocodiles...but why let a minor detail get in the way of boyhood imagination"; devouring unnamed disposable white crewmen and black native bearers by the dozen, in every Tarzan movie.

And! While genuinely worried about Uncle Jack losing his new motor, in way of testimonial to having had my child-priorities straight at all times, I quietly and to myself was way MORE concerned about us three cousins missing out on one more go at our previously hot brim hole. Distressed to real tears by the notion that our day out there fishin had apparently been brought to an abrupt halt, I was sad as Hell that catching more big brim no longer appeared a high priority to either adult.

"Then?" Well then I was shocked to hear our Dad arguing a bitter point with Uncle Jack. Based on what I was hearing, I realized our Dad was ALSO strongly opposed to Uncle Jack's proposed swimming expedition! Silently, and with great remorse, I concluded that our brim fishin was over for the day. Concluded that our Dad TOO, wanted no part of ANY kind of swimming demonstration, by anyone; least of all someone our Dad knew and loved; "our Uncle Jack!"

Keep in mind; all three of us Missourians in MY biological family; Me,

Brother Ben, and our Dad; were mere Yankees from Up North. Therefore; AS mere Yankees, our wee Missouri Family was not entirely "up to speed" regarding the relative danger posed to ordinary White Men on safari out there fishin; who might just happen to also decide to go diving for a sunken motor in alligator infested lakes. But! I had known my Dad for a long time; if Dad was worried, I was worried. "I always…100% of the time…sided with my Dad on everything! No exception. Always! Our father-son one mindedness drove my Mom nuts. Now as always…My Dad must be right…HAD to be right!"

The urgency and pitch of verbal berating emanating from everyone in the boat grew worse. But no amount of childish screaming or shrieked boy words, or our Dad's stern arguments, could dissuade Uncle Jack from making a valiant effort to retrieve his valuable motor. I learned later, MUCH later, that the dollar value of the lost motor relative to Uncle Jack's disposable, discretionary income was WAY out of proportion. Uncle Jack feared the potential of being eaten alive by a rouge Louisiana alligator far LESS than he feared the certainty of being eaten alive by our temperamental Louisiana Aunt Pinky; "IF we five men folk were to show up back in Monroe without Uncle Jack's expensive new motor…there would be Aunt Pinky H-E-L-L to pay!"

Those kinds of subtleties are never apparent to young boys. Fledgling youths who were NOT at the beginning, but who WERE (more so) by the end of our day out there fishin, transformed into becoming young MEN! BUT! Regardless of our minor or major status as boys or men; we three innocents were savvy enough to realize a genuine family tragedy was unfolding before our stunned young eyes. "Sudden death by gator…OR…slow death by Aunt Pinky…even three badly shaken boy cousins got it!"

But our massed family objections did not matter. Stripped naked, except for white boxers, Uncle Jack took in hand a small rope previously stowed in the boat's front compartment; a small hemp rope briefly used at our first stop to secure our boat to a tree limb. "Back at the first good fishin spot…the hot hole where we three boys caught two stringers full of big brim…while our Dads drowned minnows."

Once over the side and holding tight to the boat's freeboard for support, Uncle Jack realized he wasn't certain where to dive. He reckoned we had coasted past a couple of large cypress trees, and somehow said he knew where the offending stump lay hidden beneath the water; "The big stump…the one that decapitated our motor."

During Uncle Jack's disrobing phase, our Dad busied himself tying our boat to a nearby tree; a prudent move, made by a landlubber Missourian. Tying off the savagely disfigured boat stopped our steady drift AWAY from the offending stump; "our Dad's keen mind kicking back in gear"; drifting farther away from Uncle Jack's intended dive point. However! We weren't getting any closer either. Matter of fact; we weren't getting anywhere. An entirely different problem; one our adult male guardians had yet to face. Or? If indeed our Dads had come face to face with that certainty, they had yet to comment about or explain their intended solution to us scared-shitless cousins; three boys squatting silently in our half the suddenly way too small boat.

But! There WERE reasons for optimism. Uncle Jack had done a stint in the Navy. He was an accomplished outdoorsman and strong swimmer. He had a plan. And he had no difficulty reaching the point where he felt certain our boat hit the sunken stump. Predictably, Uncle Jack located a stump. Verified to be THE stump by finding fresh impact marks on the stump's upper edge, Uncle Jack prepared for making his brave dive. "Some folks later said...foolhardy dive."

First; Uncle Jack tied his small rope to an overhead limb. Then letting out a long length of line from his carefully clutched coil, Uncle Jack dog paddled to a point he believed to be directly above the offending stump. Saying he was ready, Uncle Jack executed a perfect bluebill dive; "A placid diver duck species." Placing his hands together and above his head, bending at the middle, his ass suddenly rising in the air, his feet locked together, Uncle Jack shot upwards a bit, nosed over, and disappeared beneath the black water. Then? Silence! After what seemed way too long, Uncle Jack surfaced. He reappeared about ten yards beyond the hidden stump. He was breathless and gasping, also shouting, in the direction of our boat. Saying something forgettable about the water under our stranded boat being...DEEP! "Duh...Ya think maybe TOO deep?"

Yes; soooooo deep Uncle Jack failed to reach bottom! "But don't worry...worse news would follow...things would get worse."

Another three to four similar unsuccessful dives and puffing Uncle Jack regained his wet rope from the tree limb and swam back to our bobbing, tied off boat. Not only had Uncle Jack NOT located his missing motor, he had failed to locate the bottom! "That's right!" Struggling back aboard, Uncle Jack sheepishly confessed that he had failed to ever touch bottom. Based on his vast array of practical, outdoor experiences, and the amount of rope he let out, Uncle Jack made an educated guess that he had dived straight down more than thirty feet. Unfortunately; he failed to reach bottom, touched nothing beyond festooned tree tops and thick underwater vegetation. Uncle Jack said it was too dark and murky; that he could see absolutely nothing. Said he had no real idea how far it was to the missing bottom. Partially restoring his dignity by donning his damp clothing and lighting up a Camel, Uncle Jack opined that our best bet was to flag down a passing fishin boat and hitch a tow back to the boat ramp. Uncle Jack said he would return with help and retrieve his lost motor; "What help meant…I had no idea?"

As a child of seven it didn't seem as if our protracted misadventure had taken long. From the initial crash; our Dads emptying their vaults of blue adjectives and adverbs; the imagined boy-terror of seeing Uncle Jack eaten by gators; the disappointing dives; our Dads yelling to Shanghai a passing fishin boat, explaining our predicament, hitching a ride back to the boat launch, and reloading our stern-battered, motor-amputated boat; all seemed a mere blip in time. All these many years later, after hearing the story a million times, I finally realized we were stranded out there for hours. And that eventually sunset was coming. Our Dads did NOT want to spend the night in our stranded, crowded boat, on that spooky lake. Both Dads did their manly best to hide genuine adult concerns.

"And the worst part?" Our slow, towed, boat ride back to the boat launch was horrifyingly embarrassing for Uncle Jack. Louisiana men, Real Louisiana Men, just don't go out there fishin and lose their brand new motor. "Losing his left arm to an angry alligator would have been preferable to Uncle Jack…which of course is exactly what we cousins were CERTAIN would happen…but did NOT!"

As for alligators? Well; we DID actually see a few. Later during the towed boat ride; the SLOW boat ride back to the boat ramp. The friendly Good Samaritans who towed our boat to shore were besieged by inexplicable, overpowering man-urges to point out every tiny alligator our heavily laden boat passed by; "About a dozen all total."

Five MONTHS later, Uncle Jack called our Mom to wish her Merry Christmas; "he always called our family on Christmas." During the prolonged conversation that Christmas, Uncle Jack surrendered the sad news that two local duck hunters finally located and retrieved his recalcitrant, runaway motor. Our ongoing, dual-family legend was made greater by Uncle Jack establishing the fact that his lost motor was somehow mysteriously discovered nearly a quarter MILE from where it first became detached from our boat; "Of

Brothers **"Jimmy and Benny"**. It was Christmas and we heard from **Uncle Jack**. (1955)

course that quarter mile was subject to human error...and to documented ...natural born tendencies for Louisianans to exaggerate."

It didn't occur to me as a child, and may not have occurred to you as a reader; but exactly HOW was Uncle Jack's missing motor eventually located, so many months later, so far from where he thought it lay submerged?

Fishermen and Hunters are a gregarious lot; "Most of us." Louisiana Fishermen and Hunters may just be the world's MOST gregarious lot. Word quickly spread around all of Northern Louisiana; "Ole Jack Ashley has done lost his brand new Umpty Stump motor...it's still sunk out there in the lake...and it's yours for the takin!" Legend had it that hundreds of boaters, maybe thousands, using a wide array of contraptions and search devices, probed in vain for Uncle Jack's missing motor. Every sportsman, fisherman, duck hunter, water skier, and moon shiner enjoying that stretch of lonely, alligator infested lake made it a point to make a pass at locating and retrieving Uncle Jack's drowned motor. The two men who actually found the missing motor were old friends of Uncle Jack's; the finders-keepers entitled men thought of nothing OTHER than returning the moss encrusted soggy motor. The two friendly Motor Finders somehow located the ruined motor using a crude fish finder-depth finder gizmo heretofore unheard of down in Deepwoods, Louisiana. Made initial contact with Uncle Jack's missing motor by affixing a large, strong magnet to a thin flexible rope. The Finders Keepers then attached a standard grappling hook to a heavier rope and were able to snag the sunken motor and drag its ruined body to the surface. Yes ruined. A fair amount of corrosive sludge and South Louisiana chemical erosion had invaded the new motor's vital innards. All in all, Uncle Jack's formerly new motor was beyond salvage; "Probably one reason the motor was so promptly returned to our weather worn Uncle Jack."

Decades later Aunt Pinky was still speaking in glowing terms about Uncle Jack's lost motor. "That's right!" When Missouri Yankees attended Uncle Jack's funeral, Aunt Pinky told this true story in detail at the wake.

Uncle Jack in his
WWII pilot's flight gear. (1944)

Chapter Four

Shirt Pocket Trout

[Preamble: "Although convoluted, there IS a moral to this dirty little story. I've never entirely gotten over what we did; what I did. So allow me to publicly confess for the first time, here in this book, sins that have haunted me for years; confession is good for the soul. We were in college. It was the debauchery-laced 1960s. We drank too much beer, chased too many wild girls, skipped too many classes; did unbelievable things that either flaunted or outright broke the law. There are reasons WHY some of us who attended college during the 1960s refer to those years as; the wildest time of our life. We were wild! We perpetrated lists of despicable deeds; rebellion against the establishment, all forms of authority, was our way life. Protests, especially against Viet Nam, were rampant. Burning draft cards, not bathing, using drugs, and two-fingered hippie peace symbols or clinched-fist Black Power salutes were in; our futile attempt at drowning myopic problems, common to youth. Contentious behavior escalated to levels never before seen on America's campuses. For many students, psychosis inducing new drugs like LSD or stupor inducing old drugs like marijuana saturated college life. Revolt, riot, and restlessness were common themes running through our time. Parts of the personal lawlessness described in this fishin story rank among my worst. For what I did, I am now truly sorry! Look what I forced myself to do! I lied; then I lived the lie. I cheated. I repeatedly took huge chances of being arrested. I used contraband substances to perpetrate crimes. I created an elaborate, premeditated disguise. I grubbed in raw filth, merely getting myself into position to exhibit criminal behavior. I risked pissing off my college buddies. I divested myself of respect and integrity. I conjured up, and then forced my straight-laced Dad into unknowingly helping me maintain, a dark family secret. And eventually had my sorry, sneaky, law breaking, puckered into tight little knots, scared, ass nearly arrested by The Man! All of THAT scrofulous insanity, just so I could act like a backwoods Louisiana redneck. So what you say? Well...paraphrasing Kenny Roger's hit song Coward of The County...I say to you Son, Daughter, Friend, Amigo, Anyone; Son...Don't do the things I've done. Because The Man WILL come calling, and he WILL get your ass!"]

During the summer of 1965, two wide-eyed freshmen attending the University of Missouri, Friend Scott and I, joined the same social fraternity; future home base to most of our important personal relationships. The strong, bonded friendship that developed between waterfowl hunting buddy Scott and I, described in my book "Not Your Ordinary Hunting Stories", one prime example. Fortuitously for Good Buddy Scott and me, neither of us limited our recreational endeavors to duck hunting. "Nope!" There were girls to chase, kegs of beer to drink, games of poker to play, and millions of fish to catch. "OBTW...Scott and I both graduated TOO! ...

But during spring break of our sophomore year, as Scott and I were "wandering through life" we did a few things we lived to regret; things we wished later we had never done. The story I am about to tell was just such a thing; an act perpetrated when he and I were young, wild, and didn't care. Back when we really didn't know shit from shinola.

Buddy Scott and I invited two of our pledge brothers to join us on a trout fishing trip to Bennett Springs State Park in the Missouri Ozarks. One fraternity brother we invited to go along was nicknamed 'Tagalong Ted'. "Why?" Ted had a bad habit of begging Scott and me to be included 'IN' on high powered personal plans, asking to be allowed to tagalong; even though Tagalong Ted didn't necessarily understand or even enjoy whatever it might be that Scott and I were planning. The second fraternity brother Scott and I invited to go along fishing was 'God Son Ed'. God Son Ed was given his appropriate nickname our first week of Pledge Camp; "Ed was former President Harry S. Truman's real live GOD SON!" Catching a limit of state-park-stocked rainbow trout topped a short list of special events and social activities our fraternity's fearless foursome had planned for ourselves during what we hoped would be a memorable spring break.

Buddy Scott, God Son Ed, Tagalong Ted, and I piled in God Son Ed's four door Chrysler sedan; a big, fancy car loaned to us by Ed's Dad; a nice man who had for years been Post Master of Independence, Missouri; NOT coincidentally also the hometown of President Harry Truman; "God Son Ed's Godfather!" Four fraternity brothers heading south to trout fish in the Missouri Ozark's most popular trout stream. God Son Ed and I had been there before; Tagalong Ted and Good Buddy Scott had not. No one in our foursome claimed to be a real trout fisherman. I owned the only fly rod in our group. Our foursome could have more accurately been described as bait fishermen; catfish, carp, bluegill, crappie, bass. In our group, on that trip, the coldness of our beer was FAR more important (to us) than the liveliness of our bait;

catching a few rays more important than catching a few fish; being near water doing something preferable to being away from water doing nothing. "And why did our adventuresome group have such a strong preference for being near water?"

Near the water's edge was where indigenous wildlife were most likely to appear. Local indigenous wildlife slathered up good with Coppertone; rare specimens of wildlife collegians oftentimes referred to as "Hot Chicks". And in the likely event there WERE a few wildlife sightings, so much the better for defining our trip! It was after all; "Spring Break!" And while our worrisome manhood may have been pointlessly swimming UP stream, while local indigenous wildlife were swimming DOWN stream; prime examples of local wildlife of all sizes, shapes, and favorable descriptions WERE known to inhabit green belt areas near cold trout streams. Catching a few wary trout, observing a few wary specimens of local fauna; our collegiate crew was prepared for either eventuality.

One of Missouri's largest fish hatcheries was located adjacent to Bennett Springs State Park. The hatchery supported trout fishing enjoyed within the state park, one of The Ozark's most popular fishing retreats. The trout stream that flowed through the park was a constant level, underground, natural spring; subdivided into four roughly equal sections, each section delineated by large signs. Fishing within each segregated section was based on the type bait allowed within that section.

Within the park, furthermost downstream, was the 'Natural Bait' section. Delineated by large, black and white, Natural Bait signs posted at the section's upstream end where concrete footbridges crossed the fast flowing spring; with similar Natural Bait signs posted at the spring's terminal end, one-half-mile downstream. There; a small, sandy delta marked THE spot where gin clear Bennett Springs dumped its icy water into the murkier and warmer Niangua River. The Natural Bait section was the largest of the park's four designated fishing areas. Referred to as the Natural Bait area, artificial lure and fly fishermen WERE permitted to fish within that section. However! Fishermen opting to use artificial lures or flys WITHIN the Natural Bait section, were theoretically fishing at a distinct "bait disadvantage" hardly anyone ever did it. Few lure fishermen possessed fishing skills requisite to matching the powerful attraction of natural baits.

Overall; the greatest numbers of fish were caught in the downstream Natural Bait section of the park. Older men, younger boys, rookies, first-timers, and occasional rare female fisherman, tended to fish in the Natural Bait area. Some of those fishermen knew exactly what they were doing; most did not. Over the years, whenever my Dad and I fished Bennett Springs, my

Dad would head straight for the Natural Bait section and use night crawlers hauled from home; "His Natural Bait of first choice."

Within the park, next section UP stream from the Natural Bait section was the 'Artificial Lures Only' section; clearly marked by large signs posted near low footbridges crossing the spring; one bridge and set of signs upstream, another bridge and set of signs downstream; the two sets of bridges and signs serving as 'Posted' terminal boundaries of the Artificial Lures Only section. Artificial lures, of any type, could be used within that section and could include anything from plastic worms to rubber balls; "hellgrammites to tadpoles"; rubber salmon eggs were popular. Tens of thousands of fishermen used Rooster Tails ™ or Mepps Spinner Baits ™ in the Lures Only section; "small bodied spinner baits with single treble hooks." Casual observers enjoyed watching as a wide variety of lures were cast in the Lures Only section; lures tossed hither and yon by every imaginable combination of rod and reel. For fishermen in the Artificial Lures Only section, substance prevailed over style; "And it didn't seem to really matter what type lures fishermen used…they generally caught trout." A small plastic earthworm with a few tiny red plastic beads strung ahead of a twisting silver metal spinner was typical of lures generally effective in the Lures Only section. But, on any given Sunday nearly any kind of manmade lure would catch a trout; even ridiculous-appearing lures. Conversely; some days, nothing seemed to work. "That's why they call it fishing."

Back during the 1960s, back when I irregularly fished at Bennett Springs, the most popular style lures were white or cream colored plastic grubs; "that looked exactly like real live garden variety grubs"; with single small gold hooks imbedded. But! Lures used in the Artificial Lures Only section were required to be…well…artificial! Manmade! NO natural bait, of any sort, was allowed within the Artificial Lures Only section! "A big rule that one…an ornery rule…natural bait versus artificial lures!"

And! There IS a big reason why I'm going into so much detail about the four designated fishing sections of Bennett Spring's. Segregation of those four fishing sections was based entirely on the type bait or style of equipment used by fishermen pursuing trout within those designated sections. Those small differences in bait or equipment are fundamental to the point of my story. Younger adults, men mostly, a smattering of teenage boys, and a few salty female fishermen, fished in the Lures Only section. I fished there myself, a lot; until 1966, when I was given a new fly rod for my nineteenth birthday. After which time I declared myself sophisticated enough to be graduated UP stream to the 'Fly Rods Only' section.

Within Bennett Spring State Park's third designated section, the Fly Rods

Only section, all fishermen were required to use fly rods. Any style artificial lure could be tied on; but hooks and lines HAD to be attached TO and controlled BY neophyte derelicts like ME attempting to make fifty yard casts with our ten yard abilities! By my college years I had assimilated a respectable collection of fly rod lures, wet and dry baits; of which only a few qualified as actual flys. But, like many expert fly rod fisherman, I quickly discovered that a teeny hook tied to a tapered leader and baited with an artificial salmon egg constituted one of the world's most effective artificial lures. Random colors of tiny grubs and small multicolored plastic larvae rounded out my workingman's repertoire of fly rod lures. It almost goes without saying; "NO natural baits were allowed within the Fly Rods Only section." The Fly Rods Only section, like its two downstream counterparts, was clearly marked by large black and white signs.

Back in those days, back during the late 1960s, there were a couple of distinct advantages to being a fly rod fisherman, when fishing Bennett Springs. One big edge, an unintended fringe benefit most likely lost forty years later; the Fly Rods Only section was never crowded. Relatively speaking, it was sparsely fished. By stark contrast; most days at Bennett Springs Park, rod and reel bait fishermen of every size, shape, social standing, demeanor, and physical description, lined every available foot of shoreline; filled every cubic yard of available standing space. In addition to being far more crowded, wade fishing in the two downstream sections wasn't practical for a different reason. Shoreline bound bait fishermen were extremely territorial; "They frowned on fancy fly rod fishermen strolling by and disturbing trout in their personal holes."

But! Despite pedestrian crowds and institutional canned fishing factors, during the ten years I fished Bennett Springs, the Fly Rods Only section remained a reasonable alternative for experiencing the unique thrill of catching a trout while wading. It wasn't a clear Rocky Mountain stream from "A River Runs Through It", and I wasn't Robert Redford; but it WAS wade fishing, while seeking trout, and wasn't crowded weekdays.

So! Less crowded, an opportunity to wade fish, and most important; the Fly Rods Only section usually held a few trout of above average size. The reason for that size differential was simple; "far less fishing pressure." Older and wiser trout quickly learned to migrate upstream; seek quieter shelter and relative safety within the four confines of pressurized Bennett Springs State Park.

Within the park, last upstream and MOST desirable of the park's four designated fishing sections, was the upper-most section. Most UP stream and strictly reserved for fly rod fishermen using FLYS! Hand-tied, multi-feathered, multi-colored, squirrel hair sporting, bona fide FLYS! NO lures! NO rubber baits! NO red and white bobbers! NO half-assed, semi-fly, or partial-fly…flys! Real flys only! "However!" If you WERE a fly rod fisherman capable of catching something on a genuine wet or dry fly; "something besides a bad summer cold"; you WERE awarded nearly one-fourth of Bennett Spring's entire park system. Clearer, cleaner, deeper, faster running, and UP stream; quasi virginal waters teaming with more and better upstream trout.

Fartherest upstream and final of the park's four segregated fishing sections, the Flys Only section originated where a gin clear spring spewed forth from the bowels of a rock strewn huge hole in the earth; a chasm the size of a double car garage, boiling up icy spring water from deep within Missouri's Ozark Mountains; "Bennett Springs."

Rookie fly rod fishermen…men like me…were initially dumb asses. We believed we could actually wade into a crowded trout stream…and using artificial flys only…easily catch a limit of extremely lure-wary trout…from a public stream frequented by tens of thousands of…real fishermen. Men exactly like ME! Whose true Sportsman credentials were even more suspect than my own!

Perhaps real fishermen like ME should have known better than to even TRY fly rod fishing? But! The REAL problem I had with fly fishing? The biggest truth? I wasn't good at fly rod fishing. How could I have been…I had only used my new fly rod half-a-dozen times. I had never practiced. And lessons were something Baby Sister Mitzi took from a piano teacher. So what was I…really? Easy. I was a half-sober college frat-rat…showing off for my good buddies. I didn't know a wet nymph from a wet whore. And since I was young and had years to burn…and since I didn't realize the gross manpower inefficiencies of the ludicrous uphill challenge I was facing…and since I didn't really give a rat's ass about appearing foolish…I decided to try fly rod fishing. I waded into Bennett Spring's Flys Only section and fished my skinny young collegiate ass off…all the while thinking to myself…I must be doin somethin terrible wrong…I ain't catchin shit?"

For several years my Dad and I made regular trips down to Bennett Springs. During one of our father-son trips I first used my new fly rod; whereupon I discovered what I called my "shirt pocket technique". A secret fishin method I invented for catching trout at Bennett Springs; a technique I accidentally stumbled upon. During the time when my discovery up and just happened I wasn't very smart; not yet formally edu-ma-cated. But I instantly realized I was on to something. Here's my duplicitous and sad story.

I was fishin with my Dad. I had caught three small trout in the Fly Rods Only section and had then wandered downstream looking for my Dad. He was totally trustworthy in every way; in this case referring to my Dad's absolute tendency to fish from atop a certain huge rock overlooking the deepest hole at the fartherest point downstream within the Natural Bait section. Predictably my Dad was exactly where I thought he would be; fishing away, barely upstream from the muddy Niangua River. There, practically in the warm delta waters of the exiting colder spring, Dad seemed to manage to catch his six daily trout; "Even though often wearing out the day doing it."

But Dad didn't appear to mind. More mysterious to him was how I could get trout, ANY trout within the boundaries of Continental North America, to bite on ANY type bait OTHER than one of our fresh, homegrown night crawlers. Dad considered fly rod fishing a gross waste of energy and valuable manpower; not to mention "fancy assed fly rod fishermen more style than substance...more casting than catching."

Politics aside; with my fly rod in hand and sporting a meager half-filled stringer, I approached my Dad. He was diligently fishing. Dad said he was glad to see me and ready to return to our cabin to get some rest; "As soon as I (Dad) catch my sixth trout!" Back then, during the decade we fished Bennett, the daily limit was six trout, of any size, per day. Because I lacked three trout to complete MY daily limit; and because the slow flowing waters nearest my Dad were relatively uncrowded; I decided to wade into the spring and fish next to my Dad, while he worked at catching his limit; "Jimmy... Sometimes catching that sixth trout can be a real bitch (troublesome)."

With Dad, catching his daily limit was a point of Old School pride. I never saw Dad quit until he had his limit, or park rangers sounded the 'Quittin Time' horn. Daily fishin in the big state park commenced every morning and ended every evening with an official blast of a loud horn; "Like a weather warning siren." Fishermen best not be caught allowing their hooks to touch the water before the morning horn sounded, and those same hooks better damned well be reeled in and clear of the water by sundown, when Quittin Time blew; "Or the tardy fisherman's rule-violating-ass was mud!"

"During the years I fished Bennett...Park Rangers were VERY strict! Routinely observing every where...checking every one...all at once. Watching Park Rangers politely checking and enforcing rigid state park rules got under my Country Boy skin. But then...without rules where we would be? Uncivilized? Ruthless? Running amuck? Engaging in random tribal warfare? Lunging desperately to sink a rusty hook in the world's last surviving trout? Harpooning the world's last surviving whale? And don't forget! It was after all...the 1960s. More on rules later! Much more...I'll get to rules!"

But for now, back to my discovery; I was nineteen, standing near my Dad, fishing quietly like a disciplined school boy. I had made a dozen empty-creel casts; "my most common type fly rod cast"; when Dad yelled over and asked me to hand him some inconsequential piece of tackle he lacked having in his possession. I waded over and offered my Dad the item he wanted. I was SOOO proud to have had whatever it was my Dad needed. I considered it a rare opportunity, being allowed to strut my real fisherman stuff by providing my DAD with a badly needed piece of gear; "My glory was brief…but great." I was relaxing; enjoying the favorable moment; standing idly by watching my Dad tie on the object I had just provided. Busy doing nothing; when one of my Dad's precious but still wet and slick and rapidly wiggling night crawlers dropped from his wet hands and floated near to me.

I picked up the wiggling worm and dropped it in my unbuttoned outdoor sportswear pocket. Then, with no particular agenda in mind, I parted company with my Dad and moved upstream to an uncrowded hot spot; remaining near to where my Dad continued seeking his sixth and final trout of the day. An inglorious hot spot, within the Natural Bait section, which after fifteen minutes of water thrashing produced a grand total of zilch point zero trout!

I was fishing hard, trying my best to catch up to my Dad; when the casually retrieved, still alive, night crawler began wiggling around in my oversized shirt pocket. Suddenly, like fresh kernels of popcorn bursting in red hot grease, a real fisherman's true epiphany began popping in my warped brain! "POP!" "POP!" "POP!" "POP!"

POP one; I was officially fishing IN the Natural Bait area. POP two; my Dad was currently kicking my ass five-trout-to-three in take home, edible fish. POP three; I was having NO luck and had nothing to lose. POP four; I decided trying something new and different was better than standing there pretending to fish. So I decided to conduct an experiment; decided to use a smallish portion of Dad's just retrieved largish fishin worm as Natural Bait. But! I didn't bother tying on an appropriate bait hook or putting on a tiny split shot; standard rigging when using fishin worms as bait. I instead broke off a tiny smidgeon of Dad's fat, juicy night crawler and hooked it directly on the small single hook of my artificial lure. Not wanting to cast off my experimental natural bait, I peeled off about fifteen yards of floating fly line and let it out by hand. Fly line tied to a tapered six foot monofilament leader; attached to my small artificial lure; baited with Dad's fat, juicy Natural Bait. "B-I-N-G-O! Bingo! Bingo! Bingo!"

After selecting my new hot spot upstream from my Dad; thrashing the clear trout stream with three-dozen sloppy downstream casts; clumsy as a ten week old Lab puppy in my two sizes too big brand new Redhead hip waders; I had barely gotten myself reorganized from attempting my most recent BAITED floating cast…when? Well! Somewhere six feet deep and fifteen yards downstream, my baited cast ended with a sudden thump; a definitive jerk on the opposite end of my floating fly line. Obvious even to a dull witted, rookie fly rod fisherman like ME; I was experiencing a real bite! Two breathless minutes later and the score between my Dad and I stood at five-trout-to-four. And. I had learned something. And. As Yogi Berra was purported to have said; "If somethin is worth doin…it's worth doin twice."

So! From the big worm secreted away deep in the pocket of my USMC issued outdoor sportswear, I pinched off another quarter-inch section of bloody night crawler body and baited up. "And now…forty years later…I will confess…must confess…that after that first strike…on that first worm…by that first fish…trout fishin at Bennett Springs with my Dad became one big blurry adrenaline rush!" For the balance of the day the difficult part was keeping my hopelessly impulsive and overly excitable mouth SHUT! I was absolutely dying to tell my Dad! Tell ANYONE worthy; "About my fabulous new secret." A fresh bit of Natural Bait; another sloppy, ten yard, floating line, downstream, wallowing cast; and my fly line snapped tight…again! I was in business again. "Whammo!" "Zippity Do Da Day!"

My Dad was mighty impressed; too busy to pay attention or ask solid questions. He had simultaneously hooked his sixth and final trout for the day. When I glanced his way, Dad's big smile blotted out the sun; ecstatic that he had beaten me. I smiled back, stringered up my fifth trout, and waded towards shore. Paused, then changed my mind; "What the Hell…I was two-for-two on my baited artificial lure…my quietly enhanced with Natural Bait artificial lure!" While my Dad busied himself gathering up his sundry paraphernalia and making ready to depart, "why not throw it out again…see what happens?" "POW!" "Zing!" Out went fly line in long buzzing strips. "Wham Bam Thank You Mamm!" I hooked and caught my sixth and final trout of the day. Only thing different, my sixth trout was bigger; "Nice trout…as Bennett hatchery trout go."

Dad and I stringered up our fish, cleaned our fish, iced our fish, and headed to the local café for late breakfast and hot coffee; "All managed without answering one probing question from my Dad." Once seated in the cool comfort of the Greasy Spoon Café, Dad HAD to ask; "Jimmy…Whatcha have tied on for bait over there? In all the years we've fished together down here…with me fishin there in the natural bait section…I've never seen anybody hit three trout in three casts? What were ya usin Jimmy?"

Smiling big, from the bacon grease on my lips to the buttery grits on my chin, inclined to NOT lie to my Dad, I confessed my Top Secret but perfectly legal, though highly unorthodox, accidental discovery. Dad and I laughed until tears came to our eyes. And we, Dad and I, immediately agreed; my Dad speaking for both of us when he said; "No big deal Jimmy…legal too…but most likely just a fluke…you and I've seen lucky fishin shit like that come and go all our years fishin together." Dad's initial evaluation of my three trout in three casts was reasonable. Such good fortune likely WAS a fluke. But! If it was a fluke and if in fact it was legal; it was a legal fluke worthy of additional field testing. "Or so I concluded?"

First light next morning Dad and I were back on fog laden Bennett Springs impatiently waiting for sounding of the opening horn. I headed straight downstream to the same point, near my Dad's favorite stretch of delta water overseen by his big rock perch. Adjusting my gear and sucking in cold morning air, I pinched off the same sized tidbit of fresh worm, put the juicy morsel on the same sized small lure, and instantly got the same results. A different day! A bigger trout! I WAS on to something! "It was definitely NOT a fluke…or anything like a fluke!"

But now the real challenge; "Keeping my successful M.O. a secret…not easy when two people know a secret." It was Dad's and my final morning for trout fishing. We needed to depart for Rogers, Arkansas that afternoon to meet with one of Dad's tobacco warehouse customers. But I HAD indeed learned something! Something big that I considered VERY useful! Something I was dying to try again; something I was bound to tell someone?

"Now!" Fast forward with me to spring break 1967. Fast forward to when my three Missouri Tiger fraternity brothers and I were heading south to Bennett Springs in God Son Ed's big Chrysler seeking indigenous wildlife; escaping into the unreality of spring break. Seven months had passed since my Top Secret discovery; experimental fishing enjoyed with my Dad. I was confident that I would have a grand opportunity to show my buddies the ropes when it came to trout fishin at Bennett? And. As difficult as it was at that point in my life, I had told absolutely no one, except my Dad, about my Top Secret shirt pocket fishin worm method. However! I DID tell my fishin buddies that I needed to stop and buy a few big night crawlers; "because I positively DID intend to secretly retest my discovery." So! I did, and I did. I bought two dozen night crawlers. And I secretly retested my discovery. Fishin side-by-side with my content in their naïveté, non-fly-rod-owning, Mizzou Fishin Buddies; fishin quietly WITH my friends in their downstream Natural Bait section of the springs, not far from my Dad's favorite perch atop that old rock by the silty delta; I fished for trout.

"Piss…No luck!" Not a tap, not a nibble. I was flummoxed; perplexed and discouraged in equal proportions. Baiting my lure with shirt pocket concealed worm guts had worked perfectly during my last stand in the same area of Bennett Springs. I thought to myself but did not say; "Oh well…Shit!

That's the nature of fishing. Maybe the trout just aren't biting? Maybe word got out? Maybe ever body fishin in the Natural Bait section is baitin their lure with worms?" Then, for the second time in as many trips to Bennett Springs, I was struck with a theory; which was really a follow-up, secondary theory. Just a sub-theory mind you, but potentially an add-on concept to my original concept; a concept I believed I had proven during two prior days of fishin with my Dad. Lacking success; feeling pressure to produce; "no one in our group had caught a thing"; I made a calculated, conscious decision to do something I had never before done; "Intentionally break the law while fishing at Bennett Springs!" I intended to wade UP stream to the Lures Only section and try out an ILLEGAL lure concept I had been toying with in my trout depraved mind. A concept made totally illegal by placing a tidbit of raw red night crawler on my tiny artificial lure. Oh, I rationalized my provocative behavior alright. I said to myself, again not aloud; "it's just for scientific purposes"; "just to prove or disprove my theory"; "just to shed light on something me and Yogi Berra have agreed is worth doin"; "confirm or repeat something I believed was worth repeating."

My criminal mind made up, I jammed a couple of fat, juicy night crawlers in my oversized outdoor wear pocket and headed five hundred yards UP stream. To a more refined section of the springs, to the Artificial Lures Only section; generally fished by fishermen with greater skills. Arriving in a quiet, uncrowded stretch of deep water, I stopped and rigged my hook with a tiny fragment of fresh-dead night crawler and quietly let out floating fly line; rigged the bit of fishin worm precisely as I had rigged it that first day fishin with my Dad. "Bingo!" "Dingo!" "Go Johnny Ringo!"

A fat trout grabbed my hook, my line, and my sinker; actually swallowed my small baited lure all the way down to its protruding trout asshole, on that, my first EVER illegal cast into strictly forbidden waters. I silently quipped to myself and God; "Wow God...That worked soooooooo damned well...I just better try it again." So I did. Then again...and again...and one more time...until...lo and behold...my stringer was jammed with a daily limit of six plump trout. Then I said; "Lord...Whatcha doin to me? I'm King David in the tower...lookin down on the bare breasts of Bathsheba...How am I supposed to resist?" In addition to my unilateral conversations with God, there was a lot of toe tapping quick talk explaining to do when my three Mizzou Buddies and I met up for lunch; "I had caught more trout than all three of my buddies combined." I felt guilty as Hell! But! Somehow I managed to bite my tongue and hide my gloating.

While our Mizzou Foursome sat eating lunch, it was corporately decided that I should return to the spring and assist my long faced, inferiority-complexriddled buddies in catching THEIR combined limit of eighteen trout. "No problem…glad to be of service." But! Alas! Like most greedy criminals before me; I couldn't stand prosperity. Like a previously successful bank robber who knows about an open bank vault, I just HAD to share my good fortune with someone. Just HAD to return to the scene of the crime with an accomplice, for more easy pickins! Good Buddy Scott; duck poaching, willing to shoot over his legal limit, willing to hunt from duck blinds on FEDERAL LAND he and I were NOT authorized to use, BEST Buddy Scott; first came to my mind as THE most likely guilty co-conspirator to whom I should first confess my deadly secret discovery. "Can't imagine why I thought FIRST of picking Scott?"

Good Hunting Buddy Scott and I had been through some real shit together; FAR worse feces than nibbling petty fishing rules in a state park. When told my big secret; after quietly defecating in his drawers; Scott begged to be allowed to break the law TOO! Asked me if he TOO could join me UP river in the Artificial Lures Only section, become a charter member of my newly forming trout poaching gang. Scott's was a request to which I quickly agreed. "Why the Hell else would I have told Scott what I was up to? That was the whole damned idea…I wanted a partner in crime!"

Upstream in the Lures Only section, our shirt pockets stuffed with fresh, juicy night crawlers, isolated from as many prying eyes as possible, Good Buddy Scott and I fished. Working separately but in choreographed unison, Scott and I hauled in trout like we were netting them in a seine; "Which…Looking back on it…Probably wouldn't have been any more illegal!" Four daily limits later; twenty-four total trout caught, cleaned, and packed on ice; it was time for beer, women, and anything else Stud Muffin college campus escapees could conjure up for the day; "Our first day fishin in hot water."

But what about tomorrow; or the day after tomorrow; we Four Missouri Tigers had planned to fish for THREE days; then head back to Columbia. Buddy Scott and I made a rarified, secret command decision; "If we're gonna catch so damned many trout using ILLEGAL bait…why bother stopping after merely catching a legal limit?" It made perfect sense to ME! AND to my more than slightly larcenous Buddy Scott!

Scott and I sneaked into town and bought a second ice chest. We had big plans for next morning, and the morning after next. We hit the cold spring's waters bright and early the second day and Scott and I effectively filled FOUR limits in less than one hour! Nineteen of twenty-four trout caught during that hour were caught by Scott and me; fishing illegally upstream in the Artificial Lures Only section; doping our lure's tiny hooks with small performance enhancing globs of pinched off night crawler sneaked from our shirt pockets.

"ZIP! POW and POP! ZING! FLIP and FLOP!" Scott and I caught a dozen trout in as many minutes. Thinking, and saying, out loud this time; "Shit Man Shit...This really IS some real shit!"

It was some real shit alright, and me and Scott were up to our bloodshot eyeballs in it; "No downstream shit for us Mizzou Boys." At lunch, all our second day's trout were iced and packed in our second ice chest; then placed in the trunk of God Son Ed's big Chrysler. Scott and I told our Amigos we were heading into town for more beer. While gone to town, Scott and I stashed our first two day's mother lode of trout; packed on ice in two separate ice chests; in thick brush along side the highway leading back to Columbia. Then Scott and I returned to the park with a THIRD secret ice chest and enough beer to assuage OUR guilt and keep our still totally legal Buddies from inquiring into Scott's and my profound illegal success.

Our third morning dawned bright and right; Scott and I were limited out in no time, so we rested. After lunch, after stashing my personal first limit, I unilaterally decided that I would wade upstream. Way UP stream; all the way to the sacred headwaters of the giant springs; go for broke trying to catch one of the behemoth trout rumored to be holed-up in the bottomless clear water boiling up there from deep in the bowels of Hell; "I found myself thinking a lot about Hell...Not sure why?" Oh Well! Departing Scott's good company, I headed out alone seeking personal triumph. Scott couldn't accompany me up to the headwaters; he didn't possess the requisite fly rod. I know we've all been taught 'Crime Doesn't Pay'; and 'Bad Guys Always Get Caught'. But not that day. Not that trip. Not that year. Not that gimmick. Never. Not that crime!

After a previously agreed-to lunch break, Scott and I were so emboldened by our apparent success at totally escaping detection, we, Scott and I, decided to go for broke. We changed our entire outer layer of clothing and went back out for our second daily limit; "serious poachers...pushing things FAR beyond reason." But I had privately decided that what I really wanted to do was go for one really BIG trout; that's why I headed up to the spring's headwaters alone. "Criminals ALWAYS up the ante!"

Once there I discovered the springs virginal waters were SO clear, SO transparent, my worm-enhanced fly was WAY too obvious! I had already altered my bait; forced to poach fish using a fly versus a tiny lure. "Just to be legal...HA!" Switch from my field tested baited lure, to an experimental untested baited fly; "IF I was going to pretend to be fishin legally in the Holy of Holies, Flys Only, uppermost, headwaters section of the spring?" I decided to use a wet fly; "a fly that sinks." I intended to mask the natural dark color of my contraband fishin worm; "worm flesh pinched off and sneaked aboard my wet fly…as a performance enhancing drug"; by using an even darker colored wet fly. So! Tying on the biggest, darkest colored, wet fly I owned; I fished, and easily caught my second daily limit of trout that day. Then I headed for shore, walked a mile back to our cabin, changed into a third, dramatically different colored set of outer clothing, and returned to the headwaters for MORE trout! "No one said I was lazy…laziness wasn't my sin…I was Hell Bent…on illegally catching more and bigger trout."

Finally! To perfectly punctuate THE END to my highly illegal activity, my day, and my fishy fishin story; a polite Senior Game Warden, possibly tipped off by a nosy nearby fisherman, who had observed me catching and stringering up my FIRST six trout, walked over to check me out. Checked out my license, checked my equipment, checked my daily limit, AND asked to check my mysterious trout-attracting nymph. "OK" said I! But! At the exact moment, the moment the ultra-polite game warden approached for a chat, my black nymph was drifting fifteen feet down in Beefeater clear spring water. I swallowed hard, allowing my wet nymph to sink as deep as possible in the gin, and THEN set about complying with any and every suggestion the genteel old game warden made. When all else appeared to be perfectly in order, The Warden politely repeated himself; asking again to check my fly.

Everything the Old Warden asked me to do was standard operating procedure for game wardens at Bennett Springs. Over the years I had observed dozens of wardens conduct dozens of similarly polite, and sometimes NOT so polite, shakedowns. A dozen-dozen times I had personally observed fishermen being busted for using lures in the Flys Only section; or natural baits in the Artificial Lures Only section; two of the most common offenses in the park. Fishermen routinely stood around snack bars and cafes talking about the risk involved in using the wrong bait in the wrong area. Undoubtedly one reason I found the concept of upgrading bait so thrilling. And! Of course that explains the prevailing necessity for Scott and me concealing the fishin worms in our shirt pockets. It was routine to be checked out regarding regulations, bait related items, fishin tackle functions; especially for proper lures, baits, or flies within proper sections of the crowded stream. But! I still swallowed hard. I was stuck. I had moments before hooked on an extra-large chunk of gooey, bloody, night crawler belly. In my racing mind I imagined the big worm glowing red and blinking "LOOK HERE" to the suspicious game warden! Sure my guilt showed like white rice in black beans; certain my felonious heart sparkled like a big diamond in a small goat's ass; convinced my pounding heart sounded like Edgar Allen Poe's butchered but still thumping heart under the floorboards in "A Telltale Heart"; I winced while also complying.

Anyway; the Old Gentleman Warden asked me to reel up my line so he could verify the legality of my fly; "Everything else had checked out A-OK!" And reeling up is precisely what I was proceeding to do; knowing full well my jig was up! Pardon the pun. But! God DOES protect fools. On the slightest first crank of my reel, a gigantic rainbow trout clamped down hard on my ugly glob of fly and swam away like a WW II runaway torpedo; running deep and far away from me, deep and far away from the Good Game Warden, and hopefully deep and far away from me getting caught with blood on my worm. Alternatively; I hoped the big trout had chomped down soooooo hard on my luscious morsel of REAL food, had swallowed my fly so far down into its trout gullet, NO ONE this side of a skilled CSI pathologist would be capable of retrieving or recognizing my Natural Bait as having once-upon-a-time been living, juicy night crawler.

That's exactly what happened! Mr. Deep Throat swallowed my incriminating worm, and there was NO CSI pathology! Meantime; no matter how hard I tried; "and I DID try"; I couldn't loose the freakishly big, deep running, trout; "a frisky fish that eventually tired and swam to the surface." Demonstrating the speed and nimble dexterity of thickening molasses on a cold duck hunting day, I finished reeling in my oversized trophy trout; knowing its trouty mouth would be awash in fishin worm guts and raw worm hide. But not so! Not that day. The game warden looked over my big trout, checked out my roughed up and freshly cleaned-and-gleaned empty wet fly, and handed back my trophy. Offering double entendre with his final words of encouragement, The Man simply said; "Good luck Son! You may need it someday."

By sunset that same day Good Buddy Scott, Tagalong Ted, God Son Ed, and I were Columbia bound. We stopped twice to retrieve TWO stashed ice chests FULL of incredibly illegal fresh-caught trout; "something approaching one hundred." Our group's legal possession limit was forty-eight; "Louisiana Folks might argue seventy-two"; "three days fishing times four fishermen…times six trout per day!" But! In spite of our wicked ways and many distractions, the four of us made it home to Columbia in time to celebrate at our favorite campus watering hole; lift a mug to our sweet victory over The Man!

"Good Buddy Scott and I NEVER told our less-inclined-to-debauchery, but quite capable, and way more honest, Brothers our deadly secret regarding scurrilous deep pocket fishin worm methods used at Bennett. "Hope they read this book?"

Chapter Five

Iron Bottom Bay Monster

From the halls of Montezuma to the shores of Tripoli; for more than two hundred years US Marines have been sent around the world to...fight our country's battles...in the air...on land...and sea. Once upon a time I was one of those Marines. I too was sent...to far off lands in sunny tropic scenes. And while accomplishing the NOT enviable tasks of remaining above ground and NOT assuming room temperature; while trying to NOT be killed dead by slant-eyed, fish eating, little Gooksters trying to put a ten cent Chi-Com bullet in my overly aggressive Ugly American ass; I did a few interesting things besides dodge sudden death and avoid grizzly destruction. And while surviving was our primary goal; "foremost on our minds and not as easily accomplished as one might erroneously conclude"; we also managed to carve out scraps of time for pleasure. So! In an effort to relax, I took my fair share of time OFF, to enjoy a few pleasant distractions. Healthy distractions like scuba diving and deep sea fishin in sparsely inhabited waters off the coast of Thailand and Viet Nam; ditto fishin and snorkeling in Pacific waters off the coast of Okinawa (Japan). Enjoyed several waterborne pleasures; did things I had never done; and in the process, caught or killed some strange fish I couldn't identify. And then? Well then we ate what we caught and wondered why entrepreneurs back in The World[1] didn't commercialize the culinary delights we were enjoying. In short; we did what we could, when we could, to shorten our time overseas; enjoyed life a little whenever possible. One of my personal philosophies; "Much can be said for finding treasure where no one routinely looks." I can't remember exactly who said that, so I'll claim it. Following

---

[1]Footnote: The World was a generic term. Used by Viet Nam era GIs, meaning any fondly remembered place back in the USA. In context, generally NOT meant as a reference to planet earth; more accurately meaning somewhere IN America far-FAR away from the Godforsaken Hell Hole GIs were at the moment experiencing in their personal corner of war torn Viet Nam. A common euphemism uniquely used to articulate and address GI's real time, then and there, on-the-spot, feelings of separation and loneliness brought on by their Tour of Duty serving in The Nam...while missing The World.

here are a few fishin stories I was sober enough to recall.

Not long after arriving overseas I found myself in the part-time working, part-time playing, full-time pleasant company of our rifle company's (250 Marines) gifted, motivated, highly decorated First Sergeant. First Sergeants in the Marines live life on its leading edge. First Sergeants constantly stand on the threshold of achieving God-like status; "Or dying while trying." One or two well-performed Tours of Duty as a Marine First Sergeant and a man could write his own ticket; "Provided there WAS life after The Corps?" Even Generals looked up to and admired First Sergeants. My first company First Sergeant was Portuguese; "We called him Top Honujas." Not merely ethnically Portuguese, our company First Sergeant immigrated to the US from Portugal as a child. As far back as Top could remember, his ancestors were either fishermen or farmers; "What else?" When Top Honujas (pronounced 'On-You-Us' with a silent 'H' and affectionately bastardized to "On-Your-Ass" by his subordinates) discovered I was a tobacco farmer's son AND avid fisherman; "who just happened to also be a good Marine officer"; he took an immediate liking to me. "Farmer...Fisherman...Good Marine Officer...I arrived with a lock on being accepted by Top."

Based on my agrarian heritage, and our shared passion for providing the best possible situation for our young enlisted Marines, I quickly became a natural fit within Top Honujas' comfort zone. And although enlisted Marines and officer Marines do NOT typically socialize; generically referred to as fraternizing, with specific aspects of fraternizing such as dating, gambling, or partying strictly forbidden; Top Honujas invited me to join him and his lovely Portuguese wife on their private fishin boat on a quiet Saturday morning to go fishin for red snapper and pompano; fishin off the east coast of Okinawa, where our company was staging in route to Nam. After checking it out, Top's and my private trip was deemed to be an acceptable breech of military protocol. First Sergeant Honujas was a highly respected top-notched NCO. I was a capable young officer with a good rap. No one in our mutual chain of command frowned on ONE, highly structured, enlisted Marine and commissioned officer Marine, family-style, fishin trip. "So we did it...and will forever be glad we did. America's gallant military is second to none in the world; replete with hundreds of archaic, seemingly silly-assed, meaningless rules. But! One CANNOT effectively argue with the results!

Anyway; on a balmy spring morning in 1972, Top Honujas, and Top's sweet wife, and I boarded the Honujas' twenty-foot fishin boat, powered by a single outboard motor, and headed due east out of Iron Bottom Bay, Okinawa. Iron Bottom Bay was the unofficial, semi-affectionate name given to the island's large seaport and bay located on the southeast coast of Japan's largest prefecture (state); "Okinawa." The large bay was named Iron Bottom Bay following fierce WW II battles fought there in 1945. So many US warships were sunk in the bay by Japanese Kamikaze pilots, the sea floor was said to be littered wall-to-wall with iron; ruined hulls of sunken US ships. Top Honujas knew where he was going and I was pleased to be going with him. Top had been stationed on Okinawa for three years and was qualified to lead our intimate party on its weekend fishin expedition. As incentive to go, Top promised we would definitely catch fish; "And…We sure as Hell did!" We caught and dragged home a ton of fish; the majority of which I was forced to ask Top to identify. But fishin is fishin; part instinct, part experience, part luck. I had plenty of all three; even if not entirely familiar with the venue or species we were pursuing.

Forty minutes of cap-blowing-off-your-head boating towards the rising sun; the actual sun, the bright orb rising in the morning sky, NOT the Japanese sun depicted on their fallen WW II battle flags; and Top Honujas cut the powerful outboard and ordered all hands, me and Top's lovely Portuguese wife, whose name I cannot recall, to prepare to fish. "Career Marines like Top often have difficulty stowing or staying away from using their command voice…have trouble relaxing…even in social situations. Top's barked command to prepare to fish a prime example." All our fishin equipment was provided by Top; including a Duke's mixture of fresh baits. We used large circle hooks the size of a quarter and tied on four, one-ounce bell-shaped sinkers. We fished straight down, sixty feet straight down; "Later on…nearly one hundred feet…down!"

Other than one isolated day in 1970 off the coast of Virginia, spent trying hard to NOT heave up my freshly eaten lunch, I had never fished saltwater; "There wasn't much saltwater fishing goin on back home in Platte County Missouri." My one and only 1970 excursion into the briny world of saltwater fishin punctuated by members of our charter party setting a cumulative boat record for the grand total number of times we vomited. Also remembered for the empty creel we did NOT fill while chasing marlin off Virginia's turbulent east coast. Told later by our unembarrassed Charter Captain that our Virginia Foursome's 1970 results were TYPICAL; "told later…AFTER paying our Captain for a long sobering day awash in our own vomit!"

"As result of my ONLY saltwater trip out on the deep blue sea…tryin to catch somethin big…my reticent attitude…bordering on skepticism…must have shown? Top seemed compelled to promise me surefire results. And…as one would expect…Top was correct."

As our morning progressed, bobbing about just off the coast of Okinawa in the deep blue Pacific, I picked up on a few tricks of the trade; was quickly able to hold my own when it came to baiting my hook and getting the baited hook back down to the "fish strike zone" designated by Top. Interesting to me that we did NOT fish directly on the bottom; heavy weights were required to merely get our baits down into the proper "strike zone" in a hurry; before our baits were ravaged by hoards of less desirable fish feeding several zones above the zone holding our targeted species; red snapper.

Letting down our bait too slowly resulted in losing our bait to piggy perch and rock bass the size of freshwater perch Brother Ben and I caught in creeks and ponds back home. To hook red snapper in the Pacific just off Japan's big island of Okinawa, our threesome was forced to get our bait down fast and hold on tight. "How big were the snapper?" BIG big! The largest caught that day was brought aboard by Top's wife and weighed a frac under ten pounds. I had never before caught a red snapper. I was shocked at the fish's brilliant orange-ish-red color when first brought aboard. The red snapper's bodies were shaped like that of a largemouth bass; their jerky fighting that of a bluegill. Keep in mind; we were fighting our snapper sixty feet straight down. The able bodied snapper towed around our lead weights as if cotton balls. The action was swift and tiring. Our reels were big, our lines heavy, and our weights enormous; "By Missouri freshwater standards…our lines were unbelievably heavy!" Red snapper were plentiful. After reeling up, safely netting and tossing into our erratically bobbing boat's gigantic ice chest over two-dozen snapper, everyone on board was ready for a snack and breather.

Portuguese fishermen are justifiably proud of their fishin heritage and traditional fisherman rituals; a couple of which I was introduced to that day. For lunch we enjoyed several choices of fresh sushi and sashimi, wrapped in paper-thin dark green seaweed; "Sort of like a fishy burrito." We had Japanese beer, Asahi or Kirin, and red wine orally taken in directly from a genuine leather bota; sweet, dark, heavy, red wine, swilled about in our mouth to wash down pungent cheese served with stiff-as-a-soda-cracker rye bread. And. We enjoyed ample smiles and laughter; mostly regarding my emersion into the world of offshore fishin. My rookie efforts to master proper bota technique became the brunt of good natured teasing; "But…I could not have given a shit less." We caught a trunk load of big snapper and pompano; two primary species sought by local fishermen?

Back at it after a pleasant break, I was introduced to another species. While lowering my bait too slowly I accidentally hooked a small kingfish. Next we caught a variety of mackerel, including Spanish mackerel; then a long skinny fish with a mouth full of needle sharp teeth. Top called it a skipjack; then several bonito. Not long after hooking the small kingfish, hoping a bigger one might happen along, Top decided we should change strategy and concentrate on kingfish; thought perhaps we might even snag a ling. Top told me that he and 'Mrs. Top' had even caught small sailfish while trolling large, fresh baits in the same waters of the brilliantly blue Pacific. Thrilled at the prospect, once again a boy at Christmas, I became and remained breathless for the next hour. Top adjusted our fishin technique by taking off our sinkers, except for one small slip weight. He then had us cast our baits as far away from the boat as possible, while allowing our boat to drift with the wind. Minimum drifting brought near-instant results from a wide range of fish species, seemingly lurking mere feet below the water's calm surface; waiting for our baits to randomly appear in their feeding zone.

Speaking of bait; we used fresh-dead bait prepared by Top by cutting six-inch sardines into chunks. We also used fresh-dead squid; fresh-dead meant the baits were stone dead, but had never been frozen. We also used fresh-dead shrimp and whole shad about four inches long. Our boat carried NO live bait. Top said live bait was expensive, hard to keep alive, and totally unnecessary. "Top was right about everything else...why would I question his theories about bait?" It didn't seem to matter what bait we tossed over the side, fish of some variety would snatch it up and race off on a wild tear; usually before we could settle in to relax.

And then IT happened. "Yes...IT!" If you've read any of my short stories you may have anticipated there would be an IT. I had switched back to using four ounces of weight and streaming out miles of line towards the bottomless depths of the blue Pacific in a solitary effort to catch a BIG red snapper; "Bigger than Mrs. Top's big red snapper."

"You're free to choose your own poison (bait or method)...Sir"; so said Top.

One technique I was required to master was the ability to precisely let out the correct amount of line; "without going all the way to the bottom." Have I explained why? "Snags." Top and Mrs. Top got it correct ten times out of ten; me, about half that. Proper technique involved allowing heavily weighted line to freewheel off the reel, at a steady but controlled pace, for a designated count; say five to seven seconds, depending on the targeted depth. Top did the counting for everyone. One of the first things every Marine sergeant MUST learn is how to sound out a steady, rhythmic count or cadence; second nature to Marine sergeants the day they get their stripes. "Ever see a squad or platoon of marching Marines in a movie? Who do you think is doing all that smooth... rhythmic...almost musical counting? SERGEANTS!"

Anyway; left to my own selfish intentions, and freshly acquired saltwater fishing skills, I had been doing fairly well. That's when I decided to quit trying for small kingfish and resume my pursuit of deeper feeding snapper.

That's when IT happened.

However; four to five times just prior to IT happening; in spite of Top's excellent coaching; I HAD inadvertently struck bottom. A difficult feat to accomplish I was told; in most of the places we fished, the Pacific was many fathoms deep. But! I did manage to strike bottom four to five times, and the results were predictable; I became hopelessly snagged. Top would smile, look me in the eye, and quietly say; "Stop a little sooner Sir; "Count your line out a little more carefully Sir"; "Watch your rod tip...keep it up...Sir"; Top would have bitten off his talented tongue before addressing me as anything other than "Lieutenant" or "Sir". Anyway; when IT happened, IT wasn't what my friendly Portuguese fishin hosts were expecting; nor was IT what I thought was happening; not while IT was happening!

On my sixth incorrectly timed descent of fresh snapper bait towards the Pacific bottom, several previous trips down resulting in my hook becoming hopelessly snagged ON the bottom, while I timidly awaited another respectful ass chewing from Top, something entirely different and totally unexpected happened; "IT happened!" The bottom of the ocean, onto which I had apparently become snagged for the sixth time, suddenly moved. Then moved again; then really took off; moving with what Marines call all deliberate speed; "A euphemistic way of saying hauling ass in one given direction." Even a landlubber like me was able to deduce the significance of the steady overwhelmingly powerful tug at the far end of my tightening line. Something big and unidentified had chomped down on my bait and was in the steadfast act of swimming three thousand miles east, to Honolulu. After convincing Top that I wasn't snagged again, and that something alive was indeed hauling ass with my hook, line and sinker; "my little girl squeals of joy and amazement a dead giveaway"; even salty dog Top's face lit up. Mrs. Top cast a quick knowing glance in Top's direction, and then back in mine, and our boatload of smiling fisherpersons was off on a fish fight!

All three of us were using heavy rods, rigged with forty-pound test line and thin wire leaders. The wire leaders protected our lines against rocks, corral, and undersea entanglements unique to the area; "Entanglements like sunken WW II ships and crashed planes littering that particular area of the sea floor." Our sturdy saltwater rigs were plenty heavy enough to handle fish considerably larger than any we had caught.

When IT happened, there was little need for me to set the hook; my heavy lead sinkers accomplished the trick. The unidentified something snagged on the far end of my heavy line set out swimming due east; apparently trying its best to carry my baited hook all the way to Mainland, USA! But! I instinctively set the hook, anyway. And when I did, the yet to be identified sea critter REALLY took off and the fight was really on; "The final outcome yet to be determined!"

Fishermen, real fishermen; "not people who occasionally go fishing...but real fishermen"; know instinctively when fish fighting stakes have been raised. No one ever needs to explain that fundamental concept to real fishermen. I've known plenty of real fishermen. And although at that time in my life I may not have qualified as a real fisherman; no one needed to explain to me that I had a real fish fight on my hands. Without question, Top was a real fisherman; he immediately got it. The instant Top realized that I had hooked a sizable predator fish, he reeled in our boat's other lines and quickly hauled on board our floating drift anchor. "So!" What was it I had hooked down there in the deep blue? No one knew; least of all me.

Lt. JNP in uniform... Even though I was a mere Lt.... our company First Sgt. took a liking to me . . . He was a Portugese fisherman's son. (1972)

"Except for Fine Folks from Flor-a-DUH"; once most of us learn certain simple skills, those skills survive in our minds for a lifetime. Simple stuff; like riding a bike, swimming, or simultaneously walking and chewing bubble gum. By that time in my life, fighting and landing a big fish comfortably fit on my list of such learned skills. By 1972 I had caught several big fish; a ten pound channel cat, a twenty pound carp, even a rapscallion alligator gar longer than my Dad's leg. I knew how to fight big fish. The yet to be identified fish that had apparently gobbled up my fresh-dead snapper bait, inadvertently dropped too deep in the royal blue Pacific, WAS unquestionably a big fish; "Assuming it was a fish?" Early on, during what turned into a protracted struggle, I suggested to Top that whatever was hooked on my line might NOT even be a fish? That it might instead be one of the US nuclear subs we had spotted earlier that morning passing below our fishing boat.

"That's right. Really! Straight

down…fifty feet down…perfectly visible in the clear sea water…hauling ass like a Mo Fo with its tail on fire…a large black-black US nuclear sub…moving perpendicular to our boat…hauling ass out to sea. Top said he and Mrs. Top often observed US submarines plying Iron Bottom Bay just off Okinawa's busy coast! OR! Since we WERE in fact fishin just off the coast of what was once again, by May 1972, a sovereign Japanese island…Maybe I had hooked…Godzilla?"

Heave back, reel like a man gone mad; heave back, reel like a man gone mad; heave back…reel like a…; on and on and on…and on…it went. After nearly an hour Top informed me that I was winning. One thing, among many, that young lieutenants; "men like me"; repeatedly had hammered into our egotistical, thick, officer skulls was to listen to our First Sergeants; "Especially if and when our First Sergeant was telling us we were winning…or losing…a battle." I was happy to be winning, but failed to realize I was winning. Another thirty minutes, my adrenalin rush strength had all but faded. But! My BIG quarry, whatever it was, was slowly giving up the ghost TOO; allowing its fishy-self to be inched towards the surface! "Coming surface-ward...You know…UP! I'm sayin the big bastard…Whatever the 'F' it was…Was comin UP…Comin my way!"

Near about the time of day Top had originally proposed as quittin time; when we should have been heading back towards the territorial waters of Japan; the assailant of my misplaced snapper bait finally rose close enough to the clear ocean surface for everyone onboard to get a quick glimpse. "Whoa Momma…Whatever it was…It was B-I-G!"

Top thought it was a giant grouper; "a jewfish." But Top wasn't sure; not at first glance. But! Whatever it was, it didn't matter; it WAS B-I-G! More tugging, more reeling, more sweating, more frenetic zinging out of whining monofilament against the old reel's overworked, ancient bearings, and the big, fat fish breeched; rose to the surface of the indigo Pacific and rolled over on its fishy left side. It was indeed…a HUGE jewfish. "Don't you just love saying…jewfish? Jewfish has such a poetic ring to it… jewfish…jewfish…jewfish?" To me the big jewfish resembled a fifty pound bluegill; only a different color. As Top hoisted the big jewfish aboard, shouts of joy and laughter collectively escaped our happy trio; unaware we had been a tense happy trio.

Using a short wooden handled gaff and a wide mouthed oversized dip net, Top gathered his real fisherman wits and my flopping monster fish in one grunting fell scoop. By far the biggest fish I had EVER caught; "unfortunately we never weighed it!" We couldn't! We had no scale on board. And! Our happy trio was tiptoeing around local but vague Nipponese fishin regulations.

Top reassured me that my fish, our fish, THE fish, would easily go well-over fifty pounds, maybe sixty! Then Top gutted the big sow and cut her into ice chest manageable pieces. "Top Sergeants in the Marine Corps know how to do everything. . . are prepared to fight any fight. . . win any battle. . . with whatever tools they have on hand. . . Marine tradition as old and time tested as The Corps itself."

I will never forget my Saturday morning out there fishin in deep, unsullied waters off the coast and due east of Okinawa's Iron Bottom Bay; sacred water previously fought over to the death by Japan's Fallen and America's Greatest Generation. And. Not one Marine from our company of two hundred fine young Marines went hungry that lucky weekend. Top hosted an old fashioned fish fry; did everything exactly like he always did; first class and right on time; "God Bless our Nation's military and their spouses!"

Besides fishing ... **First Sgt. Honujas** and I shared another passion ... taking care of our Marines. (1972)

Chapter Six

Searching For Viet Cong... Catching Viet Cats

No one who participated ever said being a combatant during the Viet Nam War was all pain and suffering; OR totally without pleasure. And. "Nobody ever needed to repeat themselves...ask twice...when inviting me to go fishin." Two historical facts of the matter that pleasantly converged when Lt 'Bo' Schowalter, our battalion's (800 to 1000 Marines) weapons platoon (50 to 60 Marines) commander, told me he was going fishin. Told me he had hooked up with a Papa San (old fart Vietnamese male villager with few or no teeth) and a Mamma San (female equivalent of a Papa San) who had agreed to take Bo and two buddies fishin. "Once invited...I was IN...like Flynn."

Lt Schowalter, Bo, was a fun loving farm boy from Indiana who happened to also know a lot about Marine Corps heavy weapons; "Important weapons to every Marine Corps fighting unit...crew served machine guns and mortars...good stuff we used ever day for pulling our ass outta tight cracks...stuff that really hammered the Gooks in a tough fire fight." Bo knew all there was to know about heavy weapons because during his ten year climb through the ranks; rising from the lowest enlisted rank of Private First Class up to the entry level commissioned officer rank of Lieutenant; he had learned every important detail about every infantry weapon currently deployed within the Marine Corps. After hearing only fractional details regarding Lt Schowalter's fishing plans, I jumped aboard with both sore feet; "My feet actually were sore!" I had recently been peppered with shrapnel by a VC[1] mortar round that landed smack dab in the middle of our tent; destroying a hardback tent, where ten seconds earlier, six of us bored-out-of-our-frickin-minds young officers had been sitting in our private O-Club in the jungle playing nickel and dime poker. "It was the Fourth of July 1972...most of our battalion was enjoying a day off from The War...but no one bothered tellin the VC."[1]

Actually; I was pretty badly hobbled up. Gimping around, serving on

---

[1]Footnote: VC was the common name given to Viet Cong; enemy combatant forces allied with the North Vietnamese in Hanoi.

light duty only, recovering from stitches and suppurating sores on my left foot and ankle that refused to heal; and one tiny but very deep puncture hole on the inside of my right ankle. When the VC mortar barrage first began, I jumped in the nearest fighting hole for cover. I was hit by the third or fourth mortar round that impacted near our battalion headquarters area; mere seconds after the first incoming round destroyed our Officer's Hooch; "Right where we had been playing poker!" To my own detriment, I failed to pull my size eleven bare feet down into the relative safety of the fighting hole; "To safety…along with the balance of my skinny…worm and parasite infested body." Protruding above ground, both my ankles and bare feet were sprayed with buzzing hot shrapnel the size of badly misshapen BBs. Nothing serious mind you; but enough superficial damage done to my tired and tanned hide to warrant light duty only and the unquestioned right to skip many of my routine duties for a few days; "If I wanted to?" Slide out of boring chores and instead go off with Bo on an early morning fishin trip down a little known but world class, mysterious, iconic, exotic, and without question, dangerous river. "The river wasn't dangerous…the VC dwelling along its banks…and hiding out along its shore were dangerous! It was a no brainer."

Tag along with a good buddy to cast a line in legendary catfish holes in the Mekong River; many holes miles wider and fathoms deeper than those of the scenic Missouri River that flowed passed my boyhood home north of Kansas City; or remain behind in camp with little to do, feeling sorry for myself. "It WAS a no brainer." I grew up running the muddy banks of The Mighty Mo; killing, catching, and consuming most anything I could. The Mekong is the longest river in SE Asia; fertile highway to a hundred million hungry Asians; "Forget details…just know this…it's BIG!"

"Would I enjoy going along with Bo? To drop stinking globs of rotting bait into muddy holes on a dark river that seemed the depth of the Pacific…the clean and clear Pacific where earlier that year…prior to my current hot assignment in America's FIRST unending war…I fished for snapper with my Portuguese First Sergeant? Bet your sweet ass I wanted to go! Like I said…It WAS a no brainer!"

The Mekong River is huge where it flows through South Viet Nam; deep, wide, swift, muddy, and filled with more unusual creatures and critters than you can possibly imagine. And! Home to some of earth's largest catfish; "You gotta touch them with your own hands to believe your own eyes!"

Mekong River catfish, giant catfish occasionally shown in TV specials seen these days on Animal Planet or Discovery, are sort of ugly. Which is kind of like saying a pig is sort of porky. But Mekong river cats ARE odd looking; especially about their head and shoulders; "except…catfish don't really have shoulders." Mekong cats have downward looking eyes; eyes that appear to be NOT in the correct position on their flattish heads; eyes set too far down passed the center line of their wide, grinning faces.

Like most of their European and American cousins, Mekong cats are voracious bottom feeders. However! Mekong cats run big; XL, XXL, even XXXL! They can grow up to fifty pounds in a few years; juveniles can easily be four feet long and weigh in at fifty pounds. Mommas come ten feet long and six hundred pounds; "ideal candidates for winning the title Biggest Loser on a TV reality show featuring overweight fish. . .instead of overweight pigs!"

After catching one, I kept staring at our first Mekong cat trying to determine what it was about the gaping-mouthed big fish that was so damned odd looking; "even for a catfish?" Finally it dawned on me; our Mekong cat had no whiskers! All catfish I had ever caught or seen or known about in MY sheltered life had each and all sported distinctive cat-like whiskers; "That my friend. . .is why we call them catfish!" Not our big Mekong catfish. No whiskers and no teeth. We could jam our fists in its mouth and get gummed to death. . .but not bitten. Our toothless Papa San guide told Bo and me that Mekong catfish swallow their food whole. . .and let their bulging pregnant looking catfish stomachs do all the work."

Our Euro-Asian-American, ethnically co-mingled, party of seven clustered near the Mekong River in the damp dark of predawn. We set out just after sunrise. Departing downriver from rickety wooden pilings topped with slabs of rotting boards that had been casually flopped crossways over rotting runner boards; a relic in the mist that Papa San referred to as the dock. Leaving our battalion's barbed wire fenced perimeter, a secure non combat area, venturing but a few miles down river; our fishin party was at all times hypothetically within a safe zone. And although perhaps we SHOULD have been, and in another time and place WOULD have been, neither Bo nor I nor our two companions were particularly nervous about being out on the monstrous river in the early morning dark with two virtual strangers serving as our guides. We were traversing a treacherous river, in a hostile jungle environment, 12000 miles from our happy homes back in The World; "But no more nervous or concerned about our personal safety than if we had been fishing Falcon Lake in south Texas too near the dangerous Mexico border?"

Bo Schowalter spoke a fair amount of Highland dialect Vietnamese and got on well with our skinny, toothless, flatlander Papa and Mamma San; who, at that toothless moment, were poling our shallow dugout sampans out into the powerful river's swift current. Bo was in one sampan with Papa San as his personal guide, I was in another with Mamma San as my guide; and a third much larger sampan, manned by a third and noticeably larger-sized and younger male guide, was hauling two of Bo's best Sea Bee buddies; "Sea Bees were special Navy units that performed heavy construction miracles in Viet Nam…good people…around when we needed them…to build shit we helpless Marines needed built. OBTW…I think the larger younger Vietnamese guide may have had a French Foreign Legion Daddy…from back when Din Ben Phu fell to Ho Chi Mien's raging hoards during the late 1950s or early 1960s? Son San was big…strong… light skinned…and appeared to have benefited from hybrid vigor?"

Three boats; "actually rickety shallow-draft narrow-beamed wooden sampans"; outfitted with strange looking petroleum powered outboard motors that sort of resembled a weird version of long-drive-shafted motors seen on modern day swamp craft. All of it guided downstream by hard won native intuition and the hand of the God of Fishing; a good God known to all fishermen the entire world over; a forgiving God undoubtedly present even there in those otherwise God forsaken river hamlets of South Viet Nam. Ours was an eclectic flotilla. Three tiny boats carrying an unlikely burden of four American GI invader-protector servicemen; who, on that quiet day, merely wanted to catch big catfish, drink a few beers, and come evening, be allowed to return upriver with our GI heads still attached to our GI bodies. With the final outcome of all our important GI desires depending, more than anything else, on the political points of view of three Vietnamese owning the opinions; "Our three guides!" Four giant fish-seeking Americans, seen as either savior or slayer; "I kept hoping our guide's politics were NOT ambivalent. Kept hoping our guides did NOT suffer from latent VC tendencies…whose political point of view changed every night come sundown."

But, be that as is may; our trio of floating flotsam, huddled meekly there on three wormy sampans that weren't much more than floating hallowed out logs, was directed on its way and herded downriver by three leathery skinned, mostly naked, bean pole thin, yakkety-yakking, nearly toothless, broadly and incessantly grinning, Vietnamese; one Papa San, one Mamma San, and one throwback genetic misfit Son San who was actually no more than twenty but looked fifty. "Why do toothless people look SOOOOO much older than their actual age?"

Later; during Post Op analysis of our one-of-a-kind day in Nam; Bo and I were unable to decide EXACTLY what our Vietnamese guides were using to power their tiny boat motors; gasoline, kerosene, plutonium? Most likely jet fuel; stolen from our base and mixed with some locally concocted early version of bio-diesel? Fuel many GIs had witnessed being rendered in giant iron kettles; fuel known to contain fat rendered from the flesh of wild creatures killed in the jungle; "After Vietnamese villagers did whatever it was they did with all the inedible parts?" Whatever their fuel was, it smoked like and smelled like burning Marine shit. Scientists tell laypeople that of all human memories, smell is the most enduring. I totally believe that. "Why?" If you've ever had the dire misfortune of smelling burning human shit, large quantities of it, you need not be reminded of the fact that the horrible smell is uniquely one you will NEVER forget.

"While out in the bush...we Marines sat on large boards with big holes cut in them...boards strategically placed over fifty-five gallon oil drums...and then shit into the oil drums...then burned off the resulting oozy mess...every day! Burning out the shit barrels was seriously sorry duty assigned as punishment to misbehaving Marines."

"Our Vietnamese guide's boat motors...ancient outboards the size and shape of your Momma's 1950s Sears home food mixer...tiny motors effectively used to steer our teetering boats downriver...to ineffectively and excruciatingly slowly push our boats back UP river after finishing our big day of big cat fishing...were casting off clouds of low hanging filthy-smelling smoke. Burning, shit-smelling smoke! Returning home that afternoon our progress was so slow...I kept fighting off a strong urge to get out and walk back upriver. And just might have (walked home)...EXCEPT for...big bad ass snakes... deadly booby traps...lurking VC...poisonous punji stakes...ferocious man eating tigers ...quicksand pits the size of Kansas...leeches big as your thumb...non-discriminating hostile natives never particular about who they ate...saltwater crocs thought to be NON indigenous to Nam but seen ever where...and ugly piranhas with teeth like a Macaw parrot! Otherwise...like I said...I might have grown impatient and walked back upriver."

Forty minutes of quiet skulking downriver and our guides pushed our three boats ashore on an elongated sandbar. Just upriver from where broad riffles of chocolate milk broiled up where the huge sandbar disappeared into chalky water; soupy water entirely impenetrable by sunlight. "Our grinning Papa San...Bo and I quickly took to calling him Pedi...short for Pedophile...not original...a common moniker hung on older men in Nam...because many WERE pedophiles...and if they weren't...they could have been. Their culture took a different slant on that tender subject. And! Bo and I called him Pedi because Pedi was way too smiley and attentive to our younger French looking Son San. And. Like many Vietnamese with whom I served...I was never quite able to entirely trust Pedi. OBTW...It goes without saying...If you're busy worrying about your toothless fishing guide dropping you off in the middle of a preplanned VC ambush...it's sortta difficult to kickback and enjoy fishin. But! We four GIs knew that taking a risk was part of the gig when we signed up for our private chartered fishin trip downriver.

And besides…We American GIs WERE…after all…immortal…or so we thought."

Therefore; none of that mattered. From my first day In Country I had been hearing wild stories about local villagers catching huge Mekong catfish; I wanted to catch one, or two, or a dozen. "And by God…Me and Bo…We did it!"

"Our bait?" A wretched, gag-evoking conglomeration of raw meaty effluent; large chunks of some kind of rotting flesh; leftovers from God alone knows what kind of deceased animal? And if my youthful twenty five year old nose was still properly functioning; leftovers that had apparently been gathered straight from local benjo ditches or Vietnamese outhouses. Our grinning, witless-appearing guides said the bait was a crude mixture of pig, duck, and chicken entrails; artistically woven around and upon heavy steel treble hooks the size of a hen egg. "Our guides only appeared witless…they knew exactly what they were doing. But! Remove anyone's teeth and have them smile for you…they appear feckless…AND older than they are!"

I correctly surmised that if we WERE fortunate enough to hook a big catfish, any big fish, our hooks would hold; "Our fish would remain hooked." However! I WAS worried about the tinsel strength of our worn lines. All items used that day; boats, paddles, dip nets, bait canteen, gaff, ice chest, weight scale; were clearly homemade. Except for the rusting old reels; "imagine a reel the size of a Quaker Oats oatmeal box… with a grimy handle attached." Ugly reels, with Chinese writing on the sides; "or it may have been Korean…I'm not sure?" Anyway! Our reels were huge; because our line was large. Line the same gauge as a Nike shoestring; line way bigger than a pencil lead; dark black line frayed throughout; every running foot of its twisted knotty length appearing one moment's notice from giving up the ghost as line and fraying into a million threads to be blown away in the sultry, tropical wind; hopelessly large line unspun by hand, off screeching ugly reels. Two golf ball sized weights were attached at the very end of the knotted old line. And just above the dangling weights, one large hook; held in place by an eighteen inch long drop line rigged in just a certain way so the heavy weights carried our baits directly to the bottom, while allowing the bait ball to waffle back and forth in the river current and bump off the silty river bottom. All the while, all of it held in place in the swift river; its powerful current dangerous in even the deepest eddies and holes.

Keep in mind; I was forced to pick up details of our day's activities secondhand through Buddy Bo. Bo interpreted information given him by our guides; interpreted that which was discernable to a farm boy from Corn Belt, Indiana. Between Bo's Corn Belt dialect and my Tobacco Road dialect there was plenty of common ground; so I got it. But! The total sums of what really went down that day, important subtleties, were forever lost with our toothless guides, this story subject to Country Boy errors of omission and misunderstanding; "But Bo got all he could and I got most of it...I think?"

Meanwhile Bo's perpetually smiling Sea Bee buddies, two good men, seemed overly content. Seemed lost in a world of their own; seemed unperturbed, even disinterested, in learning the subtle what fors and whys regarding what it was our party had come there to do; "Catch big Mekong River catfish."

"In retrospect I can't tell you why I bothered asking...just curious I guess... and be damned if I intended to keep trying...but at first I WAS curious about a cloud of light smoke billowing our way on the jungle breeze...carrying a sweet aroma of burning fall leaves...leaving me wondering aloud if the smoke had anything to do with the slack demeanor and woefully laidback countenance of Bo's Navy buddies? I quietly decided that making aromatic smoke was perhaps something Bo's friends routinely did while warming their morning coffee? I had never before met Bo's two Navy Sea Bee Buddies, and after that day I never again saw either of them. Later on that year I heard that one of Bo's Sea Bees was blown to bits by a booby trapped five hundred pound bomb; killed instantly driving his small bulldozer while digging a drainage ditch in an effort to help pacify one of the local friendly villages.

"The sad fact that Bo's Navy Friend died trying to help local Vietnamese villagers ...who by 1972 were supposed to have been Americanized...to the point the villagers could takeover and fight their own damned war...so we Ugly Americans could pack our noisy trash and head home...wasn't a whole lot different from what America is currently trying to do in Iraq or Afghanistan...as I sit here humbly writing this humble fishin story ...glad to be alive and in one piece...sorry as HELL we're in the shit again!"

"But back to fishin!" Bo's guide and my guide had tied their two small boats to the same fallen mahogany tree; our two boats located fifty yards across the narrow sand bar from our party's third boat; thereby hindering practical conversation between all three boats. But! Stoked or not, laidback or worse, Bo's Navy Sea Bee buddies struck oil first; their boy-like yelling scaring away every squealing monkey and squawking jaybird in the Mekong River Valley when a twenty pound Mekong River catfish came flopping over the low beam of their wobbly sampan. From where Bo and I sat, the Sea Bee's catfish looked bigger than any catfish I had ever personally caught. Growing up back in Missouri I had seen and touched a few monster catfish; mostly flatheads and blue cats my Dad's fishin buddies caught on trotlines out of the Missouri River.

But! Once Bo and I saw that it could be done we intensified our effort. Being competitive, it didn't seem right that pot smoking, soft-bodied, Navy boys could catch a big catfish while two concentrating, tuff as Hell, Marines couldn't. But! That was a mild incongruency we changed in favor of Marine occupied boats. I hooked up next; a big catfish thirty inches long; big around as a badly bloated, road killed, raccoon; fatter than an overfed slaughter pig. Our guides said my catfish would go about twenty pounds. The Mekong catfish were ugly. But then, as they say; "Beauty IS in the eye of the beholder!" What I really mean is, the Mekong River cats didn't look like, not exactly like, our channel cats or bullheads back home. They most resembled flatheads. But Mekong River catfish heads were flatter and their mouths bigger; "If that's possible?"

The Mekong cat is known for phenomenally rapid growth; several pounds per year during favorable conditions. Perhaps an unusual and significant food source HAD recently been contributing to our big fish's daily diet? The Easter Offensive of 1972, second largest enemy offensive of the ten year Viet Nam War, was mere months in history's rear view mirror? Whatever those big catfish we caught had been eating, it agreed with them; they were fat and healthy and as strong as any fighting fish I had ever caught. By quitting time that day our three boat armada had caught a total of fourteen whopping catfish. Our biggest of the day turned out to be our first of the day. The one Bo's stoned Navy Buddies hauled aboard before lighting up another unidentified smoke. Another sweet smelling smoke rising from their tiny boat, the Sea Bee's production of landed catfish dramatically dropped!"

Back at the dock, that had somehow managed to remain upright and intact for the duration of our day while out there fishin; our guides cleaned our yearling-hog-sized fish. Bo and I gave away ninety percent of our fresh filets to our guides and local villagers. But Bo dragged back to our battalion area, twenty pounds of iced down filets; filets which were in reality irregular shaped, pink salmon colored, chunks of fresh catfish flesh the size of baseballs. Dragged the slightly greasy, too warm fish flesh back to our Officer's Mess; "a hardback tent similar to our Officer's Club tent blown up on The Fourth of July." Bo had one of his Navy Corpsman buddies, a man who had years earlier served as a Navy cook, fry up fresh catfish for everyone's evening chow. Next, Bo's friend, the former cook turned Corpsman, managed to come up with necessary ingredients to bake slightly dry cornbread; "Like our Mommas baked back home…only not as good." Field Marines, especially Marines fortunate enough to have Navy Sea Bees attached to their combat unit, improvise anything imaginable. Conjuring up the correct ingredients for a down home, backwoods, fish fry was no challenge. "Honestly…In spite of trepidations brought on by watching the greasy looking catfish being butchered by filthy hands. . .the cleaned catfish's too warm. . .too long trip back to our battalion area. I told Bo that his fish was the best I EVER ate!"

Mekong River ... fertile highway to millions of Southeast Asians ... dangerous as rivers go. (1972)

Chapter Seven

Swimming With Fishes

"Not all things hunted are taken with a gun." "Not all fish caught are taken with hook." Someone who really knows their stuff wrote that; actually it was me. I opine; "Quite the contrary." One of my most memorable fishin experiences didn't involve hook, line, NOR sinker; nor boat, nor guide, nor net either for that matter. Merely stamina, courage, swimming skill, and a mega dose of youth inspired idiocy and foolhardiness. Having been young once and invulnerable to mortality, we Marines did a lot of things we should never have attempted. Sometimes we got lucky and came back from our adventure in one piece; sometimes not. "In this war story…I'm specifically NOT referring to combat."

During Tours of Duty in SE Asia, it was SOP for US Servicemen to be awarded ten to twenty days off duty. The vast majority of us traveled to pre-approved locations to enjoy a break. The term R&R, an efficient acronym for Rest and Relaxation, was a popular practice that allowed weary combatants a few days off to travel OUT of the war zone; go to a place of their choosing for a little Rest and Relaxation; join a spouse, girlfriend, or significant other, often in the combined company of fellow combatants. It was a new war fighting concept conceived during Viet Nam. There have been alternative versions applied piecemeal to modern conflicts, including Dessert Storm and our prolonged inveiglement in Iraq and Afghanistan. In Viet Nam, depending on duties and unit, there were different rules, regulations, and restrictions; but the concept applied across the board to all ranks and every branch of service.

When my R&R rolled around, I was an infantry officer attached to a Marine air unit serving in northern Thailand; "Odd Huh?" My unit's primary mission was to provide security for the planes, pilots, and support people of the air unit; protect the people and their mountain of flight paraphernalia. The planes my Marines protected were fighter bombers; the pilots were flying missions over North Viet Nam during the Easter Offensive; named after an enemy offensive begun ON Easter Sunday.

When fighting wound down to a mild roar, support personnel in units like mine were allowed to take delayed R&Rs. For a variety of forgotten reasons, a friend and I chose to celebrate our mutual R&R by driving one of our rifle company's old jeeps two hundred miles due south to Bangkok; capital city of Thailand. Other buddies were also heading south to Bangkok during that same time frame; several Marines from our unit were just returning from the mystical ancient city. A huge tropical city, that offered a Marine ever thang he could possibly desire; ever thang available at dirt cheap prices. "Five dollars bought horny Marines ever thang they could conjure up in their stressed out minds...and I DO mean EVER THANG! Got it?"

Several other lieutenants and captains; "men my age and generally members of my immediate peer group"; had invited their young horny wives, isolated back in The World, to join them for R&R in Bangkok. Never one to be outdone if I had an option, I invited my Bride to join ME in Bangkok. "That's right! First Wife Jen-Jen...who would someday become EX Jen-Jen...flew halfway round the globe to Thailand for my R&R!"

Told of it, First Wife Jen-Jen gladly agreed to join me in a South Pacific Gala. With her version of a perpetual smile on her Missouri tanned face, the two of us met at Bangkok's International Airport, and were off on one of our marriage's greatest TRUE adventures. "She and I...Ex Jen-Jen and I...had a lot of adventures...unfortunately many stories describing our best adventures were either mostly untrue or tarnished with embellishment. And...God help us...Ex Jen-Jen and I are the only surviving witnesses!"

First Wife Jen-Jen arrived on time and as planned. She and I quickly hooked up with and traveled around Thailand in the pleasant company of several other young officers and perpetually smiling wives. "I had never seen such a concentration of far away stares and whimsical smiles...reflecting such satisfaction and mass contentment... as seen every morning in our randomly gathered entourage of housewives visiting their husbands. Wives smiling at themselves...for so blatantly smiling... husbands smiling because for the first time in

Sunburned ... dehydrated ... but smilling and sippin a cold one on the way back to Patyia Beach. (1972)

months…we felt like smiling!"

After doing Bangkok and its surrounding confines; after trying out everything worth trying; including dozens of dips in a Champagne colored sparkling pool, horseback riding on massive black steeds recently imported from one of Europe's finest riding stables, consuming mountainous portions of fine Pacific Rim dining, nodding off to half a dozen native bonfire serenades, AND soiling several sets of the cleanest, whitest, finest smelling bed sheets any Marine ever soiled in his young stud muffin life; me and my group of Marine buddies and our glib wives decided we were ready to seek higher adventure; move on to greater challenges in South Thailand.

Several R&R-ing Marines decided to hire taxis and travel two hundred additional miles south to Patyia Beach, Thailand. Patyia Beach was a well known resort area located near the mid point of the long, narrow, south-stretching, peninsula of Thailand; a tropical beach resort renowned for sugar-white sand and gin-clear deep water; a paradise teaming with fish, fauna, and beautiful indigenous wildlife. "Informed of Patyia Beach's sultry tropical charm and ancient exotic lure…I had no choice…I was bound to go."

Hotel accommodations at Patyia Beach were a step down from world class suites initially enjoyed in Bangkok; "Hotel suites that cost us twenty bucks American…per night!" But local scenery and mystical magic of the remote tropical hideaway more than made up for forfeited big city atmosphere. WOW is a fair summation of First Wife Jen-Jen's Missouri-bound first look and feel of Patyia Beach. The scenery and setting were Bogart and Bacall, perspiring in 1930s Africa; Hemingway and Roosevelt busting skulls and charging up hills in turn of the century Cuba; "That would be Teddy…during the early 1900s…NOT Franklin D forty years later…for Slow Folks from Flor-a-DUH!"

Seven married couples from our loose coalition of ten couples in Patyia Beach decided to join our group's next survivor's challenge. Seven Marine officers and seven smiling spouses, signed up for an all day excursion; "be boated by private charter out to a tiny, isolated, offshore, coastal island, for an entire day…where we could go snorkel or scuba diving." Forty years later in 2010, Nurse-Wife Peg calmly said…No Shit Buck Wheat; "as if it should have been obvious to me back in 1972"; but I was genuinely shocked that not one wife in our friendly group wanted to participate in snorkeling or diving? However! Seven out of seven wives absolutely DID beg to tag along for the day to enjoy the hidden promise of adventure available on an uninhabited South Pacific paradise? Pristine, tropical wonderfulness, said to be totally uninhabited, believed to be mostly safe; estimated by toothless guides to be approximately ten miles off Thailand's rugged, jungle covered, mainland;

a bare speck of sand ten empty sea miles due east of South Thailand; ten miles out in a salty coastal sea, crossed here and there by sampans, only; in deep ocean, near the extreme western rim of the Greater South Pacific; a wide open space thousands of miles due west of Honolulu, Hawaii.

Men Folk were told our boat ride out would take two hours; but that there would be interesting things along the way for wives to observe. Fearing I might miss something unusual, I never batted an eye during the two hour boat ride out; a routine, pleasant ride out to sea; our destination. A ten acre spec of white sand covered here and there by green palms, creeping vines, and dense prickly undergrowth; "To me...our tiny islet paradise looked much the same as the lowlands of Viet Nam."

Our grinning-guileless-guides told us that small, pot bellied pigs, hairless monkeys, and a few harmless, toothless lizards were the islet's primary and only known inhabitants; "No SIR...No snakes stay he-ah...SIR!" I wasn't certain about the accuracy of the grinning guide's reassuring information; but I didn't care. I intended to spend my day IN the water off the seaward coast of the islet.

One thing about our anticipated adventure made me slightly nervous. Our guided boats, all seven of our guided boats, immediately after arriving on the pristine beach of the isolated islet, announced they were departing! That's right, heading back to Patyia Beach the minute we fourteen paying clients stepped OFF their rickety little boats and ON to the white beach. We Marine Officers; seven adult He Men; each of us in our own way individually responsible for the lives, safety, and general wellbeing of our lovely wives; were collectively shocked to discover that the guided charter boats were NOT remaining with us ON the isolated island. Someone in our convivial group immediately offered up that we had been told by our hotel that such would be the procedure for our Charter Captains; that our grinning guides in their tiny, rickety boats needed to make three round trips to-and-from different islets per morning, and three return round trips per afternoon, in order to eke out a meager living hauling tourists out to sea; "Hopefully not on a one-way ride!"

Even though we paid in advance, feeling a tad shaken down by the nonchalant backhanded method of our guides disclosing their intentions, I remained confident that our tiny boats would return. The entire booking operation promoting guided day trips to offshore islets had been hotel sanctioned; it was economically imperative to the hotel that NO tourist ever be abandoned offshore or become shark bait. Even though a mild ripple of concern swept over First Wife Jen-Jen when our charter boat actually departed, I was comfortable enough to remain. "However!" One embarrassed lieutenant and his fiery redheaded pregnant wife; "responding to a howling teary eyed pregnant wife"; were not so comfortable! Seeing our tiny charter boats packing up and preparing to leave; the newly-wed, recently-bred, definitively-red (faced) couple from Chicago, could barely wait to depart back to Patyia Beach on their returning charter.

So now we were SIX couples! Twelve young married people; six cases of cold beer; six bulging picnic baskets; six perpetually smiling wives. Six separate couples; who had formed into one, cohesive, randomly constituted group; a dozen Americans, twelve thousand miles from home, who shared one overriding agenda; "Have a good time on Nowhere Island Thailand...No Matter What!" "Five of six husbands of those who remained...every husband save one...prepared for the day by bringing along snorkeling gear...snorkeling being the primary reason for going to the isolated island?"

"Snorkeling in clean water...like the water we eventually swam in THAT memorable day...water so pristinely clean because it WAS shared with absolutely NO other swimmers...is a thrilling experience difficult to exceed!"

Somewhere along the line, every swimmer in our snorkeling party had learned to use what we called an Australian Sling; a simple three-tined fishing spear permanently attached to a four foot long bamboo pole. The four foot spear pole allowed the cocked spear to be pointed at and silently inched close to targeted fish. Swimming or drifting in close, gently approaching unwary fish, it was difficult to miss; especially difficult to miss unstartled fish. Nearly all fish in the isolated tropical waters where we dived were unstartled fish back in 1972.

Before it was finished, our day out there fishin, afloat in fins and mask, picnicking and frolicking with smiling, scantily clad wives, pretending we were castaways on a speck of South Pacific sand; turned into one of the most exciting days of my sixty-plus years of taking in and absorbing the enormity and greatness of what we sometimes unthinkingly and too nonchalantly refer to as the splendid great outdoors. "Ours was a tropical dream come true...a day to remember!"

Our planning was flawed. There was yet another kicker involved; "besides being abandoned by our charter boats." A salient point that should have, even back then, turned back five-outta-five over zealous young Marines. An agenda item that should have turned away any sane men and stopped us from attempting what amounted to an unreasonable plan. We five snorkeling Marines were expected to perform a four mile swim! "That's right!" Swim two miles to merely arrive at a highly touted coral reef purported to be the best spear hunting grounds up and down the entire, isolated Thai Coast! "You got it!" Swim two MILES before arriving at a site where our party intended to snorkel...for the day!

Unfortunately, up to the very last moment JUST before making what I later called "an oozing departure", no one in our surviving five-man group had actually articulated exactly how looooong our intended swim was going to be. Not until all five over-the-top, iron headed, iron willed, co-participants were standing ankle deep in lapping waves near the pristine beach of our remote Pacific Islet. Not until all five interlopers were standing tall, donning black rubber flippers, easing forward into the surf for our loooooong swim. Not until all five bold swimmers were in the act of departing seaward; our male egos already drowning in unhealthy doses of false male bravado, did anyone ask...How Far? What I meant when I referred to ours as an oozing departure. Although there were those among us inclined to turn back; no one DID! "Faced with a...Well we're here to snorkel ...are we mice or are we men situation...faced with the seductive challenge of...doing what we came to do...we collectively...sort of one-by-one...OOZED ourselves forward into the shallow surf...maybe like lemmings?"

"Allow me to make myself perfectly clear on one point...we should NOT have gone. Today...somehow magically given back my twenty-five-year-old Marine hard body...in perfect physical condition...but being blessed with experience and maturity...I would NEVER repeat such folly. I POSITIVELY would have taken OFF my flippers and face mask and joined Wife Jen-Jen on the sunny white beach...contenting myself to making a husbandly effort to keep a perpetual smile on HER pretty young face. I promise...In retrospect...I would NOT have gone swimming...Wouldn't think of it!"

Before readers of my true fishin story erroneously conclude there was anything approaching a disastrous conclusion to our day; allow me to quickly say this. Number one; there were few sharks around. We saw no sharks the entire day. We saw nothing large enough to eat anyone. The greatest threat to any of us experiencing real harm was perpetrated by us; five totally fit young men! Number two; five future male contributors to America's eventual decline into "Idiocracy" DID return safely at the end of our too looooooooong, adventure-filled day. This is a TRUE story! In my humble author's opinion; "humbled by a million true outdoor adventures"; a good true story is only worth sharing if told as things actually occurred. Mix in more than occasional tidbits of fiction, and worthwhile meaning in a true story is diluted or lost. But! There were moments when our idiotic lives could have been, perhaps WERE, in genuine peril. But we didn't realize it, so we didn't care! "Didn't care until later...when we eventually matured...and therein lays THE reason why warriors throughout history have been YOUNG men!"

"So! Like Marines before us had done for two hundred years...We looked each other in the eye...crossed the beach...went to sea!" After a mere two mile swim OUT, we let down a marker buoy and tied it to a small inflatable raft carried along to house accumulated personal gear. Two deeper thinking buddies brought along a floatable beer cooler. In the end, the beer cooler proved a drag and was abandoned. The envied drinkers of cold beer were barely beginning to regret bringing the cumbersome cooler along, when our leader suddenly stopped his ceaseless swim towards Hawaii and declared; "OK Men…THIS is the spot…We'll spend our day snorkeling HERE!"

Nothing resembling GPS, or anything like it, existed. We carried in our hearts and minds that which told us where on earth we were swimming. Back then; every Marine officer was forced to learn a military discipline referred to at the time as "dead reckoning". "I guess that meant if we reckoned incorrectly…we would end up dead?"

No single requirement was more important to a Marine officer responsible for the safety and well-being of his men. Some of us were considered phenomenal experts at doing it. But! During our foolish day out there swimming off the coast of Thailand, I could not have cared less about our bravado-driven, manly group's incredibly isolated position on ANY battle map. I merely swam along, one man among five; a very quiet participant.

I abandoned to someone else all worry associated with our choice of diving site and precariousness of situation; a fine young Captain who seemed to know exactly where we were; who seemed to care. We were swimming in clear, clean, entirely uninhabited waters, ten to twelve miles off Mainland, Thailand; two miles off the cost of an isolated tiny islet SO small it may not have been on maps, even good military maps; not prior to satellite photos. I was there to relax and have fun, and did. And. Our story may NOT be what you're thinking? Nothing tragic or magic occurred; or surreal, or unearthly. Just mega doses of overdone adult male idiocy; from which every participant miraculously escaped intact. However; there were near misses.

My first near miss involved a critter I later learned legitimately should have been considered dangerous; a slow moving, black and white snake the diameter of a broom handle and barely three feet long; a sea snake. As it turned out sea snakes are among the most venomous snakes on earth; but also timid. Sea snakes tend to withdraw, unless molested. "But what does that mean? How does one molest a sea snake? Especially while swimming ten feet down…two miles offshore?"

Immediately upon arriving in our designated snorkeling area we began seeing spear-able fish swimming among towering coral. Much of it stag horn coral ranging up to fifteen feet high. Underwater trees growing in forty feet of sparkling South Pacific saltwater, the woods alive and teaming with an odd assortment of strange looking, odd acting critters, mostly fish; fascinating to swim among the irregular mini forest.

I speared a large blowfish. I'm not sure blowfish is the correct name, but that's what we called it. Prickly, slow moving little fellows, purportedly considered a top delicacy throughout SE Asia; odd looking little fish said to be deadly poison if not properly cleaned before being cooked. I didn't worry about that; gave my speared blowfish to my guide when he returned; "Local custom...Proper etiquette."

During our first hour I didn't see, touch, or feel anything sinister. But suddenly I realized my snorkeling partner was gesturing, pointing! Excitedly gesturing; trying to get me to look straight down, twenty feet below the sparkling surface of the calm sea. There, fifty yards out, was a marvelous, huge school of tuna-like small fish we later learned were Spanish mackerel. My buddy and I were watching the large school of foot long mackerel pass beneath us, spellbound, when, without apparent reason or warning, the school of identical fishes exploded in a thousand directions. Into the void left behind by the darting-departing school of mackerel, swam a four foot barracuda. I swear before God, you could see the barracuda's individual teeth from fifty yards! "We had been forewarned that barracuda might be lurking in our area. And there...big and bright... WAS a barracuda...staring at my skinny ass from fifty...no thirty...make that twenty... then only ten yards away...then a flash of underwater silver...and the barracuda was in San Francisco Bay...or so it appeared. A bullet dodged."

The excitement created by the gymnasium-sized school of a million tiny Spanish mackerel, chased away by a solitary nuclear submarine-sized barracuda, had barely subsided when another reasonably dangerous phenomenon chanced by our dive area; a drifting school of man-o-war jellyfish. To me jellyfish seemed harmless; "but not so." One sting from one dangling jellyfish tentacle and our swim, our day, perhaps even our overconfident lives, could have been finished. The school of softball, up to volley ball, sized jellyfish stretched off into the distance forever; a looooooooooooong way! Our unofficial Leader of The Pack, our self-appointed Marine-Captain-Guide, declared that we should immediately move our snorkeling area. Pick up and move UP current from the drifting school of man-o-war jellyfish; avoid all contact. "So! We moved...thereby successfully avoiding a cloud of toxic jellyfish...another bullet dodged."

Anyone who has EVER visited any beach; "practically everyone in America"; has seen dead jellyfish, especially memorable to kids. Most saltwater fishermen have encountered free-floating, live jellyfish; passing innocuously by in singles, small families, or large schools. But! To be nearly naked and swimming among jellyfish, and to then discover too little too late that the jellyfish were NOT Corpus Christi Texas family-fun-in-the-sun ordinary jellyfish, was an asshole puckering bit of seriously bad news; seriously bad word that spread rapidly among five intrepid swimmers. Our Leader said; "MOVE OUT!" And. From his four followers, there was no pretext of scientific curiosity; no petulant demand for qualifying or defining his warning regarding the nature of the hazard; no lame duck equipment check, for which Marine Leaders are notorious for requiring prior to moving out; and no formal rules of dis engagement. Only one, brief, oral command; "Pair up...Stick with your swimming partner...We're moving up current...MOVE OUT!" With that, our five man group was abruptly off in a different direction for the entire DAY! Another bullet dodged."

Now! One could reasonably conclude that a random gathering of six educated, highly trained, and by that point in our lives, combat experienced Marine officers, would have had more of a formal plan; would have demonstrated more common sense. Yes SIX officers! Don't forget our sixth buddy; the one we left behind on the beach with his perpetually smiling bride. He was involved too. But! There was little preplanning and almost no common sense demonstrated; not much of either!"

"Look! We were six Marine Officers decidedly off duty! Being off duty was the whole damned reason we were out there swimmin...gettin the livin shit scared out of us. It got bad. Uncontrollable tropical diarrhea stained the clear Pacific near the back side of one exhausted and embarrassed officer...us helpless buddies looking on in empathetic despair. A random grouping of adventure seeking young men...SO decidedly off duty we weren't just out there...we were working overtime at validating the concept...we were decidedly off duty! We carried a collective huge chip on our muscular brown shoulders. We had a point to make about being free...about being alive...about being allowed to do as we damned well please! We were out to prove our point...even if it killed us! But... on the other hand...none of us out there swimming that day was worrying about the competency or grit of his fellow swimmer. All five of us assumed the other four would keep up...maintain the pace. Assumed our fellow swimmers would abide by...conform to our leader's plan...as it evolved...whatever it evolved into...however it evolved. Keeping up and maintaining the pace was what we as officers did fulltime...for a living ...only in a different more controlled setting...in combat...in a WAR!"

Here's more food for thought! Imagine replicating our group's swimming effort with that of any other random group of similar-aged male swimmers randomly plucked off; a cruise ship, or maybe a beach, a college campus, perhaps randomly selected from anywhere else in the entire free world? In our NOT so random Marine Officer case, randomly thrown together as a homogeneous group by a chance encounter in a tropical hotel, while enjoying an R&R 12000 miles from home, were five-outta-five swimming MARINES! Members in good standing of one of the world's largest, tightest fraternities; brothers in arms, bonded comrades, part of a larger team, trained to perform as one; using proven military methods that intentionally and routinely carried male bonding from normal TO extreme. All five of us were physically fit, mentally capable, loyal by definition; and although in retrospect it may not appear so, were above average bright; each of us conceptually committed to the welfare of one another in a way not fully appreciated by non-members of America's select military fraternity. The least among us would have been judged to FAR exceed today's pasty norm; if someone were forced to hypothetically choose from America's general population. As things turned out, it was a damned good thing our quintet had such extreme NON randomness going for us; our friendly school of fish faced additional challenges; "destinies yet to deny...like...."

Like? No one had given weather much thought. If they had, no one mentioned it. Weather was possibly THE most dangerous thing we encountered; something that could have cropped up and instantly spoiled our day; a danger that has ruined the day of many seafarers.

About half-an-hour before quittin time we regrouped; gathered ourselves in a knot preparing for a relatively easy return swim. Everyone appeared to be in good shape; no one seemed to be having physical problems of any kind. Wearing swim fins and face masks, knowing what we were doing, we seemed to have a solid grip on our situation; on our reality. "And then?"

Well then, in the far off distance, a Major League dark cloud began rising out of the Pacific. At first, the cloud appeared to be heading left-to-right; angling away from our gathering of warm male bodies clustered there in God's biggest ocean. But then the wind changed, picked up steam, and the darkening cloud headed straight towards our puny bobbing bodies. The only evidence we swimmers existed, that our living carcasses inhabited such a forlorn stretch of massive Pacific water, was our tiny marker buoy breaking every passing wave. A pitiful signal if you consider it, that human life existed there among troubled waters. Within minutes we realized our buoy flag was being tossed higher and farther by each successive wave. "No doubt about it...a storm was coming... we just didn't know how big...or how soon? Tropical thunderstorms come up fast...can get big and bad in a hurry...or...go poof...and be nothing at all?"

We huddled to confer. Our Leader concluded we required an hour to make the return swim back to semi-safety afforded by the tiny islet, currently inhabited by six wives and one slightly more sane buddy. Considered as a whole, as a single mobile group of five, our group had gained weight. Several of us had speared fish, all of us had gathered a few rare shells or pieces of dead coral; and our Leader had latched onto what appeared to be a corroded brass clip off a WW II fifty caliber antiaircraft gun. And while more heavily burdened than during our swim out, to offset that, we would be enjoying the benefit of an in-going, breaking tide, helping push along our tired bodies once we got near the welcoming beacon of white sand; currently occupied by what we hoped were six, still unconcerned, smiling wives and one relaxing buddy. Our Leader told us the outbound swim was always much slower and more strenuous than the inbound swim; "Thank God!" That was legitimate wisdom, provided by our Leader, who had several times before made the swim; "Turned out he was right."

But halfway home, two of our group of five began experiencing mild leg cramps; "And THAT my friend…AIN'T good!"

Instinctively pulling ourselves into a tighter formation; sort of a "worried ducks straggling gaggle"; we stopped and let down our marker buoy; checked on every swimmer; inquired about everyone's condition; had our two cramping swimmers drink our group's last two luke warm beers and eat our lone remaining orange; jettisoned some burdensome junk; tidied up our designated order of march by putting our slightly distressed swimmers at the FRONT of our column, thereby intentionally allowing the weakest among us to set the pace; and continued our long slow swim towards shore.

By that point I was beginning to worry; nothing approaching panic, but genuine worry; mostly silently, mostly to myself, we had a problem. I was feeling bad, and intuitively realized something important. That at the outset of our swim, I began the day in better shape than my comrades. And even I began feeling myself withering; feeling as if I was shrinking? Suddenly feeling as if my entire body was getting ready to implode and disappear? I concluded that I was suffering from severe dehydration or sunburn; "Or both!"

At first I wasn't overly concerned; both were normal trauma, routinely experienced during similar outings. Our current adventure group had collectively endured worse during previous outings. We expected to suffer mild maladies; mild dehydration and overexposure; brought on by the South Pacific's bright tropical sun. Both were considered tolerable discomforts; neither was thought threatening enough to preclude activities in which we were currently engaged? The day's searing tropical temperature and the duration of our immersion in the briny Pacific had both been mentally tossed off as tolerable. Nothing about our day was more taxing or more vexing than had been the case on dozens of similar day-outings conquered elsewhere;

It was ugly, piosonous to eat, and hard to come by... but it was my catch of the day... a large blowfish! (1972)

Okinawa, Nam, California, Virginia, even during the extremes of army Ranger School off the coast of Flor-a-DUH! "Ours wasn't exactly a typical day at the office...but it wasn't far from it either...not for me and my group...not at the time...not for five Marine Officers."[1]

That point made; on that day, swimming back towards shore off the tiny islet off the splendid south coast of Thailand, something bad was going on; "psychological or physical...I wasn't sure which?" I suddenly believed I was in danger of NOT making it; thought I might NOT being capable of swimming to shore. And I began experiencing leg cramps. My respiratory function began giving out; I began gasping for each next breath. My mental tank was running on empty. At the same time, I was puzzled; felt I should NOT be experiencing a problem? But I was. I WAS running out of gas, hitting 'E' a mile from shore; and couldn't decide exactly what to do about it? "Why feelings of doom and gloom?" "Who was I gonna tell?" "Who could I call...for help?" "Was one of my tired buddies...gonna drag my water soaked and sun baked ass ashore? I seriously doubted that...but...what the 'F' WAS goin on?"

Then two other swimmers began coughing and wheezing; complaining of mild chest pains and incredible fatigue. "My malady was contagious!" "What the Hell WAS going on?" No one knew; there were no obvious answers. Least not from anyone out there swimming with us in the middle of nowhere!

---

[1]Footnote: In July 1970, I departed Marine officer training in Quantico and went directly to gut-bust-ing-ly strenuous Army Ranger School in Fort Benning, GA. I was assigned to attend Ranger School as part of an experimental pilot program. After six months in Quantico and two in Fort Benning, I was in the best physical condition of my life; "good as any mortal that ever walked the planet." As "Rangers in training" we routinely jogged eight miles, swam three miles, dead man floated in the open sea for hours at a time, performed hand-to-hand combat drills for hours on end, then conducted daily PT regimens to fill up our day! EVERY DAY! "Oh...I was fit alright! I had been a strong swimmer all my life...swimming ability enhanced by tough training. Believe me...I could swim...FAR...and for hours."

God Bless the Marines who landed on Iwo Jima! God Bless John Wayne for his many portrayals of such bravery and hardcore stiff neck-ness! We five Marines found ourselves inspired by common heritage; driven by our Corps' proud history; "We WOULD land on the beach!"

Without further word or complaint, we gritted our collective sandy teeth and continued our pain-perforated, angst-bifurcated, long, slow, swim back towards relative safety; "Now less than half-a-mile to go." Less headway per flipper-enhanced leg stroke; a stronger wind at our sunburned backs; more gentle push from Mother Nature's fleeting thunderstorm; more grisly progress; less energy and willpower remaining to continue; no alternative in sight; we swam towards a distant but distinctly visible shore.

"But…REALLY…What WAS the problem?"

Finally; "none too soon based on coughing and wheezing and puking going on all around me"; first my left foot, and then my right, struck the sandy bottom of the South Pacific. I grinned a greasy numb grin. When I looked up, the tallest man among us was taking off his flippers; "He touched bottom first!" I slumped in the breaking surf, allowed my tired feet to drink the familiarity of supporting sand. "Terra Firma"; albeit it two feet beneath the salty Pacific! Two deathly silent minutes later and every tired soul from our party arrived ashore and assumed some version of standing upright in the frothy Pacific surf. Our day, which had mysteriously become an arduous ordeal, was finished.

The next day, all of us who had been out there swimming, slept in. We gathered in the hotel bar around four and began a beer-accentuated, whisky-laced debriefing; had a conversation regarding what had taken place the day before during our labored return swim. None of us had an answer, but we did come up with theories, one of which was plausible; "At least plausible…in theory…to us."

One Marine suggested we became sick because of our overexposure to tropical sun in such intensely clear water. That we swimmers, somehow or another, suffered unusual stress to our sun coping mechanisms, exacerbated by other elements of our day; dehydration, duration, alcohol, fatigue, and the overall situation.

Another theory evolved; pushed by our Leader. He hypothesized that perhaps some chemical such as Agent Orange had been dumped in the area by a low flying aircraft; aborted over the area for reasons unknown? Not a bad theory. I had actually seen that done several times. C-130 aircraft, spraying toxic Agent Orange defoliant, were allowed to dump their entire load if an emergency arose. But! I wasn't entirely buying the Agent Orange theory. I had showered in Agent Orange. It is easily detectable by its offensive smell.

Had Agent Orange been present in the pristine waters during our long swim, we most assuredly would have detected it.

I suggested yet another theory. That perhaps the enormously large school of passing man-o-war jellyfish had, somehow or another discharged a low dose of powerful jellyfish toxins in the water through which we then swam. Toxins discharged in such low concentrations and across such a wide area, so as to make our mere passing trough the unseen cloud bank of toxin a formidable task? Perhaps a toxin overly reactive or hyper debilitating to light-skinned, waterlogged, fatigued, Caucasian, Marine swimmers?

And one final theory; THE theory we Post Op beer drinking buddy officers finally concluded was MOST reasonable? That we had collectively experienced some sort of low level oxygen deprivation; even though unaware of it at the time? Oxygen deprivation similar to that experienced when mildly choked, or by holding ones breathe to the point of nearly passing out. Oxygen deprivation brought on and magnified out there swimming in a Perfect Storm of coincidental conditions; our prolonged time in the water, our strenuous swim, our nearly naked pale bodies, and our inhumane strenuous swim; at the END of an already exhausting day. Not fatigue or tiredness, not in a conventional sense; but oxygen deprivation brought on by being pushed far beyond the point of having used up or tapped out undefined trace elements critical to our overall biological systems? Oxygen deprivation, that had, in a relatively short span of time, brought on odd sensations; feelings that caused us to suddenly experience nearly identical symptoms of physical stress and a panicked state of mind; sensing we weren't capable of continuing. Feeling fear; feeling like we weren't going to make it home to our wives on the beach.

No official answer was ever forthcoming. However! When facts describing our day were later disclosed; we five, young, foolish Marine officers WERE severely admonished by senior officers within our respective chains of command.

At the end of the day; "literally and figuratively"; everyone returned safely to Mainland, Thailand. I returned to my parent unit; finished my Tour of Duty; got out of the Marines; returned home to Missouri to First Wife Jen-Jen; and eventually got on with the remaining balance of my Crazy Viet Nam Vet life. To this day no one has ever adequately explained what happened to us out there.

"OBTW...I did kill and photograph one hellaciously big blowfish while we were out there swimming. GOD...Blowfish are ugly M—— F—ers!"

Chapter Eight

Something Beyond Fishin'

I'm a combat veteran of Viet Nam with a Purple Heart and Bronze Star. However! The worst fightin I have ever experienced in my life occurred in Missouri during the summer of 1982. June and July saw the worst of it; hot shrapnel zinging back and forth. Sneak attacks and counterattacks clouding summer's stifling air; high explosives lighting up the night. Tons of munitions expended. Isolated hand to hand battles plagued our front lines. The scourge of "All Out War" was causing heavy casualties on both sides. Chance encounters, ambushes, deadly sniper fire; we were living life on the edge. Every combative action resulted in a retaliatory RE-action, all of it pointing toward one ultimate showdown. The ferociousness, impact, and duration of confrontations increased by the day; bitter tension mounted. Mad Hatter madness broke out in every sector. THE final battle was taking shape, becoming a reality in the minds of every antagonist. Fighting approached unbearable; parents, grandparents, friends and enemies, in-laws and bit players, even paid professionals. Brittle! Rigid! Everyone was so far out there nothing mattered!

So what could cause such war? It's spelled C-U-S-T-O-D-Y B-A-T-T-L-E! Battling parents; that's what! Meeting in court deciding the fate of two young boys; it was no holds barred, no quarter given. After eighteen months of sparring there was fixin to be an Old West style showdown. Nurse-Wife Peg had replaced EX Wife Jen-Jen and all Hell had broken loose. Nurse-Wife Peg and I had been ordered out of the fray by our Counselor Psychiatrist; a fine lady providing general counseling for our entire reconstituted family of four; Nurse-Wife Peg, Me, Son Chris, and Son Ladd. Our Lady Doctor had recommended that our new Family of Four take a long vacation. So we did. We booked a week long fishin trip with a top-o-the-line guide service up in Minnesota.

Real progress had been achieved reshaping our new four-person nuclear family; but the results of that effort needed air to breathe, time to expand, room to grow. I was seeking distraction; The Boys were exhibiting signs of poorly disguised anxiety. What I wanted was to reinforce a concept that Nurse-Wife Peg, The Boys, and I were a "New Family". I wanted to do something spectacular; something The Boys would enjoy, point to, and remember. To that end I went out and rented a full-sized Conversion Van; a brand new, overdone, bright red, GMC, featuring; "A real icebox and twin beds in back!" Not referred to as SUVs back in the 1980s, our van was an authentic luxury van with four individual Captain's chairs; comfy, consoled, carpeted, cushioned, and cozied-up to the max! "What a vehicle!" I also booked a spectacular guide service; featuring chartered fishing in the Canadian Border Lakes of northern Minnesota; a family fishin trip and driving vacation of the first magnitude.

On Friday, July 30th, 1982, feeling a little like eloping teenagers stealing away in the dark, our wee family of four departed quietly. Some high performance tap dancing and fancy sweet talking had been required on my part to persuade EX Jen-Jen to agree to our new family's extended vacation plans; she was suspicious as Hell during that particular war footing period in our post-divorce history! However; my dubious mission of coercing my EX was accomplished, and our new family of four awakened at three in the morning and skedaddled north on I-29. Fleeing reality in our rear view mirror, we headed north up through Missouri, on into and through Iowa, crossed all of Minnesota, and by night fall of the second day arrived in Brainerd, Minnesota

Shore lunch with guide **Tommy Chosa**. Notice large metal spike behind Tommy's right leg. That's the USA – Canada international border. (1982)

near the US – Canada Border. Many significant things happened on that fishin trip. A brief description of a few of those things warrants inclusion in this book of family fishin stories.

First; whether they realized it or not, or verbalized it or not, Nurse-Wife Peg, Son Chris, and Son Ladd, all three of them, began conceptualizing the FOUR of us as a family. Doing things together helped The Boys and Nurse-Wife Peg assimilate that important concept. Out of raw necessity Nurse-Wife Peg was forced to assume a focused and uninterrupted mothering role. Quantitatively and qualitatively our family fishin trip to Minnesota was THE perfect setting for Nurse-Wife Peg to interact with The Boys as their loving, female caregiver; uninterrupted and uninhibited mothering of the first magnitude. For Nurse-Wife Peg our days-long, family trip provided a peaceful opportunity to demonstrate tenderness and her genuine caring way; both badly needed by The Boys. All the while the four of us were immersed in an extraordinarily positive and wholesome family situation.

Rousting The Boys out of bed every morning to meet our fishin guide, getting The Boys ready for bed each night, cleaning and tending their minor wounds after a hard day fishin, and a dozen other on-the-spot parenting situations, provided Nurse-Wife Peg golden opportunities to be at her natural best. Tending cuts, scrapes, fishhook bites, sunburns, mosquito bumps, dirty fingernails, a bad case of car sickness, a dozen tiny catastrophes as they popped up, situations snipped here and there from the treasured fabric of legitimate family relationships, fell naturally into Nurse-Wife's mothering lap! Given that timely and practical super-chance to blossom as Step Mom; 'Rookie Mother of The Year' Nurse-Wife Peg came up with game day demonstrations of genuine TLC and unflaggingly did her Nurse-Wife thing. It was pure magic.

Second; from the beginning of our family's horrific bad times in 1981, I made it a studied practice to make frequent promises to Chris and Ladd; promises both large and small. Everything from, "I'll buy you an ice cream cone." To, "I'll take you on a fishin trip to Canada!" Running the spectrum, touching points of interest along the way, I made it a calculated, tactical mission to promise The Boys things. I tried to keep one or two, or a dozen, simultaneous promises hanging out there at all times for The Boys to anticipate. My theory was simple, and not actually my own; I borrowed it! "Borrowed it from a personal experience of 1952"; parenting methodology role modeled by MY Dad on my snowed out fifth birthday! My string of little things promised tended to keep The Boys minds occupied and tied to me. Gave them something positive to think about no matter what might be going on around them. There was always something positive, always something specific, hanging out there; "Always!" And THE biggest promise? Don't worry Boys! Everything's going to be all right.

As our children progress through life, we parents promise them a huge variety of things; I simply went around proactively conjuring up miscellaneous things I knew for certain I could actually DO! So! Why NOT put a big fat fancy fishin trip at the tiptop of my proactive list? The key to my methodology was keeping half-a-dozen promises simmering on the back burner at all times! And! Keeping ALL of them! Our fishin trip to Minnesota was something Nurse-Wife Peg, The Boys, and I had talked about for a LONG time! When clearly set in stone, that promised trip became a HUGE and bright expectation; hanging up there to brighten every dark night The Boys may have been forced to endure; lighting their way like an October Harvest Moon. "I promised." I told The Boys they could COUNT on it. I said we WILL do it. It was a wonderful and effective way for me to have meaningful dialogue with my young and troubled Boys; both of whom were vindictively kept separated from me for weeks at a time by a pissed off EX Jen-Jen and her weirdo parents! Ultimately, by making and keeping my promises, I was able to achieve aspects of several much greater goals; "Establishing faith in ME... reinforcing trust in adults...building respect for truth told them by adults...just to name a few." After learning details of my promise keeping technique, our Family Counselor- Doctor began referring to my methodology as "good parenting". EX Jen-Jen insisted on calling it "brainwashing". "Good parenting...brainwashing...whatever it was...it had a wonderful and positive effect on two little boys...at a time when they sorely needed it!"

Netting **Ladd's** big smallmouth bass on Basswood Lake, Ely, Minnesota. (1982)

While enjoying our once-in-a-lifetime fishin trip, Nurse-Wife Peg and I set out to accomplish a third goal; "Create as many pleasant memories as humanly possible." My personal favorite among treasured memories from our trip; rolling out of bed at four every morning in order to meet our Chippewa Indian fishin guide Tommy Chosa. Just like the big-eyed Extra Terrestrial movie character ET, Guide Tommy Chosa fell in love with Reese's Pieces. After our first day fishin, The Boys tipped Guide Tommy Chosa a two pound bag of Reese's Pieces; "in addition to an appropriate amount of cash supplied by me." No non-cash tip ever meant more to that Old Indian Guide. He actually wept. The Boys specialty candy was a rarity in the backwoods of northern Minnesota; something new to Guide Tommy Chosa, something he had never seen.

'Indian Guide Tommy Chosa Fishing Stories' became classic tales in our new family. Getting up in years, nearing the age of mild teetering, Guide Tommy Chosa had never EVER, not even one time, taken ANY kid out fishin! Not while Tommy Chosa was officially acting as 'The Guide'; not even ONE time in Tommy Chosa's glamorous legendary career! The first day we met Guide Tommy Chosa at Outfitters Outpost, he bluntly said; "NO! Not going! Will not go fishin with young boys!" Guide Tommy Chosa flat ass refused. To make matters worse; Guide Tommy Chosa was purportedly the best guide in camp; possibly in all of northern Minnesota! I was badly miffed. And, as one might well imagine, I had something to say to Guide Tommy Chosa; in a NOT timid or humble way. I stood my ground and told Guide Tommy Chosa; "Then we won't be going...That was the whole damned purpose of driving eight hundred miles...We intend to take these two boys fishin...with or without you!" Then I switched gears. I turned on the charm, best I could, and convinced the old worn out Indian that HE, The Guide, would enjoy taking the two boys out...for one little day of fishin...if he would just try it? I finally won our micro sized international debate and somehow persuaded Guide Tommy Chosa, 'Fishing Guide Extraordinaire', to...just try it! So he did.

For the next three days sons Chris and Ladd became the most intense, hardest working, most proficient, most joyful, and by far youngest guests Guide Tommy Chosa had ever guided! By the end of The Boys second day of fishin, Guide Tommy Chosa openly and unabashedly said he admired Chris and Ladd; respected their serious attitude towards fishin; their budding fishermen skills. Guide Tommy Chosa began voluntarily boating Chris and Ladd all over several huge lakes. Nurse-Wife and I were with The Boys, in the same boat, but Guide Tommy could NOT have cared less!

Breaking ALL the rules, crossing and recrossing into Canadian National Waters, where Guide Tommy Chosa's boat was NOT supposed to go, Guide Tommy FISHED! He took The Boys on a relentless international boat ride...pursuing the really big ones. Guide Tommy Chosa did everything he could think of to help our boys catch an extra fish or two; or an extra BIG fish or two! Before it was all over Guide Tommy fell in love with Chris and Ladd; developed genuine affection for both boys. On the last day, Guide Tommy Chosa came out of his stereotypical quiet Indian shell. He even warmed up to Nurse-Wife Peg and me, a bit. That Old Indian's entire, quiet, somber, stoic attitude changed. When our time together fishin was finished, Guide Tommy Chosa told everyone in camp that he had never seen such well behaved and conscientious young fisherman! Guide Tommy Chosa also said he had never been around such HAPPY boys! "Promise kept!"

Sons Chris and Ladd single handedly changed one Old Indian Guide's lifelong prejudice about having young boys in his boat. Seeing the revitalization of The Boys countenance and mood was monumentally rewarding for Nurse-Wife Peg and I. And. "Was it not notable that in the written annals of fishin history…an objective stranger… Guide Tommy…perceived The Boys to be happy and content…while out there in quest of…the really big ones? There's a real lesson of some kind in there for every one of us parents. Think about what I'm saying."

Tiny negatives cropped up a couple of times during our all-time family fishin trip; as a result Nurse-Wife Peg's feelings were hurt. The Boys and Nurse-Wife melding into a genuine nuclear family was real; "as real as life gets." But there were bound to be growing pains. Pain-to-gain interaction showed up in unexpected ways! One example; The Boys would enter a restaurant and race to sit beside me! Fight over who was going to sit beside Dad; kid stuff that had been going on since Day One, typical childish behavior. When our newly fabricated family went out one night a week to McDonald's or a movie, intermittent activities with time lapses between, The Boys seat grabbing antics were barely noticeable. Fighting for the seat next to Dad was tolerable. However! When our Family Foursome traveled together day after day, for ten consecutive days, The Boys nonstop scuffling at every meal stop, to sit with Dad and NOT with Nurse-Wife Peg, began wearing thin on Peg's nerves.

An increasingly pregnant circumstance until Nurse-Wife Peg broke down and cried. Feeling like Odd Man Out, Peg's feelings were being unnecessarily trashed. The Boys realized their actions were offending Nurse-Wife and understood why; so everyone talked about it. Even though they were young, The Boys clearly grasped the idea that Nurse-Wife Peg and their Dad had established a new and loving relationship. More importantly, The Boys got it that The Boys and Nurse-Wife Peg could ALSO establish a new and loving separate relationship! Suddenly and dramatically The Boys realized they need NOT be ashamed to show positive feelings for Nurse-Wife. Our family's emotional exchange marked the beginning of subtle but steady progress. Nurse-Wife Peg took the time, energy, and patience to plant seeds for a lifelong, life-altering relationship with The Boys; who were…growin by fishin. The Boys affection for Nurse-Wife began flourishing; nurtured by her demonstrations of love and attention as The Boys primary caregiver…while out there fishin. The Boys responded. During our trip, roots were established; relationship building became an unofficial, overriding aspect of our trip. After a few days, Nurse-Wife Peg and The Boys were able to look at each other, smile, shrug their shoulders, and say; "Oh well…That's just the way it's going to be…for a while." While we're all out there fishin.

A number of other subtleties surfaced during our extended family trip; a locked down, tight, prescheduled fishin trip that produced a variety of special interactions and opportunities; opportunities similar to those provided newlyweds on a honeymoon. NO one from the outside world was around to interfere with members of our Family Foursome. There were NO playmates, grandparents, neighbors, uncles or aunts. NO unwelcome intruders. NO virtual strangers masquerading as 'The Man' in The Boys up heaved lives. NO strange men telling The Boys what to do. NO strange men dragging along stranger kids to pop in and out of The Boys lives. NO interloper 'Boyfriends' espousing unfamiliar, holier than thou, anti-gun, Jesus Freak, dime store, philosophies! NO external distractions. NONE! ZERO! Just the four of us; isolated, and totally dependant on one another. In and out of the boat, wrestling with cumbersome mandatory life jackets; in and out of barely passable tiny beds; in and out of our cramped motel room, from which everyone was rousted in the wee hours of the morning in the cold dark; in and out of one tiny bathroom, with an always cold shower; in and out of a warm Conversion Van that wreaked of sweet food and boy smells. Four Bonding Souls, traveling for hours on end in our cozy rented van; nonstop, observing and caring for one another's most private needs! It was an incredibly huge family time; an intense family situation. An all-time great time! While we were all out there fishin.

Ours was no dainty sipping fine wine from a fragile goblet family good time; ours was a robust quaffing of cold beer from a heavy mug family good time! Nurse-Wife Peg and I created a real life all-for-one and one-for-all family good time. Our family odyssey included frequent pee and pit stops along backwoods roads and byways. We loved shopping for fresh smoked salmon, jerked walleye pike, fresh cheese, fresh baked bread, and ice cold beer or good red wine for us adults; stopping a thousand times to get sodas for The Boys. We also stopped at EVERY bait shop from South Minnesota to the Canadian Border. The Boys were allowed to wander aimlessly in and out, taking in for the first time in their lives, a fascinating fantasyland of exotic baits and lures. Many bait shops featured dramatic mounted stringers of trophy northern pike and walleye; The Boys eyes popped in uninhibited amazement! For a time, in ways they will recall, in a place of sheer fantasy, life was pure joy for two young boys. And a glowing reward for two concerned adults. Just doing our thing…out there fishin.

One non-fishin day we drove the entire length of the northern shore of Lake Superior. As only God could have willed it on such a special day we encountered classic BAD weather; dark skulking clouds rolling in low and heavy on the horizon just off the broiling lake's foamy whitecaps. A Great Northerner was blowing in; tearing across the lake in skin-crawling, bone-chilling, eerie blasts; huge waves rolling ashore and crashing with a deafening roar drenching the fogged shoreline. It was a poor day for fishin, a bitter cold day for early August, uncomfortable outside our van; but a particularly cherished day for making memories. We Four Traveling Fishermen were purposely listening to an eight-track of Gordon Lightfoot's ballad about the Great Ship Edmond Fitzgerald; how it sank during a similar storm on The Great Lake Gitchegumee. One of my favorite songs for years, The Boys picked it up and played the song over and over on our trip, and for the balance of summer. The Boys saw The Great Lake Gitchegumee at its ferocious worst, and Gordon Lightfoot's mournful ballad became our official family theme song; for a long time. First enjoyed...while out there fishin.

Our trip cemented emerging family relationships; and like coolies did in Ogden, Utah; drove a track-uniting golden spike into our co-focal family future. During coming trials and tribulations; months, weeks, days, and hours of gloom and agony; we Four Traveling Fishermen were able to look back on the full cup of our fishin trip and take from it, tiny sips of psyche preserving peace. We Four Fishermen could think back to that lakeshore, that storm lashed moment shared, and feel genuinely bound together. And, in spite of losing one precious day of fishin to dreadful winter weather, We Four managed hundreds of warm activities that awful, cold day. Pointing to that special and treasured day, We Four could say to those who might care; "That's where...when...and how...We Four bonded into a real family!" While We Four were...gone fishin!

A scant one hundred DAYS later, The Boys were formal guests in Clay County Missouri's cavernous courtroom; carefully sequestered with The Judge in his quiet Judge chambers, describing post-divorce aspects of their calamitous family relationships. Two Young Boys; caught in the open, in withering fields of fire, in the middle of a raging war. Two Wee Boys; attempting to tell The Judge who represented exactly what in their malleable minds; providing gritty boy opinions, concepts, ideas, and testimony, regarding THEIR nuclear family. Including; WHO, in their opinion, represented the Mother Figure; and, who did NOT! Two Boys; asked to describe relationships with Fisherman Dad, Fisherman Nurse-Wife Peg, and NON-Fisherman Bio Mother EX Jen-Jen. A Bitter EX, who by Show Time in Clay County Missouri, had digressed to derisively referring to The Boys wondrous Minnesota fishing trip as; "Just more of Their Dad's brainwashing."

Me, Fisherman Dad, and other informed adults with information, insight, and intellect sufficient to know UP from DOWN; pointed to the same fishin trip as an excellent example of devoted parenting! But one cannot help but wonder; "and many people asked"; if The Boys special fishin trip was somehow blessed; "Many fine folks back home in Missouri said it WAS!" Lots of good things came out of that trip. And! The Boys, being boys, ages five and seven, WERE highly impressionable. Fishin DID work wonders for their morale and attitude! I simply believe; "If you're going to do some serious politicking...or outright campaigning...regarding your point of view... PRIOR to the election is the time for politicking...JUST prior! Correct? You know I'm Right! Besides...How can a Dad go TOO far wrong...by taking his boys fishin?"

Our trip may not have been blessed, but it WAS a blessing! God worked His wonders in a far away place, in magnificent ways! According to Nurse-Wife Peg; "Healing is a process...that leads back to good health...good health is a condition. Our fishin trip helped create embryonic cells...required for the healing process to begin... which...given time...space...and the best possible environment...indeed brought about the condition we were seeking...good mental health for Chris and Ladd. Fishin was merely a medium...a good venue...but a fun one!"

Fishin was superb! For catching a smallmouth bass in excess of three pounds, Ladd's name was entered in an official log as an 'Extreme Junior Angler'; a technical classification of fishermen under the age of five; for which Ladd received an official state certificate. I had Son Ladd's smallmouth mounted; it currently hangs in our home in Texas. At the end of day three we had our ice chests FULL; pike, walleye, smallmouth, and lake trout! Peg and I cut our trip short and headed to MO! "Smile!"

Ladd's mounted smallmouth bass arrived in time for our first Christmas in Texas. (1983)

Nurse-Wife-Stepmom-Peg with guide **Tommy Chosa.** (1982)

Nuse-Wife-Stepmom Peg showed the boys that "girls could do stuff too"! (1982)

Chapter Nine

Boys Growin' Up Fishin'–1980 to 1995

When are boys considered grown up and declared men; at what age? Nurse-Wife Peg says she'll let me know when I get there. My two older sons were born in 1975 and 1977; while I was married to First Wife Jen-Jen, and the four of us lived in northwest Missouri. This chapter includes a dozen micro fishin stories. The first occurred in 1980; the balance are scattered over fifteen years. A collection of fishin' adventures survived by sons Chris and Ladd, Nurse-Wife, and ME! A critical decade-and-a-half in The Boys lives when they were 'Growin Up Fishin'.

Game Hill Catfish, Summer 1980

Approximately thirty miles north of Kansas City, one of my business partners and I owned and operated a members only private hunting club for sportsmen, their guests and families. Our business was located on a farm that belonged to First Wife Jen-Jen and me. My partner and I hosted hundreds of guests and dozens of events on our commercial game farm/hunting preserve; which he and I had appropriately named 'Game Hill'. On January 12th, 1977, during Game Hill's third year of operation, son Ladd was born. Three years later, my partner and I decided to add an amenity; "stock our hunting club's small lake with channel cat and promote Free Fishing for members." Promoted with energy and great fanfare; our inaugural effort centered on Game Hill's 'First Annual Catfish Tournament For Kids'!" First Wife Jen-Jen and I entered three-and-one-half year old son Ladd as one of three dozen eager contestants; "ranging in age from Ladd…up to twelve." Ladd's older brother Chris, age five, was also entered in Game Hill's highly publicized first ever fishing contest. Mountains of kid food, great kid prizes, and gaudy kid-induced hysteria were the order of the day. In most cases more fun and excitement was had by doting parents than by screaming kids.

My Dad, who taught ME to fish, was sixty-two that summer. He was proud of his Grandsons Chris and Ladd, and spent as much time as possible with The Boys. My Dad agreed to attend Game Hill's fishing tournament and assist The Boys. As one of Game Hill's proprietors I was busy supervising the tournament, politicking, schmoozing with members, and keeping little fishermen occupied and worry free. My Dad enjoyed his job helping The Boys. When he attended Game Hill functions, my Dad was our most prestigious FREE help. I enjoyed having my Dad on hand witnessing Game Hill's progress and special events. But! The day of our first fishing tournament, my Dad was there intent on teaching his Grandsons a few fishing secrets that might help them WIN!

Both Boys owned identical Zebco Model 99 reels, mounted on inexpensive rods, loaded up with cheap K-Mart line; both fishin rigs sporting golf ball sized red and white bobbers. At the business end of both rig's cheap line were top drawer Eagle Claw hooks. "Good hooks…tied on by me or my Dad…for surefire results." I was taught by my Dad to spend extra money on quality hooks, so I did; taught that it pays big dividends to have a good hook, when the chips are down. "I had no earthly idea what the condition of The Boys Zebco reels or tinsel strength of their line might be? But…Based on what happened that day…The reels and the line must have been in pretty damned good shape."

Our tournament began at three sharp on a Saturday afternoon. It was a timed event; three hours start to finish, with prizes awarded and photos distributed at six. Our local newspaper; affectionately called "The Weekly Wipe"; was on hand to take pictures and write a front page article about Game Hill's first-ever fishing tournament and its young winners! Game Hill was awarding three trophies and three handsome prizes; a Grand Prize trophy and prize for single 'Biggest Fish', by weight; a First Place trophy and prize for 'Most Fish', by total number; and a First Place trophy and prize for 'Most Fish', by total weight. All freshly caught catfish were immediately weighed by my partner, cleaned by our cleaning crew, and iced down for proud kids and parents to haul home. Our catfish were plentiful, hungry, and came in one-size-fits-all. Game Hill bought the catfish and stocked our lake just days prior to the tournament. Every fisherboy and fishergirl could pretty much count on enjoying the thrill of catchin somethin? There were plenty of able, willing adults on hand to help the Little Ones if any kid required help. Adults baiting up, casting out heavily-laden lines, fixing or altering kid's fishin gear, and keeping reels or crossed lines tangle-free was encouraged. Ours was meant to be a FUN family event. However! There WAS one formal restriction; "If a participating child hooked a catfish…that child was required to reel in the fish…without the assistance of an adult." Simple!

And! There was a dirty little secret regarding the catfish in Game Hill's lake; a "dirty little secret" that only my Partner and I knew. And although it was a secret, it was a totally positive aspect of our kids-only tournament.

"Our dirty little secret?" While there were plenty of catfish in the lake, most of the catfish were virtually identical in size. Therefore; it was likely going to be difficult to determine THE biggest fish. Game Hill had purchased healthy, stocker catfish; directly from a hatchery. Nearly every catfish released in our lake came to us having been hatched the same year; most of our catfish were in the two pound range, with only slight differences in weight. Some fatter, some slimmer, some shorter, others a tad longer, a few marked by nibbled tails or scars inflicted during hatchery days; but essentially all the catfish in our relatively new lake were the same size. Except for a very few!

A dozen catfish, out of approximately three hundred, had apparently managed to slip through the hatchery's size-grading system. When Game Hill purchased its first big load of prime, stocker fish we got a few giants. My partner and I saw the notably bigger fish when the fish were unloaded. My Partner and I knew for certain that the FEW bigger fish were alive and well and IN our lake; "But who among us could predict IF any fisherchild would be lucky enough to actually catch one of the Big Ones?" But! The Biggies were there; which added a shot of interest to Game Hill's featured new attraction.

Tournament fishing got off to a roaring start. Within an hour every fisherkid appeared to have caught at least one catfish; every doting adult silently hoping NO fisherchild got skunked; "especially not THEIR fisherchild!" There were five fishergirls. But mostly there were fisherboys; ranging in age from six to twelve. Son Ladd was the youngest; my banker friend's son, Steven, the oldest. By the time opening gun sounded, Ladd and his older buddy Steven had located themselves a prime spot of their own choosing. I say "prime" because the two boys combined, caught four fish before greener horned fisherkids caught one. I say "spot of their own choosing" because I was busy at the sound of opening gun; when young contestants scattered like quail and squatted in the first available spot on the lake's muddy shore; "GLAD I wasn't involved in Ladd's selection of a hot spot!"

My partner kept busy weighing each new catch. Game Hill provided a cleaning service, our way of encouraging young fisherkids; "nobody enjoys cleaning fish." I stayed busy helping fisherkids if they needed something. There were FREE fish stringers for every participant; FREE night crawlers; and FREE spare parts such as sinkers, bobbers, hooks, and fresh line. And there was priceless adult guidance; yakking to non listening fisherkids about where and how to fish. One surprising aspect of Game Hill's fishing tournament; "the gross ineptitude and lack of knowledge of a few geeky Dads." I kept thinking; "Hey Big Daddy...from Big City America...wearing fancy, too tight, Eddie Bauer, high water britches...where did YOU learn to fish?

Watching the outdoor channel on TV?"

As Game Hill's tournament wore on, newly arriving fisherkids took the place of a few who got tired and gave up; "But...Surprisingly...Most kids kept at it." His head down, never glancing up, his lips pursed in determination; son Ladd. Older Son Chris tired after an hour; and in the company of an older playmate, took off on a sidebar adventure chasing indigenous bullfrogs; but not Ladd. Son Ladd was all business; focused. "One reason?" As the tournament's final hour approached, things had taken shape; "It looked like...it might be Ladd's contest to lose?" Son Ladd had a grand total of six fish, all about the same size, close to two pounds each. Son Ladd's chances of winning Most Fish, as determined by either total weight OR total count, looked good.

But! With less than an hour remaining, another boy, my friend's son Steven, age twelve, had already caught five catfish; "fishing right-next-to three year old son Ladd." Steven went on a "bigger boy" tear. "Bam!" "Bam!" "Bam!" He caught three catfish in a row; numbers six, seven, and eight! At that point it was "all but over"; a near certainty that excited twelve year old Steven would win First Place for Most Fish.

Down but not out, showing renewed determination, decidedly put off by the prospect of not winning Most Fish, determined to not be distracted by events around him, bowing his neck, puffing out his lips, putting his head down further, son Ladd fished harder. Intending to encourage Ladd, I offered a dumb assed suggestion; "Don't worry Ladd...You're still in the running for Biggest Fish!" I had a suspicion that two of Ladd's catfish looked a pubic hair fatter than average, and one a tad longer.

Then, with less than thirty minutes remaining, Ladd did a decidedly odd thing. I was later able to determine that the odd thing was something Ladd had heard about while watching 'The Harold Ensley Show' on TV; a 1960s and '70s local hunting and fishing show broadcast out of Kansas City. "The odd thing?" Sitting on the muddy pond dam, desperately waiting for his next catfish to bite, with his Paw Paw helping him watch for the slightest jiggle of the semi-tight fishing line, son Ladd passed time by catching a tiny green-striped leopard frog; its frail, froggy body no bigger than a man's thumb nail. Maybe the size of a nickel, the tiny frog, and dozens of its froggy buddies, had been hopping out of harms way all afternoon. Carrying the tiny frog to his Paw Paw, grandson Ladd asked that the wee frog be placed on his hook as fresh bait. Even though all types of artificial or natural bait WERE allowed, 90% of the tournament's young contestants were using gigantic, free night crawlers provided by Game Hill; "Yes...and 100% of the young contestants actually catching fish were using free night crawlers."

Later on, after the tournament was finished and all winners announced, Ladd's sixty-two year old Paw Paw told me privately that he wasn't the least bit impressed with Ladd's idea of using a tiny frog as bait. To Paw Paw it appeared his grandson Ladd was essentially giving up on the idea of catching Most Fish. Ladd's Paw Paw was reluctant to reel in grandson Ladd's line and switch bait; change from surefire night crawlers, to some exotic idea Ladd said he had heard about on TV. But! Being a good Paw Paw, my Dad complied with grandson Ladd's request and did as asked. My fishing mentor, MY Dad, Ladd's Paw Paw, reeled in grandson Ladd's line and baited up Ladd's hook with the tiny squirming frog. "Adults baiting up and casting out lines WAS permitted!"

Adorned with its sacrificial small green frog, Ladd's freshly baited hook had no more than settled on the muddy bottom of the lake, before it was swallowed whole by a large catfish. Ladd's line went tight with the definitive "JERK" indicative of a solid bite, and Ladd set the hook; "A classic small boy…versus large fish…fish fight was on!"

My Dad stood by; silently grinning his approval and amazement. A sixty-two year old man with sixty years fishin experience, it was apparent to Ladd's Paw Paw that the catfish on the far end of grandson Ladd's line was no downstream ordinary catfish. The buzzer on Ladd's Zebco 99 "zzzzzzzzzzing" all the way, as Ladd's fragile cheap line was stripped off his inexpensive reel by a phantom-tastically large catfish. Fortunately for Ladd it was a small lake; free of snags, except for fishing lines belonging to other contestant fisherkids. This way and that, left then right, back and forth; the big catfish on Ladd's line swept to and fro. But! Sure as ducks quack and pigs stink, the hefty catfish was tiring; jerking and tugging on Ladd's line diminishing. But a collective gasp of horror went up from gathered onlookers when the irritating buzzing of Ladd's outgoing line suddenly stopped. Everyone thought Ladd had lost the fish. But then! A louder chorus of cheers went skyward when the eerie silence that had momentarily settled over the lakeshore, was broken by Ladd's tightening line once again squealing off his cheap reel. Grimacing forehead to chin, son Ladd reeled until his three year old tongue protruded in an Old Man and The Sea, determined expression.

Approximately ten minutes later; a potbellied, gasping catfish appeared in shallow muddy water at the lake's edge. Not one fisherkid in the tournament possessed a dip net. "So?" To the excited screams and continuing cheers of the tournament's three-dozen competitors, with his Paw Paw encouraging him all the way, grandson Ladd dragged the flopping behemoth ashore. One glance and there was no question; son Ladd, grandson Ladd, was going to win Grand Prize for Biggest Fish! At that point it was merely a matter of determining the fish's official weight. My diligent partner, officiating weigh-in all afternoon, did the honor. But; the day's final weigh-in attracted an excited crowd. Every beating heart stood wide-eyed; nary had a soul departed after son Ladd hooked his big catfish. "Four pounds...Four ounces...Exactly!" The nearest competition was NO competition! Son Ladd, grandson Ladd, was Grand Prize winner of Game Hill's First Annual Fishing Tournament; 'Biggest Fish'!

Twenty years later, at the ripe age of eighty-two, my Dad went peacefully to Heaven; never hesitating to again and again, for anyone listening, tell the happy story about; "How my grandson Ladd talked me (Paw Paw) into baiting up with a little green frog...to win that big fishin tournament out there at Game Hill."

Ladd's big catfish won the tourrnament... we all learned from Ladd. (1980)

Summer of Discontent

Many unusual events occurred during the summer of 1981. Some are described in the chapter entitled 'Something Beyond Fishin'; also in my book "Not Your Ordinary Hunting Stories" in the chapter entitled 'First Deer...Last Stand'. During that awful summer of 1981 there was enough feuding, fighting, and fornicating going on to last ten lifetimes. First Wife Jen-Jen and I were divorced in March, 1981; ending our twelve year marriage. But! Like a snake with its head cut clean off, it took our marriage a looooong time to actually die. EX Jen-Jen and I chopped off the head of our lives together, but its carcass wouldn't quit wiggling; "Not 'til the sun went down." There was a LOT of trouble. There were weeks at a time EX Jen-Jen refused to allow me to even SEE The Boys; her version of, "justifiable punishment for my bad behavior".

I did what I could to steal bits and slivers of time; anything to maintain contact with The Boys. And when The Boys WERE allowed time with me, one thing we did was go fishin. As often as possible; to places where I felt the three of us could enjoy a memorable day; to places where my boys were likely to catch something worth bragging about when I returned them to their Mom. I loved it most when The Boys had a good day fishin and hauled home somethin special to eat; back to their Mom's apartment in Kansas City. EX

Jen-Jen would complain; "Jimmy...You're just doing that (fishing) to torment ME!" But you gotta admit, The Boys begging their Mom to cook precious fresh fish; "lovingly brought home to Mom"; was a request EX Jen-Jen could ill-afford to refuse.

Anyway; "my reasoning proper or not"; The Boys and I experienced a long hot summer that year; including several fishin trips. Three fishin excursions most vividly stand out as picks of a good litter; 1) camping overnight on the shore of Cousin Joe's farm lake in Platte County, Missouri; 2) taking an all day float trip down muddy, swift Bee Creek near my home; and 3) driving down to Missouri's Ozarks to catch a shitload of rainbow trout at a pay-by-the-pound commercial trout farm. There were other fishin trips that bitter summer, several others; but for reasons described herein, those three remain firmly fixed in my mind; my "picks of a good litter".

First pick: Cousin Joe's

An overnight camping and fishin trip to Cousin Joe's well-stocked farm lake. When The Boys and I pitched our tent, the weather was windy and cool; too cool for summer. As a result of being cold all night, we suffered from lack of sleep. When dawn came and it was actually time to fish we were tired. Now that I think about it; "It may have been my greasy skillet cornbread and burned hash browns that disturbed everyone's sleep?" Or it could have been coyotes circling our campfire all night, howling like we fishermen were the coyotes next intended meal? That's damned sure what The Boys thought. Our inability to sleep, probably raw excitement? Knowing that come dawn, we were going to be blessed with an opportunity to catch a bucket full of farm pond fattened Bluegill; fun to catch, easy to fry, a joy to eat. If you haven't tried it, do so! You'll enjoy all three legs of the chore; "catching...frying...AND eating!"

When dawn came, so did swarming bluegill; two dozen pudgy fish, flopping around in our wire basket, before The Boys exhausted our supply of night crawlers. Fortuitously I had a small tackle box with me; carried out of habit, brought along for the ride. Searching for an alternative to being out of bait, I dug out a rusty trio of odd colored Rooster Tails ™; small lures with a single treble hook in back and a tiny spinner in front. I figured; "What the Hell...Let's see if The Boys can catch a few bluegill on these relics?" But they didn't. Nope! Not ONE bluegill! They were too busy catching bass and crappie instead! The three of us took home, to MY house; "as opposed to EX Jen-Jen's big city fancy apartment"; something over twenty pan sized largemouth bass...for frying. Nice eatin size; about two pounds each. And; one, huge, fat-bellied channel cat; that couldn't resist a twirling Rooster Tail ™. The Boys still talk about the bucket full of bluegill, the unexpected plethora of eatin size bass, the one fat channel cat; "AND the dozen coyotes The Boys thought were threatening to devour us alive."

Second pick: Bee Creek

The Boys and I had fun fishin Platte County's muddy Bee Creek, but mostly we enjoyed our float trip. Actually; "fishing was terrible." The big creek was running high and moderately swift, and was, as locals put it, mudded up real bad. Currents weren't dangerous, just swift. Stronger than normal currents was one reason we had chosen to go that particular day. I had been promising The Boys a float trip and knew we would enjoy an easy downstream ride. I told The Boys; "To Hell with catchin fish…we can do that anytime…let's float." And though we came home with an empty stringer, I would NOT say we came home empty handed. The Boys and I never came home from our father-son adventures empty handed.

A good mess of fish for two proud fisherboys. (1981)

I carry a loaded pistol everywhere I go. Carrying a pistol dates back to my years in The Marines. My entire year in Viet Nam I carried a .45 automatic. Currently I carry a pistol to work; "not…on the job"; but with me in my truck. Texas was one of the first states to permit Concealed Handgun Licensing; Nurse-Wife Peg and I obtained our CHLs the first year. Anyway; dating back to the early 1970s and The Marines, I have carried a pistol. That day floating Bee Creek with The Boys was no different. I brought along a .22 caliber revolver; theoretically for shooting critters we might encounter, "that might require shooting?" Large, aggressive cottonmouths were known to inhabit Bee Creek and its immediate environs. Over the years, my friends and I had encountered copperheads and cottonmouths while hunting bullfrogs on Bee Creek.

Bee Creek's funky, abnormally high post-flood-stage water carried our small, fiber glass, two man boat downstream like a child's red and white bobber caught in a gutter in a rain storm. Ours was a tiny but a fun boat. I bought The Boys the small boat to use on our catfish pond; for fishing or playing on calm, clean water, where capsizing was an expected option. That day on Bee Creek, The Boys and I were floating too fast downstream to legitimately say we were fishin; but not going too fast to return home saying we had done something useful; "perhaps more fun?"

The three of us, crowded a bit in the small, two man boat were focusing on having a good time. We had barely begun what I anticipated would be a five hour trip, when one of The Boys spotted a monster bullfrog; first spotting in what turned into THE focal point of our day. I decided that since bullfrog season was open I would take a shot. "Blam!" One shot, one dead bullfrog; its limp, floating frog body dipped from the fast moving creek with a small dip net. An hour later we had abandoned our effort to fish and were instead concentrating on spotting bullfrogs, and avoiding snakes. Higher than normal, swifter than normal, muddier than normal; mile after mile of Bee Creek's jungly shoreline appeared lined with either big bullfrogs, or a million snakes. We shot the biggest of the bullfrogs and avoided the million snakes; every last snake, regardless of size or species.

At the end of The Boys and my float trip, Nurse-Friend Peg was scheduled to be waiting downstream for our safe return. But when we three Lewis & Clark adventurers arrived at our predetermined rendezvous point, Nurse-Friend Peg was pissed; madder than a freshly kicked nest of hornets on a rainy day. Being interested in The Boys happiness; being interested in the boldness and exciting aspect of our float trip; being interested in forming a long lasting relationship with The Boys Dad (me); Nurse-Friend Peg had willingly agreed to drive my pickup and meet we three soldiers of fortune downstream; after letting us off upstream hours earlier. But! Nurse-Friend Peg made a critical error when calculating the correct time. She had been sitting there fuming for nearly three hours; all alone on a lightly traveled gravel road, near an antique bridge, high over Bee Creek. Waiting! For three hours! "Sorry!"

Nurse-Friend Peg was born in and grew up in Kansas City. Before she was ever a big city nurse, she was a big city GIRL! Nurse-Friend Peg didn't know an all day float trip from an all day bed pan. She erroneously concluded that floating explorers would show up downstream at approximately the same time as driving non-explorers. Would cover the five to six mile prescribed float trip and arrive at the preselected downstream rendezvous point, not too long after she arrived there by nonchalantly driving; Peg's definition of "not too long after" subject to a broad range of interpretations! Before departing I had emphasized, to Nurse-Friend Peg, to not hurry and not worry. "But...Peg did both!" She hurried to pick us up, thinking she was taking too long. And worried because it was HOURS before The Boys and I showed up at the rendezvous point.

A ton of bullfrogs in hand, a million snake sightings to declare, huge shit eatin grins on our muddy faces, sitting in the wet, sloppy back of my dirty old Chevy pickup, three happy boys made our way home to my farm; chauffeured home for showers and clean, dry clothes by one really pissed off, big city nurse. Thinking back on that day, I have no earthly idea, absolutely NONE, why Nurse-Friend Peg and I didn't communicate better regarding our rendezvous TIME? My only possible and practical explanation; "just a theory"; "speaking privately here...as one sane adult to another"; "Perhaps Nurse-Friend Peg and I were a tad too busy lusting...to properly listen? And. Since Nurse-Friend Peg and I were eventually married, and Peg legitimatized our relationship by becoming Nurse-Wife Peg...and she and I and The Boys lived happily ever after...my theory may indeed be sound?"

Third pick: Ozark Trout

The Boys and my 1981 fishing extravaganza to a trout farm down in Missouri's Ozarks will always rank in the top three of my 'All Time' fishing experiences. The only vehicle I owned at the time; "following my expensive divorce from EX Jen-Jen"; a dirty old Chevy farm truck, in which First Wife Jen-Jen would NEVER have been caught dead riding. "Now that I'm older and wiser...and have thought through it...is there any kind of divorce besides...an expensive divorce?"

Therefore; in order for The Boys to be allowed, by EX Jen-Jen, to go; so that The Boys would be riding in a safe vehicle, pre-approved for safety and comfort sufficient to satisfy EX Jen-Jen (burrrrrrr); the FIRST thing I was required to do, PRIOR to being allowed to depart on our road trip to go fishin, was go out and rent a clean, ecologically friendly, safe, economy car; "EX Jen-Jen and her current boyfriend were into ecology... or some such weird shit?" I didn't know squat about ecology OR economy. I was so broke I couldn't afford to pay attention; and getting broker by the day. But! I wanted to take The Boys to a special place; a fishin venue where I knew they would catch something; preferably something exciting, different enough to be memorable. However! Renting even an economy car wasn't in my budget; the only transportation I could afford was what I owned; "And that barely!" Choice of vehicles aside; "a topic about which EX Jen-Jen and I bitterly fought"; my goal was to do something special to help relieve building anxiety. Do something to distract The Boys from multiple woes befalling all three of us during what had been a sad, sorry summer filled with woe. "Arguing with EX Jen-Jen about what type vehicle I might drive...IF allowed to go fishing with my sons... one in a swarm of bees attacking The Boys serenity and my sanity that awful summer!"

But, as John Wayne said; "A man's gotta do...what a man's gotta do." I scraped together another two hundred bucks and rented a cheap car. Our small Rent-A-Buggy in hand, The Boys and I drove three hours due south to The Ozarks; a mountainous outdoor playground sprawling across the south half of Missouri and north half of Arkansas. When I was in high school, my parents took Baby Sister Mitzi and me to The Ozarks. While vacationing there, my Dad discovered the trout farm I currently had in mind for The Boys and me. I had returned to that same beautiful trout farm a couple of times during my dating years at MU. Once upon a time I took a Delta Gamma Hotty down to the trout farm, expecting her to appreciate the rustic out-backedness of the place. It was inconsequential to me that the cheap motel she and I shared that night was named The Red Apple Inn; "but it may have influenced my DG's overall opinion of me?" May have altered my ultimate chances for getting lucky that trip? But I had carefully chosen The Red Apple Inn as our destination. It was convenient; located directly across the highway from something FAR more tantalizing to ME than my Hotty DG; "Unlimited trout fishing!" However! Miss Hotty was NOT thrilled at sleeping so near the sound of a bubbling brook as it traversed a full blown commercial trout farm frequented by dozens of cars. "The exotic or natural mystic of it all didn't seem to score squat with my urbane DG? But! Good trout fishin aside…I DID catch somethin on that trip with my Hotty DG …and it took me a month to get over it!"

Fast forward fifteen years; I was sitting in the same fondly remembered parking lot in front of The Red Apple Inn. The Boys and I thrilled to be parked in our little, rented car, in the heavily forested mountains of the Ozarks; breathlessly waiting to catch trout in such an out-of-the-way, hidden-from-reality, place. An isolated haven for two, down on their luck fisherboys, and one fisherdad; a place where The Boys had been told they could catch all the trout they wanted. "Fish until their hands hurt…so long as Dad doesn't run out of dough-ray-me…CASH…Me having arrived at the Red Apple a tad short…due to being forced into renting the damned EX-Jen-Jen-mandated econo-car!"

But! Believe me; "I intended to pay The Trout Man…before others." The Red Apple Inn, solitude it provided, and nearby hoards of easy to catch trout, were exactly what I was seeking when the three of us departed Weston, MO. EX Jen-Jen and her long list of ne'r-do-well, citified boyfriends had been taking The Boys fishing TOO; had been conducting a little tit-for-tat recreational fishing on EX Jen-Jen's behalf. The Boys had been catching the living "S-H-I-T" out of various species of fish in a variety local ponds, lakes, and streams; including fish dragged from two beautiful lakes I built on farmland given up to EX Jen-Jen in our still red-raw divorce settlement. I was admittedly carrying a huge chip on my underprivileged shoulder. I absolutely detested the new concept of NOT being allowed to fish with The Boys in former favorite haunts on our former land. While EX Jen-Jen and her string of first timer, non-fishing boyfriends trekked in and out at will; the lackluster boyfriends first timers at fishing...NOT at being with EX Jen-Jen!"

But! Back in the moment! The Boys trip to the Ozarks with ME, and catching a few hatchery raised trout from a trout farm, was foremost on MY mind; an excellent opportunity to get away from it all, while fishin. There were reasons why the idea of driving down to an isolated trout farm popped into my painfully throbbing brain. The trout farm was out of town; far from the scene of bitter fighting between EX Jen-Jen and me. Fishing at a trout farm required little preparation. Catching trout provided The Boys a different type fishin experience from any they were enjoying nearer home. Their innocent minds were being whitewashed by EX Jen-Jen's threadbare string of Wannabe Daddy Pretender Boyfriends. Making the trip to the Ozarks with me was a lock; "a sure thing"; for The Boys and ME having fun...together. Certain to piss off EX Jen-Jen! And. When The Boys and I returned from the Ozarks and showed up together at EX Jen-Jen's fantasyland apartment, where I was forced to return child custody of our dirty, tired, sleepy, grumpy, stinking of fish and dirty feet, rumpled, wee boys; those boys would be lovingly, and proudly, carrying for their Mom's approval, for EX Jen-Jen's approval, one hundred, ice cold, wet and slimy, trout. "Sure to make Jen-Jen's fantasyland day!"

The Boys and I had no problem locating the trout farm. Both Boys jumped out of the car "ready to fish 'til sundown." Except; just like the Griswold's arriving at Wally World; the trout farm was closed when we arrived. The Boys and I were back at the trout farm gate first thing next morning sporting happy hearts, fresh trout bait, and new fishing poles; "Both Boys were ready to catch The Big One!" And. They did. Together, The Boys caught over one hundred rainbow trout; yearling trout, generally in the one to two pound range. I paid through my divorce bloodied nose for the privilege, but the flavor of one-ups-man-ship satisfaction IS real; "the pleasant aroma has lasted for YEARS!"

The Boys were thrilled to learn there were size differences of hatchery raised trout; sizes segregated by penning the trout in clearly marked sections of the large rambling trout farm. If Dad was willing to pay, The Boys could fish for an unlimited number of trout; "AND for a trophy trout!" Which of course The Boys immediately insisted upon doing; for which Dad immediately agreed to pay.

A third set of trout pools, located fartherest from the clubhouse, contained golden colored trout that looked like long skinny goldfish! I had never seen such trout; neither had either son. Naturally, as anyone with a brain could have predicted, the golden trout were higher priced. Conveniently; "for the trout farm"; there were zero limits on the size or number of gold trout The Boys were allowed to catch. It was going to be an expensive day for Dad. "But then ask yourself...How often...in all of life...do mortals get to do something we WANT to do...where there ARE no limits...NO restrictions?"

As icing on the cake of an emotionally charged, highly positive fishin situation, The Boys and I discovered, after catching one or two, that the golden trout were bigger; "Much bigger!" One golden trout son Chris caught tipped the $cale$ at nearly three pounds! Golden trout were not as heavily fished for by patrons of the trout farm; "The gold trout...$old off by the pound as they were caught...were too expensive to simply catch and eat as ordinary food...there had to be a reason for patrons to fish for such an expen$ive prize...there needed to be a motive...an agenda." As a result of being much higher priced, the golden trout remained in the trout farm's pools longer; resulting in them growing bigger before being caught. Stayed down on the farm longer, waiting for some tired, bruised, and desperate EX like me to happen along and catch the pricele$$ golden trophies and haul them out the front gate. Hopeless, hapless men, like me; determined to prove something to someone back home; "This world is full of millions of mind bent sucker$...who...for one $ymbolic rea$on or another...are driven to act exactly as I acted...do precisely what I did?"

Home again, toting the largest ice chest we could find, chock full of fresh trout, to account for our days permitted out of town, The Boys and I re-entered 1981's summer of discontent. Within minutes of The Boys and me unloading the swollen ice chest of fresh cold trophies on EX Jen-Jen's metropolitan doorstep and bidding her "Good Day"; adding "Have Fun"; the tenuous cease fire between she and I ended, and our "uncivil war" resumed. "Hell was Hell again... revisited. And as I drove forty miles back to the relative peace of my tobacco farm...I kept thinking about an old saying I had heard. About how...even a bad day fishin...is better than a good day...doin somethin else... including putting one over on your pissy-minded EX!"

Ladd and **Chris** at Ozarks trout farm, Mo. (1981)

Scat Cat Fishin', March 1984

"We fished!" That's right. No matter where I landed on this tired old planet; "We fished." Wherever life as a Dad, Husband, Friend, Employee, or Combatant in a war has taken me; "We fished!" (Wait 'til you read the chapter entitled 'Mekong Cats'). From being flush and fishing with Nurse-Wife Peg on a private charter off the coast of California on our honeymoon; to being broke and grubbing it up all summer out in Cousin Joe's farm pond in Missouri with The Boys; "We fished." Why would spring 1984 be different? "We fished...Merely a new and exciting and different venue for The Boys and me...Where...As always...We fished."

Nurse-Wife Peg and I took Sons Chris and Ladd down to Corpus Christi, Texas for spring break. There for a week, our new family bought inexpensive tickets aboard a half-day offshore fishing boat called the Scat Cat. Our time was limited and the weather fiercely bad. The weather SO bad, going fishing beyond Corpus Christi Bay's protective jetties was risky. As a result, the Scat Cat's Captain gave his dozen or so potential passengers two options; collect a full refund, or fish within the bay. Bay fishing would be mean greatly curtailed fishing; confined to fishing inside the jetties; limited to fishing for shallow water bay fish, most of which species were decidedly NOT at their peak season. Not at a peak as far as two, totally inexperienced fisherboys having a realistic opportunity of catching something. The entire motive behind Nurse-Wife Peg and me buying tickets on the Scat Cat was based on one simple premise; "since arriving in Texas our new family of four had yet to go saltwater fishing." "Had yet to experience even a sample of the type fishing we had been hearing so much hubbub about from Texas friends." Saltwater fishing in any size, shape, or form was still a mystery to The Boys. An incongruity that would soon change; and when it changed, would change forever!

Back aboard the Scat Cat that spring day; all twelve stalwart souls on board opted to go fishing; opted to NOT remain in port. So The Captain put out to sea; approximately a thousand yards out to sea into murky shallow waters of Corpus Christi Bay. As far as The Boys were concerned we might just as well have been rounding the Cape of Good Hope off South Africa; they loved every minute. During the Captain's initial stop for fishing, ninety-five percent of his paying patrons caught nothing. A couple of small saltwater drum, a few hardheads, and a bucket full of bait stealing piggy perch; named for their appetite, not their appearance.

But The Boys stood in awe of their day, mouths agape. The Scat Cat was more enormous than any fishing boat they could have imagined, much less set foot upon. And. Neither young son; ages nine and seven; had ever encountered the likes of such colorful people as those with whom our family embarked aboard the Scat Cat that fine spring day. Nor had The Boys ever even seen such frothy coastal waters, into which they repeatedly plunged oversized baits weighted down with golf ball sized chunks of lead. Nor had The Boys ever sampled such subtle romance in life in such a foreign setting; an alien environment that included salt air and saltwater in horizon to horizon proportions; a whole new world, filled with a plethora of salty fragrances The Boys had never before realized existed. A seafarer's smorgasbord of salt air, dead fish, and rotting seaweed; accentuated here and there along the way with diesel fumes from the chugging Scat Cat.

Nurse-Wife Peg and I weren't disturbed that zero edible fish were reeled in by the real fisherman onboard; "Not one good fish was had by anyone. . .not until the very end." The Captain was about to give up; preparing to return our happy-go-lucky flotilla of sun bleached but safely embarked tourist ashore; when a Hefty Hispanic Man, with a fishing rod the size of my forearm and a reel the size of a gallon bucket, hooked something. A half-hour later the badly sweating Rotund Mexican hauled aboard the previously skunked Scat Cat a forty pound black drum. Everyone aboard was electrified by the soaring energy and raw thrill generated by Senor Mucho Grande's whopping catch. I was amazed that such a BIG fish could come from such shallow water. I was also amazed that our companion fisherman, Hunky Hispanic Hombre, had used a live crab as bait.

As soon as Big Old Boy from Tijuana's monster black drum was secured on ice; Scat Cat's only respectable fish of the day; El Jefe Fisherman was back in the shallow water fishing, using his twelfth and final live crab for bait.

"Ziiiiiiiiiiiiiinnnng!" In less than one minute, Big Old Boy from Tijuana hooked another monstrous fish! The

Scat Cat Fishin

A big fish on a big boat and both boys were happy to be there. (1983)

second fish was also a black drum, which weighed in at nearly FIFTY pounds! In less than one hour, in two consecutive casts, one BIG man, using two live crabs, and oversized T-Rex sized gear, had successfully hooked and landed nearly one hundred pounds of fresh game fish. "And I saw it happen...believed it. And the wide-eyed Boys...Well...They sucked up the excitement of the day like cold chocolate malts on a hot summer day! Took in and absorbed every last drop...like gallon jug sized sponges deckhands were using to mop up the Scat Cat's bloody deck...bloodied by the second of only two keeper fish...both black drum...caught and hauled aboard that day. And even though The Boys didn't catch much besides bait...no one else did either. The Boys...Nurse-Wife and I experienced our first day of saltwater fishing! Perhaps inexplicably...considering our total lack of actual fishing success...I was...Nurse-Wife Peg was...The Boys were...all four of us were...hooked on saltwater fishing. And the last time I checked; "We still are!"

White Trash White Bass', April 1985

We had fished the white bass run in 1984 and had developed a respectable technique for catching the prized fish there in our stretch of the Guadalupe River. Coinciding with the bluebonnet bloom across The Great State of Texas, white bass make their spring spawning run out of the lakes in which they thrive, into clear rocky bottomed rivers that feed a dozen sizable lakes in Texas. It's a bona fide annual spring ritual here in central Texas; creating thousands of one-trip-a-year fishermen. Experts, nimrods, and novices alike; dust off seldom used fishin poles and have a go at sackin a mess of whites.

White bass are smallish fish that somewhat resemble crappie. Maybe a little fatter bodied with a tougher hide; and definitely put up more of a good fight when hooked on the opposite end of a light crappie rig. One important attribute white bass bring to the table and have in common with crappie; succulent white flesh, tender as your eye when properly deep fried. Cornmeal breaded white bass fillets washed down with copious volumes of ice cold beer have brought streaming tears to the eyes of many tough Texans on balmy spring evenings. "Come April...It's damned near a religious experience."

When white bass spawning run is in full swing, fish become concentrated in the rapids of clear, shallow, tributary rivers feeding into the lakes. And when any species of fish; "good eating or bad"; becomes concentrated enough, it's a sure bet that carloads of fisherpersons will quickly follow. "I've seen grown men nearly drown trying to hand-catch large carp trapped in a muddy irrigation ditch. "In late spring...in places where there was adequate fishing space for twenty fishermen...I have personally observed one hundred...lining the rocky Guadalupe River just upstream from Canyon Lake. Hoards of white bass fishermen…lining hot stretches of river bank…fighting for dominion over some of the better known honey holes. It can become an untenable zoo."

And. "God…Please Forgive Me!" Whenever I think of white bass fishermen, I involuntarily think of white trash fishermen. "Generally speaking…of course." That convoluted thought process is based on several fishermen The Boys and I encountered during the 1985 white bass season fishing on the Guadalupe River. Wherever The Boys and I tried fishing that spring for spawning white bass, we encountered clusters and gaggles of white trash; attempting to catch white bass. "An inevitable…acceptable price paid for the opportunity to gather freezer bags full of succulent fillets from the extremely seasonal fish!"

Few white trash fishermen fished with lures; even fewer trolled up and down the river in boats. White trash fishermen using a boat to fish for white bass were a distinct minority; a footnote to greater hoards of bank running white trash fishermen who fished for white bass by thrashing the Guadalupe River until its clear, swift waters were turned dull, milky white by unending white trash casts made in an attempt to throw live natural bait; "minners…drowned by the millions"; in search of catching elusive white bass.

Standing IN the water; floating ON the water; running barefoot OUT of the water; scratching chigger bites ON the shore; toothless or nearly toothless white trash fishermen fished for toothless or nearly toothless white bass.

Constantly chattering in unrecognizable native languages; jammed shoulder-to-shoulder, beerbelly-to-beerbelly, too-small-halter-top-to-too-small-halter-top; crowded breasts perfectly aligned shoreline-to-shoreline, waterline-to-skyline, trotline-to-pee line; male and female; white trash hoards showed up in unbelievable herds and prides and flocks every April to catch and haul home dump truck loads of white bass. According to local custom; artificial lures, boats, proper clothing, bathing, peeing in private ON shore, and properly covered breasts were a waste of time, energy, and Texas natural resources. "Getter Done Bubba…Momma's got a hankerin fer sum white bass!"

Local lore held; "The only thing a body needs for catchin a nice mess a white bass iz old tennis shoes…to keep yer feet offin the broke glass…and some old raggedy throwed away clothes for wadin the river." Based on what The Boys and I observed, that fairly summed up ever thang needed; except, of course, a huge supply of appropriate beverages for "quenchin a body's high noon thirst." It gets a might hot down in Texas come April. And. It goes without saying; a huge bucket brim FULL of frisky minners; the bigger the bucket the better, the more minners the better. "Yes...I said minners!" That would be one hundred percent correct enunciation. A white trash word meaning, "small fish used as bait", pronounced 'minners' in Backwatersville, Texas. And. "You sure as HELL better come with a big bucket...a holdin plenty of minners...fer sharin with yer neighbors on the river." Or; "It was your ass...in small chunks!" Only disgusting, uppity, Yankees fished with minnows; REAL Texans, local toothless REAL Texans, fished with minners.

For Chris, Ladd, and me, 1985 was a record year for catching white bass ON the Guadalupe River, while spotting white trash IN the river; "Hoards of white trash... chasing hoards of white bass!" A top drawer white bass year; sprinkled here, there, yon, and all about, with memorable white trash highlights.

One exceptional day, The Boys and I floated the same remote stretch of river twelve different times. We would put in the river, float a mile downstream through a series of red hot but scattered current-swept holes; then get out and hand-tow our small fiberglass boat back upriver. "The same small boat we used for floating muddy, frog and snake infested Bee Creek up in Missouri." We would tow our tiny bobber of a boat all the way back to our original point of entry; then repeat the process. On typical days we made six to eight trips; that one big day we made twelve. Onshore fishermen became fatigued just watching our up and downriver effort. The Boys and I, floating by in our bobbing little boat, caused white trash Wanna Bee Fishermen to wish out loud that THEY had access to similar flotation devices; while we smiling floaters, crowded together in our tiny boat like fat triplets in a skinny woman's womb, swept by the stranded white trash standing on shore, wishing for a boat. "It caused The Boys and me to feel down right privileged. We caught lotsa fish as we slipped by...tossing a Kiss Our Ass wave at throngs of landlocked white trash...as we bobbed our way on downriver."

Fairly rapid downstream movement helped quickly pinpoint reddest hottest honey holes. Best spots in the river were too shallow for anything resembling a real bass boat to emulate our simple method. If the river rose or flowed more swiftly, spawning white bass instinctively moved upstream to escape fishing pressure; conventional boat traffic was unable to pursue the bass in shallower water. But! Believe it or not...suit yourself. The Boys and I WERE smart enough to follow the white bass. Fish moving upstream meant back to square one for conventional bass boaters loaded down with tons of cumbersome equipment and fishermen. Upstream became sanctuary where fishin masses couldn't go; became our secret fishin holes.

Wade fishermen fared better, but the sheer labor involved in wading excluded ninety percent of all potential waders. Semi dangerous deep pockets of swirling water and bad ass snakes excluded another nine percent. That left me and my two young sons; ages ten and eight; and an adventuresome one percent of the general public, an elite one percent, as sole and exclusive proprietors of vast stretches of the Guadalupe River. The Boys and I continued our success until we literally outgrew our midget boat. Wading, or using the tiny boat two at a time, didn't appeal to any part of our trio, so we moved on; to deeper waters; Lake Fork, Choke Canyon, Falcon Lake, and vast opportunities promised by Texas saltwater bays and The Gulf!

During one of our little boat float trips down our favorite private stretch of river; I hooked a monstrous flathead catfish. I was using four pound test leader, tied to six pound test spool line, rigged with a quarter ounce lead head jig; to which I had affixed an average sized minner, skewered directly onto my jig head hook. SOP bait for The Boys and me. The Big Ole Flathead; "I got one reasonable glimpse of him in the shallow semi clear river water running under our bobbing boat"; took out most of my tiny open-faced reel's hair thin line. Then, ever so gently, the big fish began actually towing our bizarrely buoyed-up boat UP STREAM! We made nearly one hundred yards headway upstream in fairly deep, and therefore fairly slow moving water, until our tiny boat reached a much shallower and more pronounced current. My spider web thin line could no longer stand the strain and snapped. "Bye Bye Fish!" "Hello lifetime memory!"

Gleaned from years of white bass fishing, our absolute best and most enduring family memory is actually a quote; something Nurse-Wife Peg, Son Chris, Son Ladd, and I all four simultaneously heard said. A proclamation made by a white trash mutterer of his intentions. Our family has laughed about the white trash threat and jokingly repeated it a million times; "as a quote." I mentioned that "white bass fishing" and "white trash fishing" are similar sounding. In our family, the two white phrases are synonymous. I don't say that without reason. PWT characters The Boys and I encountered on our stretch of the Guadalupe River lived their lives one notch below the TOP of life's all time 'Interesting But Strange' chart; normal only if lines defining "normal" are badly blurred. "Family history and family heritage were questionable issues for several regular white trash folks we encountered...I mean white bass fishermen we encountered." It was readily apparent to Nurse-Wife Peg that a few older male fishermen our family encountered on the lonely backwoods river banks of the Guadalupe were without question "Daddy Uncles". Men who were both "Daddy" and "Uncle" to passels of pale skinned, chinless children running amuck along the crowded river! "Think about what I'm saying! It's like with those women from El Dorado Texas...seen on TV dressed in identical pastel dresses...with identical big hairdos...Ladder

Day Aints...that are said to have begotten a few offspring...by way of their own begetters...daddies fathering daughters...with their own daughters...fathering babies who are daughter-nieces!"

It is skin crawling but happens. Meantime; Nurse-Wife Peg and I saw a couple of those toothless Wonder Dads pissing in the river; trying to get themselves awake for the morning run; "The white bass run AND the white trash run...both seemed to always go on hot runs just at sunrise." A dozen PWT Men Folk, wearing badly stained wife beater T-shirts, and their chinless inbred clans, had slept on the river bank. I didn't say camped on the river bank. I said slept on the river bank. Directly ON the seepy, wet ground; directly IN the cold, spring, night air; no tent, no tarp, no sign of any amenities beyond dirty, stinking, badly stained, wet clothes; probably not due for a good washin til NEXT Sat-day. The morning we heard THE great quote, OUR family of four had intentionally arrived on the river at first light; careful to pick our way through areas along the river still littered with sleeping carcasses of PWT.

One of the meaner looking Daddy Uncles kept bellowing instructions; repeating himself over and over and over; focusing his verbal ire on one of his biological offspring. The offspring's genetic markers were indistinguishable from his Daddy Uncle's genetic markers; neither the sire, nor the sired easily identifiable in what was an obviously none too crowded but shockingly shallow gene pool. Same missing teeth; same large, flappy ears, chinless faces, pointy head skulls, drooling grins; same withered, round-shouldered, thin bodies, lacking muscle definition on bent limbs. The Daddy Uncle was gutturally yelling for his grinless, chinless child to "Get the Hell down here" and wade far out into the cold, swift river to fetch the clan's small, white, mixed breed dog. Get the wet, shivering, nearly-drowned dog OUT of the Daddy Uncle's favorite fishin hole. But! No one in Daddy Uncle's clan seemed interested in wading into the predawn, chilly river to capture the clan's errant, twenty pound cur; a silly dog named Scooter.

So! Daddy Uncle commenced yelling louder and louder; cussing the wretched white dog's mother, and the dog's apparent tendency to have consanguineous sex with its own momma dog? It was a wretched white dog only because it was forced to go home every night with such flea bitten, lowlife humans. The shivering dog, Scooter, was way too frightened to dare move. Scooter was obviously the terrified dog's Godless given name. Another dozen yells at shivering Scooter to "GETCHA ASS over hear" and Daddy Uncle, tired of his own cigaretty voice, upped the ante by saying; "I'M SAYIN...Getcha ass over here Scooter...or...I'm gonna...!"

At that precise moment, Daddy Uncle yelled what quickly became our family's All Time favorite fishing quote; yelling a threat through clenched,

We floated the hottest holes... then dragged our little boat upstream and did it again. (1986)

tobacco stained green chili smelling, teeth. "Scooter…Get yer f—-in ass over here…or I'm gonna stomp yer head offin yer skinny body…and shit down the hole!"

To YOU, an average reader of this story, a PWT lowlife stomping off Scooter Dog's head, might seem more than a tad unreasonable, as one possible retaliation for the pitiful little dog's mild misbehavior. But it didn't seem unreasonable, or too far fetched, to me. Nope! Once-upon-a-time, during the late 1970s, one of my male tobacco sharecroppers up in Missouri DID indeed stomp a helpless animal's head. The helpless animal was the sharecropper's helpless WIFE! And the head that got stomped was her otherwise lovely sharecropper head! The toothless tobacco tenant husband stomped his chinless tobacco tenant wife's head until she nearly died! "True story!" One of my BEST tobacco tenants literally stomped his skinny, little wife unconscious on Main Street of our small hometown. The unfortunate wife's name certainly wasn't Scooter, but I will always think of HER when anyone in our family, me included, for whatever reason, irreverently says; "Scooter…Get over here…or I'm gonna stomp your head!"

One Doctor…Three Reds, Summer 1986

By 1986 our not so new migrant family of four was beginning to feel right at home in our adopted country of Texas; "Which…by the way…IS a State of Mind you know…Texas IS a whole 'nother country!" One reason I so readily adapted to paradise we lovingly call Texas, is because as far back as the late 1950s; way before Tammy Wynette or Barbara Mandrel were singing about it during the 1960s; before people were tying a yellow ribbon round the old oak tree in the 1970s; I WAS country. And the result when it was finally politically correct? My friends hung a sticky label on me; "Jimmy… You were country…when country wasn't cool." Disparaging? Unfair? Inaccurate? Or? Definingly right on? Doesn't matter; either way you go, I owned the rap.

Fortunately for me, most of my adult life I have naturally just fit in; some of us do, some don't. I did. When our new family first arrived in Texas, my fit in factor was working better than average. I anticipated it might be; while serving in the Marines I had met and known many good Marines from Texas. I was looking forward to life in Texas. The Boys were seven and five when our family moved to Blanco County. The Boys didn't know any better; as kids they assumed life was good ever where! When Nurse-Wife Peg first found out I had accepted a high powered real estate career and we were moving to Texas she squealed with delight. She didn't much care where we lived; so long as on warm summer evenings there were plenty of longneck bottles of ice cold beer to drink. So long as on quiet week ends, sitting at home on our patio, there was spicy Mexican food to eat. So long as ever day, all day long, there were eight hundred glorious Interstate miles between our new family and EX Jen-Jen! All in all, after studying on it for three decades, I would say moving to Texas was one damned good move.

Not that our first-ever real Texas neighbor would have EVER uttered such a filthy word as DAMN! "Nope...Not our new neighbor...Not Doctor Doug!" When our family of legal immigrants moved across the street from Dr. Doug back in 1985 he was ten to twelve years younger than me; and one of the world's finest practicing dentists. After one successful visit to his office, Dr. Doug became our family's permanent dentist. Dr. Doug, and his lovely wife Vicki, and their two talented daughters, remained our good neighbors for five, pleasant, neighborly years. Among other things, Dr. Doug, was in 1985, and still is, a world class fisherman; really and truly one of the most capable and experienced fishermen I have ever known. He has fished ever' where. Dr. Doug has caught record brown trout from the White River in northern Arkansas; landed behemoth cod from the frigid waters of the Bering Straights; snatched giant salmon from the jaws of a grizzly bear on the frozen Alaskan tundra; "Just outta sight and over the hill from Sarah Palin's front porch...the one Sarah can stand on and see Russia." Dr. Doug has caught big; "I mean really big"; genuine trophy fish from every major game fish family and popular species. And. As my good Daddy from Missouri always used to say; "That man (any man, but in this case Dr. Doug) has forgotten more about fishin (or farming, or working, or playing cards, or managing baseball, or any manly endeavor in which one might comparatively or competitively be engaged) than most men will ever know!"

That was our new neighbor Dr. Doug! Sometimes his KIA attitude could wear a tad thin on the unknowing. But many people weren't patient enough to appreciate the entirety of Dr. Doug. Many folks allowed themselves to become peeved before ever learning the finer aspects of Dr. Doug's only mildly offensive KIA personality. Part time or short time, or casual passers-by, didn't get it when it came to dealing with Dr. Doug; a man of genuinely solid character; a good man; a decent man. A good father; who cared deeply for and attended well his two young daughter's menial girl-child multiple wants and needs. "I don't think I can ever overestimate God's blessing of having been given ONLY male children to parent! Thank You Lord! Thank You Lord! TYL!"

In addition to being a devout Christian, Dr. Doug was also a loyal husband; near slave to his Church Lady wife, Miss Vickie. During the years our family has lived in Blanco, Miss Vickie and Dr. Doug have nearly run First Baptist Church. Dr. Doug has served on every committee worth serving on, and has pretty much run rough shod over our humble church's revolving door deacons. Some people gripe about Miss Vickie's and Dr. Doug's ubiquitous presences within our church. But I defend Miss Vickie and Dr. Doug, saying; "Somebody has to do it......?" And IF Dr. Doug wasn't around to hear me, I would add; "......... I don't see you're a-s-s (the person griping about Dr Doug) up there volunteering to do s-h-i-t (s-h-i-t meaning not one thing)." I always spelled out "a-s-s" and "s-h-i-t" because normally I was talking to a church member!

First Sunday our new little refugee family ever walked in Blanco Baptist Church, Dr. Doug swarmed us; "like he does all new families." Most of his rushy-gushiness was genuine. No one really minded being flattered or having a fuss made over their presence. If our church doors were open, Miss Vickie or Dr. Doug were there; period, end of story, further comment or editorializing regarding our church not required.

Dr. Doug was fascinated by my Marine history and service in Viet Nam. One of the few times Dr. Doug personally offended ME was when he rudely asked me to show him scars created when I was wounded; multiple scars for which I received two Purple Hearts. I'm not sure, but I think Dr. Doug thought my relatively minor scars were NOT egregious enough to have warranted a Purple Heart? "But...I reminded Dr. Doug that he wasn't there with me...gettin his skinny ass shot at...when I earned them...he laughed...I laughed...and I forgave his KIA skepticism."

Anyway! Our two sons, and Dr. Doug's slightly younger two daughters, we two husbands and our two wives; all eight of us living across the street from one another, all of us members of the same church; all of us sharing the same values, principles, ethics, and religious beliefs; were a natural to fall in together and become friends. It wasn't long before Dr. Doug and I were swapping fishing stories and declaring one another real fishermen. Such would be expected.

However! A discernable separation in "neighborly sharing of mutual enthusiasm" for fishin and an abrupt schism in shared conversations about the sport of fishin between Dr. Doug and I occurred when Dr. Doug unilaterally decided my family's inexpensive fishing gear was barely serviceable; was inadequate for real fishermen. And said so! To me! Actually said; "Jim...You and The Boys must not be TOO big into fishin...or you would own better gear"; fairly typical of KIA Dr. Doug to be so blunt. In rebuttal to Dr. Doug's erroneous observation regarding my family's inadequacies, I felt compelled to point out that our meager family fishin budget had to be divided three ways, split equally between two boys and one Dad; was diluted by providing for three fishermen, versus one; as in Dr. Doug's myopically lived, narrow mindedly perceived, all-female family situation. "I must have made my point?"

One fine day right after church; "our family saw Miss Vickie and Dr. Doug nearly every Sunday"; Dr. Doug walked across the quiet, dead end street separating our house from his and handed me a brand new rod and reel. It was a nice rod and reel. Expensive equipment if judged by standards of the time, elegant equipment if judged by our family's humble standards; humble compared to Dr. Doug's. I suppose the everlasting gratitude I felt regarding the gifted rod and reel are partially responsible for Dr. Doug being included in my book? I was flattered. I was flabbergasted. No one had ever walked up and just handed me such a thoughtful gift; a nice fishin rod, no strings attached. The rod and reel were both "perfectly practical" and "practically perfect" as a gift for me; one in the same. As he presented the rod and reel, Dr. Doug quietly said, and I will always remember; "Jim...I have many rods and reels...you have so few...I want you to have it." Dr. Doug meant what he said, so I accepted the gift and did what my Mom would have wanted me to do; I politely said "THANKS"!

Within a year of becoming his neighbor, Dr. Doug took The Boys and me fishin. Dr. Doug also loaned The Boys and me his small bass boat a couple of times. "I already said Dr. Doug was a good neighbor." Our first fishin experience with Dr. Doug was for redfish at a manmade power plant lake located southeast of San Antonio, Texas; Lake Braunig. Neither The Boys nor I had ever caught a redfish. Actually the proper name is red drum; a saltwater game fish that was stocked in briny Lake Braunig and thrived; along with Tilapia and saltwater shad. Redfish are shaped like and look like freshwater carp or buffalo. Redfish are carnivorous game fish, bright golden red to deep blood red in color, and nearly always have a distinctive black spot on or near their tail fin; "Sometimes several spots...sometimes huge spots." Lake Braunig is a power plant lake just briny enough to sustain saltwater fish.

Anyway; every Tuesday, his day off, Dr. Doug made a practice of leaving early in the morning and coming home late in the afternoon with a small boatload of big redfish. Dr. Doug eventually heard my none-too-subtle hints and got around to inviting The Boys and me to go along with him; "Next time." So we did; one week later. The four of us; "Dr. Doug...The Boys and me"; departed late in the afternoon, planning to fish all night. Dr. Doug had the boat, the bait, the proper equipment; "more importantly"; Dr. Doug knew the exact correct spot to catch redfish; "One EXACT Spot!" Five to ten feet; "the length of our boat"; either way off The Spot and we caught nothing. Properly anchored in The Spot, we caught a boatload of wonderful memories.

Redfish grow big; up in the forty to fifty pound range in the Texas Gulf; "not quite that big in Braunig Lake." However! Any redfish over twenty inches is considered a keeper in Texas. Trophy size begins at around thirty inches. Currently, in Texas, any redfish over twenty-eight inches is considered a trophy, affectionately referred to as a 'Bull Red'. Fishermen are required to tag Bull Reds with a paper tag provided with their annual fishing license, and are limited to catching a maximum of three redfish of that size or greater, per year! "Hell...I had never even seen a live redfish...much less caught one!" The Boys and I looked up redfish in their Encyclopedia Britannica; "Remember those big fat dusty books no one hardly ever looked at?" We wanted to learn a few critical details before going out with Dr. Doug; less we embarrass ourselves.

So! The Boys and I went fishing with Dr. Doug, seeking redfish, and we were NOT embarrassed. Internally, within our family, even one of us catching a redfish was our family's FIRST goal. One redfish for each boy was our family's second goal; a goal Dr. Doug predicted. Beyond that, we Rookie Redfishermen had no agenda or bloated expectations. Part of my personal definition of being a good fisherman, certainly a characteristic attributable to Dr. Doug, is having realistic expectations. Having and keeping one's feet planted squarely on the ground regarding what might or might NOT happen on any given fishin trip. Dr. Doug, The Boys, and I fished until midnight with ZERO success; but weren't discouraged. Dr. Doug had warned The Boys that big redfish didn't normally bite until after midnight. We were there for a redfish, preferably BIG redfish; "there", using as bait, huge live shad the four of us had earlier that evening seined out of Braunig Lake. Our boat was filled with four believing Christians; two boys, two Dads. "We sure as HELL weren't sitting out there on a damp, dark, summer night drinking beer and talking dirty about having adulterous sex with wild women. NOPE! Deacon Dr. Doug would have been offended...The Boys were only ten and nine...and somehow or another...even I managed to get by without cold beer.

When the first of our four baited rods went off, Son Chris, our designated hitter, set the hook and a fish fight was on! "Our first problem of the night?" Rod number two went off in less than one minute and our boat, loaded with two excited boys, began fighting a protracted two front battle, to land (bring in) two attacking Bull Reds.

"Our second problem?" A third rod went off, and I was forcibly called out of retirement to perform a function Dr. Doug and I had intended for The Boys to perform. Inside two minutes, our boat had three bent, dancing rods, each of which had been carefully loaded with heavy monofilament; the rods all but ripped from the fierce grip of two, wildly excited, young boys and one mildly excited, young Dad. Fortunately our boat's fourth rod didn't go off. Dr. Doug reeled in the extra line, clearing our fish fighting field for battle. A three-way, combined battle; that, start to finish, lasted nearly thirty minutes. Accentuated now and then by the hair-raising fact that; Dr. Doug was out in the dark of night, in a crowded little boat, tending the needs of two slightly frightened boys, fighting the biggest fish of their fisherboy lives! While I, customarily an attentive Dad, was lost in combat; "Fighting a battle entirely my own…NOT particularly giving a rat's ass what happened beyond the tip of my OWN doubled over rod! Not that Dr. Doug or Miss Vickie would have EVER said…rat's ass!"

Three fishermen... one big redfish... happiness obvious on both boy's faces! (1986)

When all was said and done, and all four Redfishermen were home in Blanco, and Saturday morning's sun was blinding our overtired squinting eyes, we weighed our three monster redfish. The infinitely interesting point of The Boys and my memorable redfish story was buried in TWO minor details; "The devil is always in the details." Not that Dr. Doug would approve of me mentioning the devil. Detail number one; all three redfish were identical in length; twenty-seven inches, measured down to the one-quarter inch. Detail number two; all three redfish were exactly the same weight; eight pounds two ounces, weighed down to the one-half ounce. "We took a lot of pictures…celebrated as loud as we dared for that time of morning…rousted out our sleepy wives and Dr. Doug's sleepy daughters…and drank a morning toast to God and Good Fishin…an alcohol free toast mind you.

Choke Canyon Spinner Baits, Spring Break 1987

By spring 1987 our Texas fishing routines were well established and expanding as rapidly as time and money allowed. Expansion included hiring professional guides; both salt and freshwater guides. We three; The Boys and I; were a bit schizophrenic about saltwater versus freshwater fishing. We found ourselves in a real loyalty bind; one that many, mind-warped, split personality, fisherpersons eventually cure by thrashing the living HELL out of one type water, while altogether abandoning the other. Born in Missouri, The Boys and I weren't quite ready for that bold step; "totally abandoning freshwater fishing?" And because we did suffer bifurcated loyalties regarding salt versus freshwater, The Boys and I were still hiring freshwater guides in 1987; Lake Fork guides for bass, Lake Buchanan guides for stripers, Canyon Lake guides for crappie and bass.

To satisfy our freshwater urges, to retain a hand in both pots, The Boys and I hired a well known freshwater guide to take the three of us largemouth bass fishing on Choke Canyon Reservoir located in south central Texas; the guide's name, Sonny. Older Son Chris was twelve, younger Son Ladd ten. We arrived in Three Rivers, Texas in hot pursuit of a trophy largemouth bass. For their ages, both boys were proficient bass fishermen. Both wanted nothing more complicated out of life than the chance to catch a trophy sized largemouth bass; "Say eight to ten pounds…or greater?"

The three of us; The Boys and I; had been to Lake Fork several times pursuing big bass. Lake Fork is located in the piney woods of northeast Texas. There was one particular, egocentric guide up on Lake Fork that The Boys and I used every time we fished Fork; Guide Tony. On the other hand, The Boys and I fishing Choke Canyon and hiring Guide Sonny was a totally random shot, fired in the dark. We hired Guide Sonny from a newspaper ad. There was no Internet back then, and no one I knew personally fished Choke Canyon; except for trot lining channel cat. In the end, The Boys and I chose a name out of the newspaper and were pleased. Guide Sonny turned out to be a real colorful character, which can be interpreted to mean a lot of different things.

"But the truth?" Guide Sonny was a man WITH character, which he chose to mask with a lazy sense of humor; part of the color in his character. He was a bit of doozie, but not in a bad sense; merely unorthodox. Guide Sonny was professional, hard working, had the proper boat and equipment for the job, but fought hard with his own image to NOT come across as a doozie. Guide Sonny was a field-hand-looking redneck cowboy, trapped in a professional role; a combination that made for a lollapalooza dose of dooziness. He was loosey goosey; sort of a caricature of more serious, more stiff guides like Tony up at Lake Fork. Sonny was NOT a classic textbook professional guide, not like a lot of guides; many of whom tend to take themselves WAY too serious. Sonny was NOT the kind of guide that a lot of too tense, too uptight, artificially hardcore, bitchy because they are paying a big fee to a guide for little or no fishing success, wanttabee big time, bass fishermen often prefer. Guide Sonny wouldn't have made it up at Lake Fork, and wouldn't have made it hosting a TV show. "But you know what? In retrospect. I'd say Guide Sonny fit The Boys and me to a T!" At the end of the day, we all three loved Guide Sonny, and have quoted him for years; Guide Sonny's best quote is included in this story.

Our first inkling that an abnormal day might be in the making, and insight into Guide Sonny's colorful personality, occurred during breakfast at the Antler Inn Café in Three Rivers. The Boys and I were waiting out front when the owner of the café turned on the lights. The Boys could barely wait to get going. We rushed in to patiently wait for Guide Sonny and have a bite of breakfast. While enjoying breakfast and the pleasant company of a dozen or so local yokels, who wandered in for endless free refills of coffee and free chit chat, I happened to mention that we three, The Boys and I, were waiting to meet our fishin guide for the day; Guide Sonny. When I said "Guide Sonny" four to five colorful locals burst into spontaneous laughter. No amount of throat clearing or amended statements could erase said local's original laughing opinion of Guide Sonny. Like I said, local opinion of Guide Sonny wasn't bad; it was just that Guide Sonny seemed to own a universal rap with the native population. Every local in the café was quick to point out; "Oh...Don't worry...Sonny's a GOOD guide alright...It's just that......!" And then, in no particular order, four to five redneck celebrities from the Antler Inn Café added favorite personal stories describing wild misadventures or oddball things that happened when they, or someone they knew, hired Guide Sonny to fish Choke Canyon.

When Guide Sonny finally showed up; "about thirty minutes late"; he was a nice man. Nice as any you would hope to encounter in a small cafe in a small town in south Texas. Using colorful language from the get go, carrying a sizable beer belly that bounced with frequent laughter, issuing new stories every five minutes for wide-eyed boys; "who sat spellbound in the breakfast booth next to me"; our jovial guide, Guide Sonny, was the right man for our party, our day, and the transitional time in our lives!

And; by the "time" our two-vehicle entourage actually made it out to the lake and had our gear loaded in Sonny's fancy bass boat, bright morning Texas sun had warmed the spring air to shirtless warm for both suntanned boys. Guide Sonny looked around, yelled for everyone to "Hold On", and roared off as fast as he could go; heading to the middle of nowhere across a large flat lake. But seconds before departing the confines of the state park dock, Guide Sonny told The Boys to tie on standard spinner baits; any color or combination of spinners and skirts they preferred. During his bellicose breakfast spiel, Guide Sonny had made it perfectly clear that spinner baits were our best bet; "The Boys and I ALWAYS listened to our professional guides...NQA!"

We first stopped and tried a few deep holes and structure-filled ravens; no results. By noon, the four of us; "Guide Sonny was thrashing the water as wildly and as often as his three clients"; had a grand total of ZERO keeper bass. Son Ladd, who can catch fish on a dry gravel road, was the only person who had caught anything; two, small, eight inch, spring spawn, yearling bass from that year's hatch. Guide Sonny, Son Chris, and Dad were skunked; shut out, zippo for zippo. Disregarding the pitiful outcome of our morning's fishing; zero decent fish caught; Guide Sonny told The Boys to hang tuff and assured The Boys that things always picked up after lunch; "Which of course…they did NOT!" By three p.m. all four of us in Guide Sonny's glistening clean bass boat were still skunked. We were growing weary of casting spinner baits at hidden unseen structure.

No matter where we went; "and I assure you…we went MANY places"; Guide Sonny told The Boys; "Cast over there…aim for structure." Insisting there were submerged trees, fencerows, rock outcroppings, tangled ditches, and creek beds ever where (structure); all of which were allegedly hidden structure, at which The Boys were instructed to cast! Sonny constantly reassuring my boys; "Bass love structure…can ALWAYS be found IN or NEAR structure this time of year." By the end of the day I'm absolutely certain Guide Sonny used the word "structure" at least one million times; maybe two? As our blazing hot afternoon wore on, The Boys and I grew restless with hauling in NO fish…one after another! NONE is what our boat caught.

So! We clients jumped all over the idea when Guide Sonny asked if we would like to explore up the Frio River; where Guide Sonny said he had been having success during late afternoons. I was ready to try almost anything, and the swift boat ride upstream would provide welcome relief from heat and tedium. But! The Boys and I were terrorized by our trip upriver! When Guide Sonny said; "Let's make a quick run up the river…and see what's up!" He meant; let's make a QUICK run up the river! Wide open, going as fast as the huge motor would push his boat, Guide Sonny thrilled The Boys, while scaring the living dog shit squarely out of me; swerving to and fro around hairpin elbow curves and narrow, swift bends in the muddy river; a murky river that grew shallower by the hairpin curve! Finally! Guide Sonny cut the roaring motor, declaring; "This is the spot Boys…Get em!"

The Boys did as told. Cast their lines until their lines were threadbare; "Nada!" Guide Sonny, in what I saw as a lame attempt to distract The Boys, from the irritation of NOT catching any fish, all day, lowered his voice, for effect, and warned The Boys to keep a sharp eye out for alligators. Guide Sonny said a few really big gators had been spotted hanging around the upper end of the lake, in the Frio River; spotted in the area of the lake-river where our boat was currently beginning a slow drift downstream.

Once we arrived upriver, Guide Sonny's infamous hidden structure looked good. Way better than hidden structure I had been hearing about all morning but had not been able to see in the deep clear lake. "I'm not saying structure wasn't there...like Guide Sonny said it was...I'm just saying I couldn't really ever see any structure." I may have been MORE optimistic, except for ten thousand gar that exploded on the funky surface of the nearly stagnant water; spooked by our drifting boat. I'm not saying good bass water and sleepy, loafing gar are mutually exclusive; but things just didn't look bassy to me.

Guide Sonny kept chattering about the potential for encountering a big alligator; too much yak, too little fishing; nearly preaching to The Boys about keeping an eye out for gators, about being extra careful. Sonny was frustrated too; conducting a full blown "gator watch" WHILE reminding The Boys, for the umpteenth time, to cast towards structure. "I had NO idea what we were supposed to do if we did indeed spot a gator?"

"BAM!" Like lightening in a bottle, something grabbed Guide Sonny's spinner bait the instant it hit water; as it landed near a rotten stump just offshore in milk, murky, stagnant-looking water. Sonny called it gar water. "Splish Splash...I'm taking a bath... I'll be damned if Guide Sonny didn't have on a big Bass...a really BIG BASS!" A few minutes of spellbound fish fighting and Guide Sonny proudly netted our day's first sizable bass! Guide Sonny weighed the fish on his pitiful, rusting, spring operated, scale; seven pounds ten ounces! "Nice Fish...for gar water!"

After his lone bass was properly weighed, photographed, and carefully released; Guide Sonny proffered to us three clients; Chris, Ladd, and me; what has since become our family's second most repeated fishin quote; second only to our first, "Scooter...Get over here...or I'm gonna stomp your head!" Guide Sonny, with a straight face and heart of pure fisherman gold, looked The Boys dead in their boy eyes and said, seriously said; "Boys...Keep usin them spinner baits...Looks like the ONLY thing they're (bass) gonna be hittin on today...is spinner baits!" That was a profound suggestion if you think about it. After a collective ten million cast of spinner baits, during thirty-two combined man hours of fishing, spinner baits had produced exactly ONE nice bass! I suppose an optimistic guide could call that a trend?

Guide Sonny's "looks like the ONLY thing" brilliance could easily have served as the natural ending for our day. We could have quit bass fishin for that day with a feeling of contentment and a light heart, thought mirthful thoughts, enjoyed the wry grin on our collective chin; except NO! There was one more special moment to be shared by our boatload of True Grit bass fishermen. One of those frozen snapshot pictures trapped forever in your mind; one that decidedly trumped Guide Sonny's stellar advice to "keep usin them spinner baits."

About ten minutes after Guide Sonny's Catch of the Day had been released; "our boat's ONLY Catch of the Day"; son Chris did a remarkable thing; did the unthinkable. Standing at the front of our boat near the trolling motor; due to fatigue, malaise, boredom, or just plain old boyhood haplessness; carefully following very specific instructions from Guide Sonny; son Chris made a sterling cast towards shore, plunking down his spinner bait within inches of precious structure pointed out to him by Guide Sonny. For a briefly suspended instant, everyone in the boat smiled with glee; group affirmation and acknowledgement of Chris' fine cast. However; within the same instant, everyone in the boat realized Chris had committed one of fishing's top ten worst sins. During his otherwise perfect cast, Chris' rod and reel had slipped from his right hand. "You got it!" All eyes blinked as Chris' rod made a big splash in the vodka clear lake water, about ten feet towards shore, in what appeared to be ten to fifteen feet of structure-less water.

Just before he did it, but not before hesitating long enough for ME to realize he was GOING to do it, Son Chris, Sir Lancelot Chris, the son who always does the right thing; jumped! Looking at me, looking at his sinking rod, Chris belly flopped into the warm, gator infested waters of Choke Canyon Reservoir! On purpose! Intentionally!

I saw Son Chris staring in horror at his sinking rod. I saw him sneak a glance back at me. Then I saw Chris make up his mind. A parent, this parent, could literally see the wheels in Chris' well-endowed brain turning. Without a second glance, fearing the loss of his rod more than the loss of a limb or his life to big gators, INTO the clear deep water went Son Chris! "I can honestly say…I can tell you for real…I could hear Chris' tormented mine asking its self. Whatta I do? What about my expensive Calcutta reel? What will Dad say? What will Sonny say? What will those big gators do to me? That… and more…flashing across Son Chris' brilliant eyes in one mille-micro-nanner second!"

When Chris jumped, everyone in the boat was astonished; "Everyone except me and Ladd." I wasn't surprised in the least that Chris jumped; just amazed at his chutzpa for doing it without permission. Guide Sonny was incredulous; although I doubt Sonny knew the meaning of the word. Standing nearest to Chris, Son Ladd watched as his older brother's rod slowly sank out of sight. Younger brother Ladd was frightened for Chris; recalling at least two hundred alligator warnings issued by Guide Sonny; but Son Ladd instinctively just knew Chris was going in after his treasured rod. Following the giant splash, Son Chris swam underwater to his rapidly disappearing rod. He reached the rod as it was disappearing into the dark; grabbed it and emerged from the churning water wearing one of life's biggest smiles. As if to say; "Hey…Look what I got!"

We didn't catch another fish. Fact is; after Chris' big splash we didn't really much try. We also didn't see an alligator, or get eaten by an alligator; although, over the years, we have discussed that possibility with Chris. We didn't catch or see a bass worth talking about save one; the one Guide Sonny caught on his spinner bait. But we did have a good time. And we did learn something useful. The Boys and I learned, and have since tried to teach others; "When all else fails…simply look your problem in the eye…ANY problem…look it square in the eye…and say with a straight face and a dash of sincerity …Boys…Looks like the ONLY thing they're gonna be hittin on today…is spinner baits!"

Lake Fork Largemouth, Spring Break 1988

Sons Chris and Ladd were a year older, a year wiser, and several typical fisherman years more proficient at catching fish than when the three of us fished with Guide Sonny on Choke Canyon. But! None of us; The Boys nor I; had come even close to catching an elusive Texas trophy bass; something each of us desperately wanted to accomplish. Individually and as a trio and we had been working long and hard; spending a lot of time and money but having no success at landing an actual trophy bass. During the interim; between Choke Canyon 1987 and Spring Break 1988; I would estimate The Boys caught something approaching one thousand fish; five hundred of those thousand fish were bass! "NOT one of my wild exaggerations…a legitimate estimate." The Boys fished nearly every day on the Blanco River, which was loaded with smallmouth and largemouth bass; even a few Guadalupe, white, and striped bass. Not to mention bluegill and channel cat by the stringer-full. Local ranch lakes coughed up a few nice bass and occasionally the Blanco River produced a five to six pounder. But realistically; a Texas trophy bass wasn't likely to come from any of our routine local venues.

Catching a trophy bass would require a professional guide and long drive to a real bass lake; a real bass lake like the one The Boys and I fished during Spring Break 1988; Lake Fork Reservoir located in northeast Texas. At that time Lake Fork was considered Texas' number one trophy bass lake. For several years, something approaching eighty percent of all the largest bass caught in Texas came out of 'Fork'. The Boys and I had decided to give it another try; "Once more into the breeches…seeking The Big One!"

Lake Fork Reservoir is a Corps of Engineers lake first flooded in 1983. "And…I can count it among one of my trivial but interesting experiences…that I was standing there!" I mean literally standing right there on the lake's shore when the gates were officially closed and the lake began filling for the first time. Unbelievably; "Ripley's Believe It Or Not unbelievably"; my family's small real estate company owned a full section of prime land on Lake Fork; six hundred forty acres of ranchland with approximately one mile of timber enhanced lake frontage. Lightly wooded slightly rolling picturesque grass pastures made up the bulk of the ranchland; purchased by our family's small real estate investment company back in 1983. Our company developed the ranch into one of five RV Parks that we owned at the time.

Five RV Parks that were part of 'The Great Texas Land Scam' that originally lured Nurse-Wife Peg, The Boys and I to Texas in 1982-83; part of the chain of five RV Parks that included the big one in downtown Johnson City, Texas; where Good Buddy Wayne and I initiated our Texas Duo duck hunting on the Purty Pedernales River. Part of the same chain of five RV Parks that included wilderness riverfront property on the Guadalupe River less than thirty miles north of San Antonio; where Bubba Bob and I and a host of cold blooded characters from Missouri killed a truckload of deer on an old abandoned golf course; also part of our family's investment property; part of the same chain of RV Parks where The Boys and I took advantage of our property owner's rights every spring to fish for white bass in the clear swift water of the Guadalupe River.

And. Unbelievably! Part of a chain of five genuinely first class RV Parks our family investment company went broke attempting to build. Legitimately and accurately build. Build according to specifications and wild promises made by a small army of gold chain wearing, gaudy jewelry sporting, fancy Cadillac and Lincoln Continental driving, pushy, backroom inhabiting, high pressure, Jack Lemon emulating, Tin Man clones. Paid by the deal, land tract peddling, hyperactive, fast talking, always short on cash, raw land development salesmen, realistically portrayed in the hit movie "The Tin Man". Part of a much larger and prosperous, rapidly growing, affiliated RV Park concept called Camp Coast To Coast; a nationwide chain that included over one hundred similar parks.

Our family's five park chain was going great guns; until the mid-1980s, when the oil and gas industries went belly up here in Texas and our market for timeshare and resort properties collapsed. In what was, compared to today's much greater national economic problems, an inaudible peep. Our investor owned properties were a peripheral part of a get rich quick 1980s mentality that evaporated in the ashes of Texas' scandalous 1987 savings and loan debacle. Our family's parks were part of a sound concept; until every last one of the one-of-a-kind golden opportunity properties were lost in a cascade of lawsuits filed by disgruntled investors clamoring for someone's hide to be nailed to the barn wall; "My hide among many hides for which there was investor clamor!"

But, back in 1983, back before the first public boat ramp was ever built, within weeks of the Army Corps of Engineers closing the gates allowing a flooding process to begin, which quickly filled Lake Fork; The Boys and I, not realizing how unbelievably fortunate we were at the time, launched a small aluminum bass boat directly onto Lake Fork from our family's lake front ranchland. No boat ramp, no fishing dock, no road to the water's edge; The Boys and I drove across the ranch's grassy pasture and unloaded our small boat with the help of Louisiana Cousin Larry. We fished all day; I tied our boat to a fresh stump whenever and wherever The Boys and I felt like coming ashore.

Within days of the floodgates closing in 1983, landowners and local fishermen lucky enough to own or have private access to rising Lake Fork waters, immediately began catching large bass; lucky landowners and local fishermen like The Boys and I. Wisely, as it turned out, Texas Wildlife and Fisheries experts had for several years been pre-stocking tens of dozens of small impoundments; private lakes, ponds, and deep holes in big streams. When rising Lake Fork waters inundated the hundreds of smaller bodies of water; giant sized, extra healthy, acclimated, already relaxed and spawning, large Largemouth Bass swam free; slowly and periodically escaping into the greater environment of Lake Fork's rising water. It worked like a charm and bass fishing on Lake Fork remained superb to great for many years thereafter.

By spring break 1988; "when The Boys and I hired Guide Tony"; bass fishing on Fork was reaching its natural peak. But! All five of my family's investment properties, including the ranch located on Lake Fork's shore, had been lost to foreclosure and our investor money lost to gross mismanagement. Out of necessity I became a rookie sales agent with a large business brokerage company located in Austin, selling small privately owned businesses all over The Great State of Texas. Continuing to perform in that role for that business brokerage company for the next two decades accounted for my family's additional exposure to countless personal adventures; spawned many travels and travails while I was out and about hustling a decent living for my legal immigrant family hailing from Missouri. Ten thousand duck hunting stories emanating from Falcon Lake and our discovery of Stink Tank near Pearsall, Texas are prime examples of treasures unearthed during my business broker travels.

Back to Lake Fork! By 1988 The Boys and I had begun spending a few precious dollars on professional guides; trying our best to catch ourselves a trophy bass. "I refuse to define a few precious dollars." But! There was good news lost in there somewhere for Scrooge-act-alike Nurse-Wife Peg. When she and I were first married, we put our heads together and made a solemn deal regarding The Boys and I hiring fishing guides. Nurse-Wife and I agreed that IF I would give up my lifetime goal of buying a fishing boat; IF I would agree to NEVER purchase a boat, and cease bugging her about the subject; then The Boys and I would be allowed to hire fishing guides up four times per year, each year, for the coming decade; or until The Boys graduated high school and went off to college. "During which time Nurse-Wife and I were lucky to afford food and shelter…considering the high cost of having two boys going to A&M at the same time."

NOT buying a boat wasn't a bad deal. Fact is, not buying a boat and NOT driving Nurse-Wife Peg nuts about wanting to buy a boat, in lieu of being allowed to hire a series of professional fishing guides, was a deal I faithfully honored until both Boys graduated from A&M. But then, in 2002, my burning lifetime desire to own a boat overcame the remaining remnants of my good judgment. After our agreed-to decade expired and there WAS money enough in our meager family budget for something besides, "beans and rice…and rice and beans" to quote financial expert Dave Ramsey, I finally was allowed to buy a modestly nice hunting and fishing boat. Nothing extravagant, just nice; an eighteen foot Grizzly Tracker with a forty-horse four stroke Mercury outboard. Perfect for The Boys and their friend's low key fishing expeditions and Preacher's and my Falcon Lake duck hunting.

Anyway; by spring Break 1988, The Boys and I were back on Fork for the umpteenth time; scheduled to fish with our favorite Lake Fork guide, Guide Tony. In addition to hiring Guide Tony to take ME and a few close friends and business clients fishing, The Boys and I had hired and fished with Guide Tony six to eight times. Fact; Guide Tony much preferred guiding ME when I brought along The Boys. And. When fishing with The Boys and me as a trio, Guide Tony MOST preferred fishing right next to Son Ladd. Guide Tony much preferred Son Ladd's company to either Son Chris' or my company. Guide Tony was gifted. He owned an instinctive ability for determining true fisherman genius. Ladd had it, Chris and I lacked it. Family passions run deep in our entire family. All three of us; Son Chris, Son Ladd, and I; have plenty of passion for fishing, but only Son Ladd showed real promise of genius for bass fishing, sufficient to catch and hold the devotion of Guide Tony.

Guide Tony paid tribute to Son Ladd's genius factor when placing us

Guide Tony loved **Ladd**... and taught him way more than he bothered even telling Chris and me. (1988)

three clients in the boat. Three members of one family; one hopeful Dad, one competitive older Brother, one fishing genius younger Brother, each of us carefully placed within Guide Tony's boat relative to our ability. Strategic positioning in Guide Tony's boat, that provided more of OR less of an opportunity to catch a genuine trophy bass according to our differing and demonstrated fishing skills; placement that was accomplished as diplomatically as possible but dealt with strictly according to fishing acumen.

Son Ladd was always up front; always put in the correct spot within the boat to make that first critical cast into the hundreds of new hot holes, flooded creek beds, deep crannies, shallow pools, and quiet backwaters Guide Tony explored on behalf of our family. Anyone who has ever fished from a boat, any kind of fishing from any kind of boat, will appreciate Guide Tony's placement theory. No one minded, least of all ME! "Guess which of the three of us was consistently awarded the most inopportune spot in the boat...given the least desirable spot from which to make that critical first cast...ME!" Not only did I not mind the affront, I prayed for The Boys to catch a big bass; and they did; a lot of big bass. Back during the late 1980s and early '90s, finding a good hot spot and pitching the correct lure in the correct manner on Fork was tantamount to success.

Also! Guide Tony insisted that The Boys and I use whatever artificial lures were hot; "NEVER natural baits!" Fishing pressure was far less back in The Beginning and using live bait to catch a Texas trophy bass would have been unthinkable to our family trio. According to Guide Tony, two biggies coalesced to ruin Lake Fork; twin death knells that eventually doomed the incredible trophy bass fishing for which Fork initially became famous; the use of live bait by massed crowds of meat fishermen, catching and keeping oversized spawning bass; both unsportsmanlike like conduct fouls coming together to dethrone Lake Fork from an incredible run it enjoyed as THE preeminent bass lake in America. A premier bass lake status Fork held solely and exclusively for ten years; lost to greed, laziness, callousness, and shortsightedness; according to Tony.

But; getting back to 1988, and us four fishermen in a boat seeking a trophy bass; we were hard at it. On the second of our family's two day fishing trip, Guide Tony showed up early and stayed late trying everything he knew to provide at least one of us a genuine shot at landing a trophy. The Boys and I caught six to eight nice bass, in the five to six pound range, with each of us getting at least one bass worth writing home about; but no real trophy. Then Guide Tony did something for which I shall always be eternally grateful; he decided to keep The Boys and me out on the water until after dark. Not sunset; we had stayed out until after sunset before; until after DARK!

The Boys had been casting spinner baits part of the day and a combination of Carolina rigged plastic baits, affectionately called French Fries, along with Slug-Gos. Slug-Gos had been around for less than a year. The Boys and I learned about Slug-Gos through Guide Tony, months earlier when he guided me and a friend. Standard sized ivory-over-grey colored Slug-Gos were the only ones available at the time. The soft plastic lure was brand new and sizzling hot. So! It should come as no surprise, that's exactly what The Boys were using when Guide Tony suddenly cut the motor and eased his boat up into a long narrow flooded creek bed. A deep channel filled with ancient standing dead trees and floating debris; body sized submerged fallen trees and limbs.

Sensing the opportunity, seizing the moment, fishing genius Son Ladd, of his own volition, without seeking permission from Guide Tony, explicit permission always sought in all other instances, quietly cut off his Slug-Go and tied on a Bomber Long-A; orange and green striped over black. A medium sized top water lure with two sets of treble hooks. Daylight was fading. Guide Tony told The Boys and me that we would fish only to the end of the flooded creek channel and then stop. Moving around on the lake in the dark wasn't a good idea, but Guide Tony said we would slow-fish the backend of the heavily wooded creek where it dumped into the lake. Guide Tony said if we didn't catch anything there we would call it a day and head to the dock.

It was getting dark; the creek channel had narrowed to ten yards across and was filled with dead trees and floating structure. With the skill of a Master Cellist pulling his bow at the Philharmonic, Guide Tony eased our bass boat into position, then practically whispered to Son Ladd; "Cast there…into that tiny open pool…just THIS side of that submerged log." Guide Tony emphasizing just THIS side of the big log.

Son Ladd did as instructed; gently tossing his Bomber Long-A so it would land gently just THIS side of that submerged log, in clear water. "Then?"

Well then there came a quick loud...SMAAACK! A BIG SPLASH! AND MORE AND BIGGER SPLASHES! The lake's surface exploded in a series of roaring cascades the size of buckets. At first I thought Ladd had hooked an oversized gar, or maybe even a small alligator. We had seen plenty of gar in other areas of the lake and I easily recalled Guide Sonny warning The Boys about gators in South Texas on Choke Canyon; especially when it had gotten close to sundown.

But sundown on Fork had come and gone; it was barely light enough to see the submerged log and the structure in which Ladd was now fighting some sort of big fish. It was obvious to me why Guide Tony had emphasized just THIS side of the submerged tree. Exhausting every last drop of his eleven year old's strength and stamina, squeezing the last bit of daylight from our waning day of professionally guided fishing, genius Son Ladd fought and was able to land himself a Texas trophy bass; hooked and retrieved from just THIS side of that submerged log.

Son Ladd insisted on keeping the huge fish; how could ANYONE, including Guide Tony, have faulted an eleven year old boy for wanting to keep his fish? Back at the dock Son Ladd's BIG bass weighed in at an amazing TEN pounds-two ounces! My Friends; I DO believe THAT qualifies as a Texas trophy bass in nearly anyone's book! Using my Kodak disposable camera, the classic fisherman's smile frozen on genius bass fisherman Son Ladd's face, was recorded for history. The moment, the day, the year, the lifetime reputation of Son Ladd as our family's Best Bass Fisherman was assured; likely forever? Although, perhaps not? Ladd's brother Chris and Ladd's Dad are not exactly downstream dough bait fishermen. Chris and I have a few fishing stories and mounted trophies of our own. None however more dramatic, more satisfying, more absolutely astonishing in detail, than Son Ladd's big one that did NOT get away...making HIS day!

Smiles say a lot... big fish cause big smiles! (1988)

Saltwater Fishin With Captain Fred, Summer 1989

For better or worse, transition and change are an inevitable part of life; sometimes for the better, sometimes not. So it was with The Boys and my transition from being primarily freshwater fishermen, to becoming primarily saltwater fishermen; a positive change for our three man, family team. It was nearly inevitable; "our family threesome's transition from fresh to saltwater." Eventually initiated and fast forwarded by one man; a tough, old, crotchety, longtime, highly respected, saltwater fishing guide who fished exclusively out of Port Mansfield, Texas; saltwater fishing guide extraordinaire; Captain Fred. A living legend giant of a man; a six-foot-five, two-seventy-five giant of a man; leather skinned from a million days in the sun and a command voice that resonated a stern unspoken warning; 'You better listen when I tell you something…cause it's important… whether YOU think so or not'!

No fish finder, no depth finder, no off the shelf Walmart electronic gadgetry to help locate and catch fish; Captain Fred found fish the old fashioned way, by working at it. By watching for feeding gulls and sea birds, by watching for changes in water color, watching for oil slicks and streaks, watching for other boats enjoying success; watching for anything and everything that might reveal the whereabouts of fish he was seeking for clients. Captain Fred fished every day, all day long; in every legal, moral, or ethical way; except one. Captain Fred forsook the use of natural bait. When it came to saltwater flats or shallow bay fishing on the Texas Gulf Coast, Captain Fred unintentionally set aside or inadvertently forgot more about fishing than most fishing guides will ever know.

Through no fault of our own; other than an honorable heritage and birthright rooted in the hills of northwest Missouri; The Boys and I began our fishing lives together as freshwater fishermen. Growing up in Missouri, I was barely aware of saltwater fishing. Saltwater was what my Mom forced us kids to gargle when we had sore throats. But when our reconstituted new family of four permanently moved to Texas in February 1983, it was only a matter of weeks before the Boys and I tried our hand at saltwater fishing. However! Because The Boys were very young when we arrived in Texas, and because most venues for saltwater fishing were relatively expensive, there were limited opportunities for meaningful improvement in our saltwater fishing-stunted lives; nothing that significantly altered our heretofore saltwater-less lifestyles.

I experienced a touch of offshore saltwater fishing while serving in The Marines; offshore in Virginia, California, Okinawa, Viet Nam, and Thailand. "But that's a whole 'nother story." Generally speaking I enjoyed myself, but also had a couple of bad experiences; "Like paying $600…along with three other Marine Lieutenants…to go marlin fishing out of Virginia Beach Virginia."

Of the four Marines on board that day, I was the last man standing. The only client aboard our charter boat that did NOT vomit up a small hairy knot of fleshy material, which in my Brother Marine's three cases turned out to be their puked up assholes! Six hundred bucks each, to heave up our guts and not get one single strike; "I'm told that's common when marlin fishing?" But the Charter Captain of our marlin boat didn't bother telling us Marines that tidbit of useful information; he was too busy counting our twenty-four hundred dollars; "A month's pay each...from four Viet Nam-bound Brown Bars."

A year or so later, while serving in Okinawa, a Salty Old Marine First Sergeant invited me to go offshore fishing. The First Sergeant's Father and Grandfather were Portuguese fishermen and his wife was an immigrant from Portugal. First Sergeant and I caught tons of small fish; including pompano, Spanish mackerel, and red snapper, and one big jewfish; but also got lost in a squall and were nearly swamped by high swells. I was relieved to return alive and happy about catching fish, even though most were species I couldn't identify. The fishing that I did (slightly) offshore of Viet Nam was highly illegal and involved high explosives and dip nets; "But I guess it still counts as fishing?"

In 1982 while on our honeymoon, I took Nurse-Bride Peg deep sea fishing on a charter out of San Diego. We caught a shit load of mackerel and bonito, but Nurse-Bride became seasick and decided she was suffering from a sudden case of flu. Even though she is now, and was then, a highly skilled RN, I had a difficult time explaining to her that she was merely seasick. I'm still not sure that she believed me?

The highlight of our honeymooner's day out there fishin was NOT the fifty to sixty mackerel and bonito we caught. THE highlight, second only to figuring out a way to temporarily cure Nurse-Bride's seasickness, was a jet black nuclear sub that passed directly under our sixty foot charter boat; about thirty feet down and perfectly visible in the clear sea; "It sent cold chills up my spine thinking about where that sub might be heading and what it might be up to...and we cured Nurse-Bride Peg's untimely seasickness by having her sip leftover Champagne."

Generally speaking, prior to moving to Texas, I never really paid much attention to saltwater fishing; had never genuinely experienced it; except for one empty creel day aboard the Scat Cat described earlier in this book. All in all, my personal saltwater fishing experiences were limited in scope and return per hours fished. Not void of fun and pleasure, just spotty.

At the far end of our Missouri family's eight hundred mile move to Texas, we became neighbors with a fine young couple who had one son. Our new Texas neighbors; Husband Buster, Lovely Wife Karen, and their extra-fine eight year old only son, Jason; were all three avid shallow water saltwater fishermen.

The BIGGEST reason for our new neighbor's strong proclivity for saltwater fishing; guide extraordinaire Captain Fred Wagenfehr; Captain Fred was Husband Buster's Daddy! Husband Buster and Lovely Wife Karen and Son

Jason had enjoyed saltwater fishing, at its best, properly done, all their landlocked Texas lives; in the productive company of one of Texas' best EVER professional guides. Our new neighbors had their own private mentor. Captain Fred!

Our new Texas neighbors' son Jason was classmates with and became best friends with our son Chris. As the years unfolded before them, our three boys; Jason, Chris, and Ladd; literally "grew up together fishing…the livin crap out of the pristine Blanco River." New Texas neighbors, Husband Buster and Lovely Wife Karen, owned a large ranch with about one mile of wooded river frontage directly ON the Blanco River. By the time our two boys and their son Jason started school in September 1983, the three sons had become friends and fellow fishermen.

As years in Texas rolled by, our new friends became our BEST friends; same interests, same church, same youth group, same ski trips, three top notched sons, all three sons separated by only twenty-two months total age difference, two of our three sons in the same grade, same little league teams, same football teams, same everything, all the way through high school

Within a year I was taking three sons hunting, camping, and fishing; Husband Buster doing the same. Eventually Son Chris grew up and was Son Jason's Best Man when Son Jason married in 1997. Our three young boys became three young men, living one similar lifestyle.

From early on, through years of inter-family fellowship, our good friends insisted that The Boys and I would enjoy speckled trout fishing with Captain Fred; Husband Buster's Daddy. Somewhere along the line The Boys and I invited Son Jason up to Lake Fork a couple of times to go bass fishing with our favorite freshwater guide; Guide Tony. So! As said; it was inevitable that our friends, Husband Buster and Lovely Wife Karen, would reciprocate the honor by arranging a trip for all THREE SONS and I to go trout fishing with Captain Fred; seeking speckled trout out of Port Mansfield, Texas.

Captain Fred had guided along Texas' fertile coast for thirty yeas. He knew all there was to know and kept the best of it to himself. The four of us; Me, Chris, Ladd, and Jason; were booked for two days in July. We were going out with Captain Fred; to fish for trout in inter coastal shallow saltwater flats either side of, north or south of, Port Mansfield.

The first day out everyone in the boat caught and kept a legal limit of ten trout each; keepers were required to be over the state minimum size of fifteen inches.

Actually the four of us caught well over one hundred trout that first day, and released whatever fish weren't clearly over the minimum; "Until we each had ten keepers." Captain Fred was a stickler for details and discipline.

Likely one of the reasons Fred's son, Husband Buster, and Fred's grandson, Son Jason, turned out so damned well? "Finer people...you never met."

Our second day fishing was an instant replay of the first; only the trout were bigger, greater in number, and biting like there was no tomorrow and they had never seen a tout. A 'tout' is a small shrimp-impersonating soft plastic lure, fished on medium sized hooks and quarter ounce lead head jigs; a rough, crude lure if compared to today's detail-fixated shrimp-imposter lures, but quite effective during the tout's decades-long reign as one of Coastal Texas saltwater flat's most favored lures. "Did I say lures?" Captain Fred would have snipped the line from your rusting reel had he EVER caught you fishing with live shrimp or any natural bait. The idea of using bait was repulsive to Captain Fred's fine tuned guide skills.

Halfway through our second day, Captain Fred decided to make a ten to twelve mile run south to search for better sized trout; routine for him. When we stopped and resumed thrashing of the salty surf for trout, it was mere seconds until Sons Ladd, Chris, and Jason each hooked a trout; at the exact same moment. I stood watching with a big grin on my sunburned chin; but was brought back to reality when Captain Fred yelled for me to grab the dip net and help the boys; while Fred was busy easing our boat into the wind; "So the Three Sons could fight their fishes." OOOOPS! The boat's dip net, Captain Fred's treasured, twenty year old dip net, had blown overboard during our long run south. It was clearly MY fault! Beginning with the first fish of the day, I had intermittently been assigned Net Boy duties; and had been doing quite well. That is, had been doing quite well after an hour of persistent coaching from Captain Fred. "Somehow or another...netting a large frisky saltwater trout...was entirely different from...netting a large frisky freshwater bass...at least that's what I was told...at least a dozen times...in NO uncertain terms...by Captain Fred."

By the time we made our long run south, and Captain Fred's priceless net blew overboard, I had relaxed a bit at my Net Boy duty station. Perhaps relaxed a bit TOO much? But! I had relaxed only AFTER netting something approaching two hundred trout! Thus far, every trout netted without major mishap or fundamental f—k up; nothing serious enough to piss off Captain Fred. Then? Well then! I really f—ked up...big time! Losing Captain Fred's dearly departed net did wonders to lower Captain's Fred's opinion of ME, and nearly cost me my seat in the boat! Don't get me wrong, I messed up bad. The net had its proper place for high speed travel, and I had failed to return it to its place in the boat.

When our day ended and we were back at the dock, I walked straight in the bait house and bought a new net as near in size and shape to Captain

Fred's as I could find. I presented the new net to Captain Fred when I paid and generously tipped him for two great days of fine fishing. But! I despaired. I thought all was lost in my sincere effort to gain Good Guy status with Captain Fred. Despaired; until weeks later when Husband Buster and Lovely Wife Karen informed Nurse-Wife Peg and me that Captain Fred had privately bragged on me and complimented our landlubber sons on their rookie saltwater fishing skills and determination to learn something new; "Trout fishing in saltwater."

Every parent of every child appreciates a sincere compliment; atta boys coming from Captain Fred made my day, my season, my year. And! Captain Fred's honest evaluation of The Boys as novice saltwater fishermen helped convert the three of us TO saltwater fishing while weaning us OFF freshwater fishing; truly launching our family effort to become genuine saltwater fishermen. And. Do not misunderstand affectionate criticism of Captain Fred. My descriptions and comments regarding The Man are simply my way of paying respect to a fine man who knew his business and went about doing his business professionally; always keeping foremost in his mind the best interest of his clients and those around him. "To me…the quality of Captain Fred's fine family is living proof of Captain Fred's skill as a man…a father…and fishing guide extraordinaire."

The Blanckitty Blanco Spring…Summer… Fall…and Winter…1983-93

Our transplanted family's first temporary home in Texas was a native

A look of approval from **Captain Fred** was difficult to come by... but the boys earned one! (1987)

stone antiquity located five miles east of downtown Blanco and directly on the Blanco River. Once we settled into our adopted country, the Great State of Texas; "and had been granted permanent work visas"; we began making new and interesting friends. First and foremost among our new Texas friends were our nearest neighbors Husband Buster, Lovely Wife Karen, and Bright Son Jason; three fine people given their début in my book a couple of chapters back. During our first month in Texas, Sons Chris and Ladd, and our new neighbor's son, Jason, took off running out the back door together to fish the Blanco River…and never looked back. One afternoon fishing together; "three grade school chums disappearing over the river bank trying to catch a few perch"; the three boys continued fishing together every year, year after year, for a span of fish tale years currently going on thirty. Every river, lake, tank, slew, pothole, bay, tide pool, land cut, saltwater flat, deep or shallow eddy, sand bar or saltwater grass bed; any place our enduring threesome encountered potential fishing opportunities, freshwater or salt, they fished.

Allow me to make a point of conjecture; think about this hypothetical. If I were able to determine the cumulative grand total of every adult man hour that ALL adult males in Blanco County spent fishing on the Blanco River during that same decade, 1983 through '93; ALL that combined adult fisherman time, multiplied by ten, would NOT equal the grand total number of boy man hours our three boys spent fishing the little river during that same decade; "During their childhood!" Ninety five percent of their boyhood fishing time spent on the same ten to twelve miles of their favorite, most available venue; the Blanco River! "No S - - t!" "Seriously…NO S - - T!"

Three young catchers of fish; Son Ladd, youngest and most studious fisherman of the trio; Son Chris, older brother to Ladd and moral conscience of the dynamic fishing trio; Son Jason, oldest and quietest of the trio, and possibly the nicest young man I have ever encountered. "Cause…IF Son Jason would have been anything other than polite and decent…his Lovely Momma Karen would have skint his burred blonde boy head."

Beginning in late February 1983, with the coming of first tolerable days outdoors, continuing unabated and generally uninhibited for the next decade; "until Chris and Jason went off to college in fall 1993"; our three-pack of boys, or portions of it, fished the Blanco River. Fished the river to such an extent we four adoring parents feared our trio might create an extinction event among fish species found in the small, rocky bottomed river. After the three boys; "Our two and their friend Jason"; were grown men and gone from home, I began reflecting on their once-in-a-lifetime, non-replicatable achievement; "Taking every available opportunity of a singularly unique situation in their lives…that fortuitously allowed the three boys private access to fish the Blanco River. So often fish ...so proficiently fish...so consistently fish...the clear clean and pristine...and during those years...isolated waters of the Blanco River." I shall begin my effort at describing the fish-fry-producing trio's effort by saying this. "If I had ten dollars for every fish my two sons and their friend Jason cumulatively caught out of the Blanco River and cleaned for their two Mommas to fry...I could retire tomorrow!"

I have no idea how many TOTAL fish that might actually be; "But way more than you might imagine." Not a day went by; "not one"; when at least one of the tripod, or all three legs of the fishing trio, didn't drag home fresh fish for their Mom's to clean and cook. Typically the trio's catches were small in size but large in number; prolific catchers of small-to-medium sized fish found in most small Texas rivers. Ninety-five percent of the boy's fish were caught on lures; ninety percent of the ninety-five percent were caught on Rooster Tail spinners; "A particular type and size lure." Channel cats were the one fish species The Boys and friend Jason regularly sought using natural bait; usually night crawlers or blood baits. And even though fishing with natural bait represented a tiny fraction of the trio's overall effort, it usually resulted in the three boys catching nicer fish for their Momma's skillets.

By the trio's high school years, most, if not all, their Blanco River trophies were being routinely released back into the river...to be caught again come spring. However! Several small private tanks and lakes around Blanco attribute their initial stocking to healthy brood fish The Boys and friend Jason caught and released, free of charge, into the private waters. The trio spent most of three summers catching buckets full of fingerlings for the specific purpose of releasing the small fish in private impoundments. The different varieties of fish species our trio of boys caught included, but wasn't limited to; both large and smallmouth bass, Guadalupe bass, rock bass, striper bass, white bass, crappie, bluegill; goggle eye, sun, rock, and striped perch; yellow, blue, flathead, appaloosa, and channel catfish; carp, buffalo, gar, and freshwater drum; crawdads by the tub full; minners by the bucket full; and turtles of every imaginable size, shape, color and creed.

There were also enough snakes killed and enough snake sightings reported that if all the snakes our trio actually encountered had indeed been killed, skinned, and tanned; the resulting snake hides could have easily covered a giant recliner. Big, little, short, fat, skinny, one at a time, in breeding bunches, or in slithering pods coming out of winter hibernation, the boy-trio's list of snakes sighted or killed included, but wasn't necessarily limited to; innocuous water snakes, NOT water moccasins; an occasional fat rattler with its highly valued tail noisily abuzz; a dozen common garden variety pasture snakes such as garter snakes, blue racers, and black snakes. But mostly; harmless, green, slithery, little, low crawling critters, that unbeknownst to the critters, were soon to be sent on their way to snake Heaven by a trio of rambunctious overachieving young outdoorsmen. And. "According to and in keeping with the true Bible story about Eve"; snakes were considered by our trio of boys to genuinely BE one of God's damned creatures. Therefore; snakes were sent to Snake Promised Land as often as possible and as prematurely as possible by Blanco's dynamic fishing Threesome.

There were also millions of float trips, both long and short; thousands of overnight campouts, both hot and cold; hundreds of all day excursions, both dull and exciting; dozens of wild weekend river events featuring none, a few, or many guests; and a partridge…or two…in a pear tree. All that recreational boy time and young man effort focused on and centered on catching or attempting to catch a few wee fish from Blanco County's only legitimate river. And while normally a relatively small river, it is also a flash flood-prone river that can be absolutely terrifying during notorious Texas downpours. "Anytime it rains more than an inch or two…folks downstream better keep an eye peeled upstream."

"The Blanco River circa 1986?" Sheer cliffs overgrown with bright green mossy outcroppings; cold springs tumbling off gigantic rock formations; bubbling tributaries entering here and there making their token contribution; deep holes haunted by giant beady-eyed fat-bellied catfish; shallow rapids filthy thick with channel cat fry chasing water bugs and hellgrammites; shady, twisting, turning rapids spilling into quieter and amazingly deep crystal clear swimmin holes; broad straightaways where perch and bluegill schooled by the hundreds or thousands. "And above all else?" Known honey holes where The Boys and friend Jason could count on finding a nice bass just waitin to be hooked; most of which bass were returned to spawn another year.

For many years running, our three boys, all three of them individually, or one against the other two, competed to see which of the trio was King Fisherman. Determine who among their trio could catch, photograph, or show up at the other's doorstep with the biggest smallmouth or largest largemouth. I'm not certain which of the three eventually left home declared King; "Maybe it is a contest yet to be settled?" I do know from personal, firsthand observations; "that means real shit I've actually seen with my own two eyes…and touched with my own two hands"; that over the years, the Blanco Threesome caught some pretty fair specimens of local fish species.

I saw several six to seven pound largemouth bass. Son Ladd caught the biggest bass I personally ever saw come out of the Blanco River; approximately eight pounds. "Here's a tip"; Ladd caught the bass on a small black and silver Rapala, fishing two miles east of Blanco, on Ranch Road #165. Over ensuing years, Friend Jason and his Dad Buster had an edge when it came to catching the most LARGE individual fish; they lived their entire lives ON the river. But! Jason and his Dad's historical geographic advantage was outdone by The Boys when it came to grand total number of fish caught. During their last two to three years of fishing The Blanco, our three boys dominated fishing up and down the erratic winding river; from three mile west of Blanco to seven miles east. "I know for a fact...Son Ladd caught more fish out of the Blanco River during that time frame than ordinary fishermen could count! Don't ask me HOW I know...I just know!"

The Blanco River ceases its tortured flow during dry years; Texas dry. Two different years while The Boys and Friend Jason were living at home, the Blanco River entirely quit flowing; went totally dry in 1984 and again in 1987. Flash flooding two to six times a year; "during every heavy rain"; the schizophrenic fifty to sixty mile long Blanco River doesn't sustain large enough a flow during our hottest, driest Texas summers to allow appreciable water to spill over the ancient cement dam located within Blanco's popular State Park that is surrounded by the city limits of Blanco; "The ONLY state park in Texas located entirely within the city limits of an incorporated town."

During very worst bleached bone dry years, 1984 being one, 2008 and 2009 being two more; the Blanco River went stone dry. In 1984 and again in 1987 The Boys and I were able to hike up and down the dry river bed enjoying some of the best dove hunting ever experienced. Doves sought water in small pools and stagnant holes remaining on the decimated river. While walking the dry riverbed dove hunting, The Boys and I came across a million parched and sun bleached fish carcasses; skeletal remains of every major species known to be indigenous to the forsaken river. It broke our outdoorsman hearts: "But...We killed a truckload of thirsty doves." During those awful, driest summers; riverbed potholes were doves' primary source of water.

Dry year or wet, snakes abounded. Blanco's Boy Fishing Trio encountered and killed their fair share. Rattlers, copperheads, an occasional coral snake, and a dumpster load of harmless non-poisonous snakes. In the big scheme of things, snakes were merely part of the Greater Texas outdoor landscape; to which our Fishing Trio reacted appropriately, when and if necessary.

In spite of inherent dangers; "and there actually were a few"; by the time Blanco's Fishing Trio reached middle school, we four watchful and good parents had pretty much turned our three boys loose; on their own to wander the river's shoreline in search of whatever critters they could rightfully kill, capture, or catch. They were an honest and trustworthy trio of young men. We allowed them many freedoms. Encouraged them to come and go as a trio, to NOT be on the peaceful river alone; "one reason the boys logged so damned many fishing hours." Sometimes the trio carried fishing equipment; sometimes they carried guns. Once in a while, they simply carried on!

Spanning one decade, 1983-93, in addition to routinely catching and cleaning edible fish, then bringing the freshly caught critters home for dinner; our three boys dragged home an impressive list of additional dead, dying, or crippled creatures. The bounty hauled home for parental inspection, identification, authentication, validation, and in many cases, assistance in cleaning and cooking, was impressive; "Even by Country Boy standards." Take a quick look! There were raccoons, opossums, armadillos, jack rabbits, cottontails, snakes, turtles, skunks, muskrats, nutria, abandoned fawns, two nearly drowned calves, three baby goats, sacks of bullfrogs, several lizards of unknown species, shellfish of a dozen known species, big salamanders, live quail, young turkeys, a million doves, a dozen different species of sick or wounded song birds, two coyote pups, one fox pup, four baby ground hogs; two litters of baby squirrels, one red, one black; chipmunks, crows, buzzards, owls, hawks, porcupines, feral cats, feral hogs! "And a half-frozen feral Mexican child...just kidding...although entirely possible!" On top of THAT lifetime list; one additional, very large and totally uncivil critter that more or less defied identification, which our tired Boy Trio dragged through the tattered screen door of our Texas back porch. I think, although I will never be certain, that the large, lumpy, unidentifiable mass, drug home by our indefatigable Trio on a late foggy night in early fall, was my Mom's oldest Brother; Uncle Slim? "AND THIS TIME...I AM NOT KIDDING!"

Chris makes a big cast while dog **Gretchen** & friend **Jason** ham it up. (1985)

"Huge" catch and happy boys on the Blanco River. (1985)

Chris and **Jason** proudly display a typical day's catch! (1985)

The boys made up in "volume" what they lacked in quality or size! (1985)

The sun never set on the boys effort to fish the scenic Blanco River. (1987)

A wopper bass by future **Captain Jason**. (1986)

Chapter Ten

Calcasieu Mistress

There's an ancient puzzle concerning life; one that, at one time or another, is applicable to most of us. Raking in chips at poker, cashing in at the race track, winning a victory or championship in sports, being successful in business or politics, enjoying good health, even succeeding at romance, are examples of lifetime successes that involve recognized but difficult to measure doses of either luck or skill. "Or Both?"

We've all had an experience that stimulated the question; "Were you skillful...or just plain lucky?" Catching a trophy fish is precisely the kind of noteworthy happening I'm talking about; an event that often stimulates the question. Try it! Go out and catch a giant trout or bass and see if people don't ask you; "Well Stupid...Was it skill...or dumb assed luck?" And while there's room for honest debate, truth is, many of life's notable accomplishments involve healthy doses of both; "luck AND skill!" Catching a big fish, a genuinely big fish of any popular game fish species, is certainly not an exception to this age-old quandary. For many of us, luck and skill seem to remain elusive benefactors. For other folks, the popular duet of Lady Luck or Lucy Skill seem to croon a constant lullaby; appear to stumble over delicate lady feet delivering success to the fortunate, while ignoring the unfortunate. "OR? Should I say...delivering success to the skillful...while ignoring the unskillful?"

Since this book is primarily about fishin, I want to discuss the precarious balance between luck and skill in terms of fishin success. Offer an opinion regarding how either, luck or skill, may impact fishin success. Describe how I, during my humble but prolific fishin life, personally field tested history's ancient luck-vs-skill controversy and arrived at a conclusion. To that end allow me to share two real life anecdotal proofs; where it was either "benevolent luck" or "mastered skill" that played the dominant role. My first example involves catching a monstrous black drum in a shallow lake in south Louisiana; my second, landing a monster striped bass in a flood stage roaring Texas river. Here are my two stories. Readers are allowed to draw your own conclusion, encouraged to decide; "Which was it...predominately luck...or mostly skill...that played a greater role in the final outcome of my fish stories...BIG fish stories?"

I opine; "Catching fish in general...catching BIG fish in particular...involves both Lady Luck AND Lucy Skill. But let's take a look."

****

Ever since my fifth birthday; "the one back in 1952 when my Dad promised to take me fishin...and DID...even though it snowed eleven inches the night before...and the next mornin out there fishin it was colder than a witch's breast in a brass bra"; members of my immediate family have celebrated birthdays by going fishin. Goin fishin on your birthday was common practice growin up in Missouri, a concept I enjoyed as a boy and continued as a husband and parent; a family-friendly, sixty year tradition eventually shared with my sons, their friends, and city girl Nurse-Wife Peg. April 11th 2005 was one of those goin fishin on your birthday days for ME! Second Son Ladd invited me to accompany him and a friend on a guided fishin trip over in Louisiana on Lake Calcasieu, pronounced 'Cal-Ka-Shoo'; "To celebrate my fifty-eighth birthday!" Ladd made the arrangements. Ladd's friend brought a ton of homemade beef jerky and luscious day-provisions secured from the friend's iconic restaurant in Schulenburg, Texas. "And in keeping with longstanding family tradition...I paid for everything."

"That's right...I paid for everything." Was then and is today an important subtlety associated with accompanying Son Ladd on huntin or fishin adventures; "Dad pays!" No matter! The three of us; Son Ladd, Ladd's Friend, and I headed out. We were bound for Lake Calcasieu, located in salty bayou country north of Louisiana's share of The Gulf. And. Even though it's called a lake, Lake Calcasieu is actually a shallow saltwater bay. A vast bay, choked down in three separate places to narrow passes that allow the lake to rise and fall with every incoming or outgoing tide; strong Gulf tides continuously feeding in and out of the bay near romantic getaways such as Cameron, Louisiana. There, in that expansive, nutrient rich, continuously renewed, shallow bay; in Lake Calcasieu, a lake that's not really a lake; sport fishing for large redfish and trophy speckle trout rank among some of the best found anywhere on earth. Guides are available and recommended; "IF you intend to land a trophy...which of course we did."

Our plan was simple. Hire a good guide. Fish hard one day, my birthday; "the only day all three of us had available"; come home with a trophy trout. Big trout are most abundant in spring. Catching a twenty-eight inch trophy trout stood near the top of my personal bucket list; "GOD...I loved that Jack Nicholson-Morgan Freeman movie... Bucket List!" Ladd knew about my bucket list wish. Ladd planned our trip and hired our guide accordingly, hoping I would land my trophy spec ON my birthday. By day's end, Ladd was magnificently rewarded for his effort to aid and abet me in achieving my goal. I did indeed land a trophy, a genuine Lake Calcasieu trophy; a spectacular trophy currently adorning the sacred Wall of Fame in my office. Here's the story.

Ladd and his good friend Mr. Robert Bezetsny, 'Mr. B'; "father of one of Ladd's fraternity-brother-best-friends from up at A&M"; and I arrived early on the evening of April 10th. The three of us joined other guests for a pleasant dinner served in the dining hall of legendary Hackberry Rod and Gun Club. A historical facility strategically situated on one of the back-alley sloughs of monstrous Lake Calcasieu. Hackberry's lodge wasn't crowded that night but dinner conversation was lively; every nuance and implication having something to do with fishin; "Can you imagine anything else?"

Sunup brought fog, and a flurry of guide-client pairings and peripheral activities. Interestingly, actually startling to me, two prepaid fishin parties, four men total, all four men present the night before during dinner, failed to show up to meet their assigned guides? "Lost souls…How could ANYONE fail to show up for fishin?" The Hackberry Guides were real Pros; but jaded. The guides said they were half expecting the missing clients to be 'No Shows'! "That's right!" Hackberry Rod and Gun Club is located in Hackberry, LA; thirty minutes driving time to Lake Charles, LA. Lake Charles is home to a cluster of fancy casinos that thrive on the protected shores of Lake Charles. Many a wandering Hackberry client has gone off the reservation and failed to return next morning from a hard night of gambling and drinking; has failed to show up to go fishin or huntin. The guides may have been disappointed, but were also accustomed to MIA No Show Clients. The guides merely sighed and went about their guidely business. "No refunds to prepaid No-Shows".

No such worldly distractions for Son Ladd, Mr. B, and me; we were there to fish and fish hard. All three of us had turned in at first dark. I had difficulty sleeping beyond three; SOP for me, no matter where I am or what I'm doing. Having planned ahead for just such an eventuality, I quietly got up and fetched myself a rod and reel and a pack of quarter-ounce white plastic jigs and slipped out into the dark to try night fishin off Hackberry's lighted dock. I caught three keeper flounder before first light; one big boy over twenty inches. While taking my leisurely "four in the morning" stroll, I spotted dozens of flounder billowing about in the silt, in shallow water beneath Hackberry's lighted dock. I decided the feeding flounder was fair game. My fellow fishermen at breakfast were astounded; "Except for Ladd…He assumed I would be up and on the prowl WAY before dawn…tryin to catch somethin."

Our party of three; "Ladd...Mr. B and Me"; was assigned Hackberry's Number Two Guide. Well-run, professionally organized huntin and fishin lodges such as Hackberry always have a predetermined pecking order for their guides. Big or repeat clients are afforded better known high profile guides; new or onetime clients are assigned whichever guides are available, on a first come first served basis. Usually unofficial; such ordering and pairing of guides with clients is one of life's subtle but more powerful unwritten rules. Because Ladd and his many affiliated, sundry, tagalong parties had been previous and frequent guests at Hackberry, our three man group automatically qualified as a repeat client; "Believe me...No one from Blanco County Texas had been to Hackberry more often than Son Ladd."

Our Guide was thirty-five. Salty for his age, he had spent half his life boating around the shallow saltwater bay Good Folks from Louisiana somehow decided to call Lake Calcasieu. Psychologically, Our Guide was up; knew in advance he was in for a top notched day guiding experienced clients. Ladd had laid out specific instructions for Our Guide; told the guide our party wanted to concentrate on catching large fish, possibly a trophy. Keepers are more readily hooked using natural bait and keepers are more likely caught using different techniques than those our guide intended to employ for our trophy seeking party.

Casting off lines and heading into the thickening fog, our four person party; "Guide included"; was as high as grown men can get while sober and wearing clothes. I was no exception to the mood or moment. I had made it known to every living soul with whom I had fished during the last five years that I was determined to catch a trophy trout before I expired. The term 'Trophy Trout' is a casual label. Totally arbitrary and often intentionally ambiguous; an undefined and unofficial size designator, to his best Fishin Buddy. Generally speaking, in relative terms, avid saltwater fisherpersons usually consider trophy size for speckle trout to commence at twenty-eight inches. Few speckle trout are caught between twenty-eight and thirty inches. VERY few trout are caught above thirty inches. Trout greater than thirty inches are SO rare the likelihood of catching one disappears off us normal fisherperson's Hopes & Dreams Chart; "Don't forget about the possibility of it happening...but then don't hold your breath expecting it to happen either."

My personal and publicly declared definition of Trophy Trout was twenty-eight inches, or greater. I had previously caught two wonderfully big trout; both carefully measured with multiple eye witnesses present. Both previous big trout were precisely twenty-seven and three-quarters inches long. "Both of 'em!" Both big trout were clearly within legitimate cheatin range, but both were also one rat turd short of my goal; clearly NOT genuine twenty-eight inchers. "Hell's Fire...If I was willin to pay five hundred bucks to have a fiber glass replica of my trout made...I sure as HELL wasn't gonna lie to myself and fudge the final quarter inch! Who lies about their golf score...or weight...or height...or monogamy...or drinking habits...or poker winnings...or personal income...or about their taxes? Sorry! I think by digressing I may have miserably failed to make an otherwise valid point? Which IS...I have not and will not mount a speckle trout and hang its replica on my office Wall of Fame and call it a Trophy Trout...unless it IS carefully measured...with eye witnesses present...and found to be safely beyond the magic goal of twenty-eight inches. And with that lofty goal in mind...off we went in search of glory."

Fifteen minutes of wide-open-throttle boating into blinding fog and Our Guide suddenly cut the boat's roaring motor and proclaimed what all good guides everywhere always proclaim; "OK Men...Let's try this spot for awhile...Fishin has been great right in here (in this general area) for the past few days... There are some big ones workin this area." No one ever need tell me twice to fish. I was on my feet casting by the time Our Guide was able to put out our small drift anchor. We were fishing in shallow water.

It was my first trip to Calcasieu; I was astounded to learn that most of Calcasieu is extremely shallow. It is told by local Cajun Guides, as pure Gospel, that tall Louisianans routinely walk the length of the huge lake; "which really is NOT a lake at all...but a huge saltwater bay...do I need to keep sayin that?" I wasn't certain the Cajun legend was true, but WAS perfectly capable of determining the depth of water into which I spent my morning casting lures; "two to three feet...MAX!" I merely stuck my rod tip overboard each and every time our boat stopped in a new spot; which, as things turned out, was often. We were having a difficult time locating a concentration of trout.

Never more than four feet deep; never beyond easy reach of my inquiring rod tip; the choppy lake water appeared milky-white and impenetrably murky to my untrained eye, "almost dirty." Because Calcasieu sets due north of The Gulf and is benevolently exposed to the wider expanses of The Gulf; because, relative to its immense surface area, Calcasieu IS so dramatically shallow; Calcasieu often appears to be in a broiling brackish state of unfit turmoil. But such is NOT the case! The lake's shallowness and the strong in and out tides that wash the lake are part of what help maintain its eco-system and the thriving dynamics of its water; what help make the large shallow bay a genuine hot spot for catching large, spring-breeding, heavy-feeding, sow trout. Precisely why our party was there during spring of the year; exactly the kind of fish our party intended to catch.

Everyone in our boat was well-rigged; light seven foot rods, sporting lightweight line, loaded onto good reels. I was using a Calcutta 200 GTB filled to the brim with ten pound test, low visibility, monofilament. I studiously kept a quarter-ounce jig tied on the business end of my line most of the day. I never used any sort of leader or swivel system. I tied all my lures directly to my main line; "less efficient use of tying time when switching lures…but sturdier in a tough fish fight." Ladd and our Guide, two men with far more experience and knowledge than I, were using a leader and swivel system; which included six pound, and sometimes even four pound test, leader line. I thought their choice of leader line was ridiculously lightweight. But later, towards the end of our long day, I certainly admired their results. Both younger men enjoyed what turned out to be a ten-to-one strike ratio over either Mr. B or me. "Poor old Mr. B and me…we were definitely older but NOT wiser. Not when it came to fishin. Given the option…Mr. B and I insisted on using ten-to-twelve pound test lines…without leaders. He and I got snagged a lot…would have lost a million lures if we used light leaders…like Ladd."

I realize that line test-weights and reel brand names and leader configurations are technical gibberish; innocuous details typically omitted from heart stopping excitement routinely found in my more traditional fishin stories. But in THIS story, a few industry standards and factoids are critical to making a bigger point; a point I want to be certain of making. There's a reason I'm trying early-on to emphasize line strength and lure size. And while both, line strength AND lure size, are seemingly of minor significance going into this story; both eventually had huge impact on a long day's loud results. Lure size and me using heavier line than recommended held great sway over the final outcome of that day's fishin success. Two innocent choices, brought on by MY hardheadedness and ignorance; "Mine alone." Two innocent choices, that eventually held in their hands, during a totally wild fish fighting experience, the difference between a sad defeat or a marvelous victory; a once-in-a-lifetime fish fighting experience that happened to occur at the extreme, tippy-tail end of a conventional day out there fishin. "Light lines…light lures…light rods…and in MY case… featherweight knowledge of what I was doing. But! It was MY birthday and I intended to enjoy it… turn it into a memorable day by catching myself a trophy. We'll see how that reasonably admirable quest turned out."

As our noisy motor was throttled back and silence filled the void, I immediately stood and quickly let fly our boat's first cast of the day. Bombastically declaring as I cast; "Gentlemen…If you intend to catch the first FISH of the day…it may be of value to make the first CAST of the day?" So why all the artificial urgency? Mr. B, Son Ladd, and I, had put up fifteen dollars cash each, prior to departing the dock. We three had made a friendly cash wager; had created ourselves a three-way CASH jackpot!

"So what were our three friendly bets?" (1)First Fish of the day, (2) Largest Fish of the day, or (3) Most Fish of the day. I intended to win something; one portion or another of the three categories on which we had bet. We'll see how that turned out too!

"Ziiiiiiiiiiinnnnnnnng! Out went my soft-bodied tiny trout jig...a long and perfect cast to the exact spot Our Guide had indicated...our boat's first shot fired!"

"Splash!"

"Three silky-smooth cranks of the oversized handle of my golden Calcutta reel... quickly taking up sea breeze induced slack between me and my lure...and WHAM!"

I had a smashing strike! So powerful a strike it caught me off guard; nearly resulting in my rod and Calcutta reel involuntarily being jerked from my hand and landing in Calcasieu's troubled waters. "Only by the slimmest of margins did I avoid a fisherperson's MOST embarrassing moment for any fishin day...of MY day...out there fishin. We've all seen it happen...watched in astonished silence as one of our fishin partners cast his or her rod out of their hand...or had their rod jerked away by a powerful aggressive fish. According to ten dozen guides ("NOT") queried while researching this highly technical book ("NOT")...collectively speaking...it happens... Lost Rod Syndrome happens...more often than individual fisherpersons realize."

But I recovered; hooked and quickly landed a smallish but aggressive male trout that imprudently struck the lure offered up on my first cast. It was a fine trout; a hard fighting eighteen incher. Six inches longer than the minimum required by the sovereign state of Louisiana; two inches longer than the minimum required back home in Texas. Odd to me; Louisiana and Texas share hundreds of miles of Gulf Coast, and trillions of cubic feet of saltwater sport fishing areas, along a common combined Gulf Coast. However! Louisiana allows more trout to be caught and kept PER DAY than Texas; fifteen as opposed to ten, "even five in restricted South Texas waters." But! Size minimums are even more puzzling. Louisiana allows fishermen to keep twelve inch trout; versus sixteen in Texas! "I'm here to say...a twelve inch trout barely makes a good stink in the skillet. Is barely legitimate eatin size for a grown man! But then...as we know...a starvin Cajun[1] will eat anything...any livin crawlin climbin diggin runnin swimmin flyin critter...no matter its size...species...home of origin...or orifice from which its tiny critter body may have just been shat!"

"But of first and foremost importance?" The contest for First Fish was done! First Fish was mine! Undisputed! Unchallenged! Unalterably! Mine!

"And of secondary but interesting importance?" Our boat's first trout of the day, MY trout, turned out to be my LAST trout of the day! "No Shit!" And for a long-long-LONG time; for hours on end; that eighteen incher was my ONLY fish! Until; "Has anyone reading this story guessed that MY last fish of the day...might also turn out to be ...our entire party's last fish of the day?" That's correct. I caught our Hard Rock Café quartet's First Fish of the day, during six long hours of professionally guided out there fishin; in some of the best speckle trout waters on earth; and then fished my Missouri Born Yankee ass off without catching even one, tiny, nother trout! But then...DID manage to distinguish myself, managed to make MY day, by hooking and landing our boat's LAST fish of the day! Catching absolutely nothing in between! "NADA!"[2]

Minutes after my First Fish, Our Guide caught a great trout; a twenty-one incher. Next; Son Ladd ripped off five nice keeper trout in a row. An obvious sub-contest soon broke out between Our Guide and Son Ladd. Because Mr. B and I were so clearly outclassed, we humbly retreated to the far end of the bobbing boat and enjoyed hot peppered beef jerky and ice cold beer; "Cold beer at ten in the morning IS an acceptable substitute for a fisherperson's unquenched thirst for fishin success."

"Our day wore on...and on...and on...and on...and...well...I think you get the picture." Immediately after Our Guide announced that we would fish for another half-hour, Mr. B finally managed to catch his first, and ONLY fish! His fish was a smallish sheep head, the first of that species Mr. B had ever caught. Mr. B smiled and reached for another desensitizing cold brew. I snapped a picture of Mr. B's inglorious 'Catch of the Day' and renewed my personal thrashing of Calcasieu's murky waters; with greater intensity. "I was enormously frustrated!"

And while Mr. B; "bless his gentle Czech heart"; quietly and stoically accepted his second class citizen status, smiling and sipping his twelve-teenth beer in his happy-go-lucky, carefree way, I conversely rebelled. Bowed my red neck against my ineptitude and impotency and attacked Calcasieu with renewed gusto. When Our Guide proclaimed that The End was drawing nigh, I immediately became a madman driven; became Hell Bent on producing

---

[1]Footnote: "Before you Ragin Cajuns get too bent outta shape...try remembering that my Dear Mom...currently still standin tall...still kickin Yankee ass and takin Yankee names...at the ripe old age of NINETY...was...and for all practical purposes still IS...a Cajun! Born...reared...and married to my Dear Old Dad near abouts Lake Charles Louisiana way back in 1940. So forget your Cajun letters of protest and your Cajun bitchin about my slanted perspective regarding Coon Ass Cajuns. It's useless. I love Cajuns. I AM one. Sort of? Kind of? Ifin' maternal parenting counts for anything?"

[2]Footnote: "For real Yankees...NADA means nothing more caught by me."

success. I had come to Louisiana and Calcasieu to catch a trophy trout, and by GOD I intended to catch one! Or wear myself into a frazzled nylon knot trying. Meanwhile; Ladd and Our Guide filled the boat's ice chest with a respectable number of keepers. We had a nice mess of Louisiana eatin size trout, that I knew would taste exactly the same as Texas eatin size trout; "Only smaller!" However! Other than the twenty-one incher Our Guide caught shortly after my First Fish, our boat appeared to be coming up empty handed as far as catching a trophy.

There are surefire things The Boys and I learned over the years while out there huntin and fishin. One vital thing learned had come to us years earlier, while fishin with largemouth bass fishin guide Sonny Harmon on Choke Canyon Reservoir in sizzling South Texas. I quote Guide Sonny; "Boys...Always make one final cast...If I (Sonny) had a hundred dollar bill for ever damned bass I caught on my last cast of the day...I could give this damned boat to the Salvation Army and play poker ever night for the rest of my born days." That sage profundity provided to us by the one and only Guide Extraordinaire, Sonny D. Harmon, from Three Rivers, Texas; recently deceased.

Well! If it was true; if it really DID work for Guide Sonny; why not apply such wisdom to our speckle trout fishin expedition in a foreign country like Louisiana? Our Guide, our current Calcasieu Guide, yelled clearly and definitively; "We need to pull in our (canvas sea) anchor...and reel in our lures...and be on our way back to the dock." It was nearing three; Hackberry's guides preferred to be off the water and totally finished with fish cleaning and parting-company-with-paying-clients chores by four.

"OK Men...Let's go!"

Our Guide's words had barely broken the plain of my addled brain before I quick replied; "OK...But I gotta make one final cast...For Sonny." I actually spoke the words. Critical words; made noteworthy by events that followed. Those were Sonny's words. Not mine. Not originally. I'm glad there are living, sane witnesses. Why the need for witnesses? Because the results of my final cast for Sonny were staggering.

Out went my Salt Water Assassin ™; a small artificial lure sailing downwind as if shot from a gun. A lure picked over all other lures from Academy's mind boggling array of millions upon millions of lures; a lure setting sail all alone in the milky white capped shallows of Calcasieu; a lure disappearing in a barely audible bliiimmmppphphph at the far-far away, invisible end of my far-far too lightweight monofilament line. "BINGO! No. Not a strike. That would have been too predictable...a more mundane outcome."

My lure snagged on the oyster shell-littered bottom of Calcasieu; got hung tight for the ten thousandth time…that day. "Shit!" That's about all I could say. There I was. Making a ceremonial final cast for Sonny, and I get my frickin lure snagged on the frickin bottom for the millionth frickin time. "OH Well…Frick it!"

Just as Our Guide announced our imminent departure, he also began hauling in our anchor. Southeasterly Gulf winds had come up during the day. By quitting time, onshore winds were creating tiny whitecaps all around our bobbing boat; a normal sea during a normal day of normal fishin on Calcasieu. Our sea anchor effectively slowed our boat's drift to a manageable scud, allowing us to cast in front of ourselves; cast in the same direction we were drifting; cast WITH the steady wind; keep the wind at our unsteady backs. But when our drift anchor was lifted free of the water, our boat immediately picked up steam. Our boat's rate of movement across the lake's choppy surface, towards my snagged lure, accelerated. Calcasieu was so vast, its surface so featureless, our boat's rate of drift across the lake's skyline-to-skyline water so slight, had it not been for an intrusive signal, none of us landlubber clients would have realized we were actually moving. "Except!" There WAS an intrusive telltale signal!

Except? As we came near to, or even to, the shelly spot where my tiny lure was snagged, but then continued drifting on past my lure, at an accelerating rate, there was an audible signal; a loud warning that alerted everyone on board to the fact; "our boat was picking up steam…being swept across the lake at an increasing pace." The except? The intrusive tattletale signal? ME! Yelling at the top of my impolite, landlubber lungs.

Shrill yelling, that immediately gained everyone's attention; particularly Our Guide's. Emphatic yelling, that caused everyone onboard to be acutely TOO aware of the critical fact my snagged line was now being emptied from my reel; critical to me! Senseless yelling, about being hopelessly snagged on the bottom; about being in dire need of Our Guide's immediate assistance; pointed comments demanding Our Guide start up his motor and chug over to where I was snagged; thirty yards out and four feet down in the gloomy, opaque waters of Calcasieu. "Oh yes…My yelling got everyone's full attention alright!" Undiminished loud assertions, that our boat was drifting too fast; that our boat was drifting the wrong direction; that my line was being stripped off my reel faster and faster by the uncontrolled drifting boat; my incessant yak took firm hold of everyone's thought processes. Increasingly stern oral demands, that Our Patient Guide do something fast and professional; "Because…Dammit…I'm still losing ground…still losing line." In short; my childish blithering was creating a confusing situation, within a confusing situation; making matters worse, not better; distracting the undistracted.

I WAS confused; the urgency of my snagged situation had taken temporary grip of my sanity? Mr. B was confused; "Budweiser…The King of Beers" had seen to that? Ladd was confused; my absurd yelling for "Help" regarding loss of my lure seemed out of character; "Dad…usually just breaks off"? Our Guide was distracted, and confused; his reasonable instructions, shouted to me from the back of the boat to the front of the boat, were seemingly being ignored; the meaning of his emphatic instructions apparently being lost in the noise of Calcasieu's rising wind, or bouncing off the incredible thickness of my landlubber-client-skull?

A confused and distracted foursome, for whom matters were about to be made worse, not better; Our Guide, Mr. B, Son Ladd, and Me! Four fishermen, riding safely in a sound boat, fixin to head in and call it a day; when our fine and properly loaded, swiftly drifting boat inexplicably began doing a curiously remarkable thing. "Inexplicable?" "Curious?" "Remarkable?" Our skittering, scudding boat came fully abreast OF but then passed on BY, a few yards astern OF and then on BY, the spot where my lost lure was so firmly snagged on the immovable bottom of milky Lake Calcasieu. "And then?"

Well then, all Hell broke loose. Caught broadside by a stout Gulf wind, set free of any-and-all control provided by our previously regained drift anchor; our boat took off, "as if Jet Ski propelled." From a point just THIS side of where my line was snagged, our boat seemingly jerked forward; appeared to suddenly lurch forward, IN the direction I was facing; and curiously began racing further downwind. And! Our wee, snug boat seemed to be moving distinctly faster; gaining speed as it and its three onlooking passengers were swept beyond the point where my line disappeared into sudsy Calcasieu; a small, alone boat, rapidly passing BY the otherwise nondescript spot where my lure had become hopelessly snagged on oyster shell. Four, sun drenched, frustrated fishermen; in a bobbing, little boat; that seemed, all at once, to be plowing through whitecap-choppy-wave after whitecap-choppy-wave. A busy boat; swiftly moving across a vast ocean, its movement fostering an uncanny, irritating zipping off of and emptying out of every last precious foot of my valuable new line, which I had been working SO damned hard to regain. "My Calcutta reel was screaming at everyone. I was screaming at Our Guide. Our Guide was screaming at me. Ladd was gawking in stunned silence. And good ole Mr. B…Well…Mr. B and Budweiser were beaming!"

No doubt Our Guide was a good guide. One of the best I am told. One reason Our Guide was considered good was because he had been guiding for a long time. He had seen a lot of different things; experienced a lot of different happenings. He was quick to react to my earnest plea to start and stop the boat. He realized client fishermen can sometimes be quirkily sentimental about favorite lures. Therefore; from the first instant I began yelling about being snagged; insisting I needed immediate relief; Our Guide had done his Guide best to start our drifting boat off in the correct direction. "Great Fisherman I…Snagged for the millionth time! Frick! Frick! Frick!"

Meantime; our vexed boat continued drifting with the stout wind. Realizing our boat was drifting beyond my snagged lure, Our Guide did his guidely best to stop the boat. Slowed our boat to a skidding-mosey, a near-halt; by hurling out our boat's small steel anchor and heavy anchor chain; did his guidely best to cause the heavy anchor to drag our bobbing boat to a quick, bottom-scraping halt. Our good guide reacting in the manner he did because he was indeed a good guide; "he thought anchoring and stopping our boat would keep it from overrunning my snagged lure"; would allow me reasonable opportunity to ultimately retrieve my precious line and valuable snagged lure.

But! Our Guide's best efforts were to no avail; slowing, and then finally stopping our boat in the choppy sea seemed to do little good? I didn't gain relief. Line continued disappearing off my reel faster than mice flee cats. I was frustrated; unreasonable. Worrying more about a boar hog tit worthless lure, on which I had caught diddlysquat all day, than the integrity of our boat. The full spool of fresh valuable line, placed on my reel the night before by dedicated fisherman son Ladd, gave me additional ammo for complaining; more so than the cheap lure. But I was being irrational! I hung the hat of my demands on the flimsy excuse of saving my spool of new line and cried out to "Guide Almighty" for relief. Our boat slowed, I reeled faster and faster; fast as I possibly could. I looked like a crazed madman scratchin a hundred chiggers, pickin a million nits!

Without so much as glancing up I continued reeling, at warp speed. Our heavy steel anchor dug into Calcasieu's shell-littered bottom, our anchor chain tightened, and our slightly crowded fishin boat jerked to a lurching halt. Reeling fast as I could, I was barely able to take up the little slack gained during our boat's sudden lurches forward; during our boat's slow, protracted, anchor-dragging stop. And then; MORE confusion! What precious little line I HAD managed to gain while our boat was moving in the correct direction; the bit of line retrieved while our boat was drifting towards my snagged lure; suddenly began disappearing off my screeching reel. My line began tightening again; straightening rapidly, as never before. Then really tightening, clickity-clicking line back OFF the drag of my carefully set Calcutta. I thought to myself, but did not say; "Evidently our anchor has shifted again…we're drifting again? DAMN!"

I also thought to myself, but did not say; "Our Guide is so preoccupied gettin ready to head in…he has somehow or another allowed our boat to drift beyond…drift farther away…annoyingly away…from the hidden snag holdin my lure…and now… DAMN IT TO HELL…more of my high dollar line is disappearin off my reel."

Then, without thinking, I did say; "DAMMIT Man (Guide) can't you stop this frickin boat? I'm losing my line again! Shit Man (Guide)!"

Before I could fully assimilate all the boat drifting, anchor shifting, wind blowing, guide cussing, here-there-and-yon boat bobbing, and get myself organized, get myself focused on MY circumstances; MORE, fresh, clean, valuable line began zipping off my noisy reel at a rate not yet seen. Losing fresh, clean line meant I was cutting deeper into my finite supply. In utter frustration, I turned face-to-face and yelled more obscenities at Our Guide; telling Our Guide, imploring him, in NO uncertain terms; "PLEASE stop the boat from drifting away from my snagged lure"; uttering those or similar soft spoken words of advice, genteelly suggesting Our Guide fix things. Ugly words, which really meant; "Fire up the f—-ing motor and steer our f—-ing boat forward towards my f—-ing snagged lure…so I can retrieve my lure…so we can get the HELL on home! And in the process…IF you don't f—-ing mind…IF you got f—-ing time…I would like to retrieve my valuable f—-ing line! You f—ing idiot!"

I was irritated. Had finally allowed our long, tiring day and our virtually empty ice chest; nearly void of keeper fish caught by Mr. B or me; to get under my sunburned, frustrated, inept-fisherman skin. The last thing I wanted to do was donate three hundred yards of high quality monofilament line to the seepy bottom of Calcasieu Lake. I thought Our Guide seemed preoccupied; too busy getting ready to head back to Hackberry Lodge to pay attention to his client's desire; "to retrieve my precious lost lure and line." Result; I had turned to have a real word with Our Guide. Actually; "I had turned ON Our Guide!" Became a borderline lunatic because I thought Our Guide was casually, carelessly, and callously allowing our misguided, malfunctioning, and misdirected boat to drift away from my snagged line. Drift too far, too fast, and without good reason.

Well then there occurred to three client occupants of our boat, an epiphany, a jaw dropping revelation; that created long lasting, red faced embarrassment; from which I shall never be set free. A hallmark moment in my adult fishing life and in the lives of my companions, Mr. B and Ladd; and in the noticeably earnest and intent life of Our Guide!

Our Guide's guidely response to my feeble tongue lashing was swift, effective, and above the fray; a retort, calmly delivered to my out-of-place berating of Our Guide; a guidely reply, that took a bit of time to soak through my sun baked, salt dried, thick skull. "Uh…Mr. Pepper…(I realized Our Guide was pissed…he had only called me Mr. Pepper one time the entire day…early that morning…before I had insisted he (Guide) use my first name)…Uh…Mr. Pepper…Uh Sir…Hmmmm…I'm sorry Sir…But our boat is NOT moving. Uh Mr. Pepper…Uh…Your line is going OUT Sir…Because…Well…Because Sir…You have a fish on the other end of it…Pulling it out…Sir…? Sir…? Sir…? Mr. Pepper…? Sir…I think you should……….!"

"Holy Shit…He's (Guide) right! Ladd…Grab the net! I think I just hooked our boat's Last Fish of the day!"

I was ecstatic. I had indeed hooked Last Fish of the day. And judging from the relentless pull on my tightening line; judging from the rate at which line was zinging off my reel and being dragged away into the murky shallows of Calcasieu; I judged a big Last Fish of the day! Additional cash for Biggest Fish might also become mine; along with cash for First Fish; "IF…By some residual professional miracle…I can get our uppity Guide to quit bitchin at me…and HELP?" I thought to myself, but did not say.

Point; our boat was currently NOT drifting anywhere, at any rate of speed.

Point; we had never been drifting; not much since I first alerted Our Guide that I needed his guidely HELP!

Point; after our steel anchor went overboard, our boat remained virtually stationary. We weren't drifting away from the snag; the snag was slowly swimming away from our boat!

Point; having quickly sized up his client's situation; Our Guide had indeed been preoccupied.

Realizing from the get-go that I was NOT snagged on the bottom; Our Guide had been busy preparing our boat for battle; busy firing up his trusty outboard; busy weighing anchor; busy securing loose items within our little boat so we could give chase; busy trying to help me catch…Last Fish of the day. As I began assimilating the actual facts of my situation, additional yards of precious line continued spooling off my tightened drag; the definition of precious in terms of monetary value, now supplanted by a suddenly FAR more rigid definition of precious in terms of the scarcity of the commodity disappearing off my reel. My Calcutta was singing a sweet-sweet melody; crooning a lovely tune. I may not have known much about hooking delicate-mouthed, nibble-feeding, spring sow trout in a shallow, salty lake; but I certainly knew how to fight big fish. Our Guide, as I have already said, obviously a Top Pro on Calcasieu, was about to discover what I did or did not know about fightin a big fish.

Before all hope of avoiding dreaded spooling; "loosing 100% of your line"; seemed lost; when fewer than six-to-ten turns of delicate line appeared left on my reel; Our Guide had dutifully and silently gotten our boat's motor fired up. "And our once-upon-a-time drifting boat...that was never actually drifting beyond my snagged line... was chug-chug-chugging steadily and directly towards my hooked fish...that I had no idea was a hooked fish!" A hooked fish that, somehow or another, Our Guide had instantly realized was a really BIG hooked fish; precariously attached to the far end of an apparently unaware or totally inept client's line. Seeing NO valid reason to do so, Our Guide did NOT bother asking ME my opinion about chasing down the hooked fish; he merely set about, setting out, to, Just Do It! "So...I reeled." Our boat was going to go TO the hooked fish; as opposed to me fighting the fish with nonexistent line, 99% of which had already been spooled off my reel. "It would've been useless to attempt bringing the fish TO us even if I HAD known what I was doing...which I really didn't."

Our Guide sensed that. Had he not reacted when and how he did, my BIG fish story would have ended there; "Did I mention that Our Guide was a Top Pro...which of course I never doubted?" Within a minute or two, reeling like a man with his pants on fire, I regained nearly half my lost line. Our Guide continued chugging quietly and forthrightly towards what was obviously a very large fish. My heart began racing. Ladd's voice began exploding. "DAD...I think we may have just gotten you that Bucket List trout you been wantin!" I was certain Ladd was correct; IF I could land the trophy fish? Had on what unquestionably would be our day's Biggest Fish; IF I could..........!

Plenty of freshly RE-acquired line back on my reel; a bit of coaching from Our totally calm, Top Pro Guide; a lot of whooping and hollering by my boat mates; and I was feeling better. The shock of realizing I had hooked; that a fish had gotten hooked; that our boat had hooked; that a really-really large fish was somehow or another hooked; on the far end of MY line; was beginning to soak in. I dared not anticipate a victorious end to my, to our boats, fish fight. My total knowledge of fighting speckle trout the enormous size of the "Big One" hooked on my line ranged between "little and none". My lifetime trout were half the size; or so I judged from the steady, weighty pull currently offending my manly sense of fisherman propriety. Meaning; "I was already in the dampening-down-my-expectations-process...convincing myself how IN-opportune it would be for a dedicated fisherman...someone like ME...to hook such a monster once-in-a-lifetime trout...and then not actually succeed in landing it." To lessen my building anxiety, I did something we used to do in Nam during fierce firefights; "I began praying." Seriously! Then I began praying out loud! Then Ladd joined me in oral prayer. Then Our Guide joined Ladd. "I never heard Mr. B pray...but he swore later on he was honking down on a Catholic version of Lord...Help my Good Buddy Jim Gitter Done!"

Fish are fish. Fish fight to live. Fish fight to swim away and fight another day. My BIG fish did it all. Did every BIG fish thing it could have done to remain free. Did its fish best to NOT become another BIG fish hanging on Hackberry's historic Wall of Fame? Long runs; erratic short runs; dives towards the boat; hunkering down and refusing to move, even when our gyrating boat passed too near; in two cases passing directly over where my giant fish was holding tight to Calcasieu's shell strewn bottom. No matter how much line I took in; no matter how often Our Guide fired up his boat's motor and gave chase; the exalted quarry on the far end of my line seemed determined to outlast me; win the contest he and I we were having. But I wasn't tiring. This wasn't like battling the giant striper along the roaring river bank over rusty cables and truck sized boulders. I was comfortable. I was casually chatting with Ladd and Mr. B. I was receiving occasional tips from our glued-to-the-exciting-moment Guide. "I had it made."

One thing I will always remember about my fish fight; Our Guide telling me at least a thousand times to NOT allow my thumbs, either of them, to inadvertently lie upon the line, trapping the line. NOT to put even slight pressure on the line by squeezing my thumbs down against the top portion of my rod. The part of the rod handle where the cork is located, the part just below the line. It was an old, old habit of mine to squeeze smaller fish down; an effective method for slowing small fish down towards the end of their fight; NOT a good idea, perhaps a fatal method, when dealing with a giant fish. "Don't touch that line Mr. Pepper"; there he was (Guide), back to calling me Mr. Pepper.

Meanwhile, it was quittin-time-plus; "plus about half-an-hour!" Boats, two dozen of them, were passing by the general our area of our fish fight. A few boats, five to six boats, dropped anchor and pulled up an easy chair to hopefully observe history in the making. No one knew for certain, but it was entirely possible, that I was hooked up with the biggest trout of Hackberry's entire spring season; certainly hooked up to a fish beyond my limited-in-scope personal Bucket List goal of twenty-eight inches!

And then it came; a sobering realization. A different guided boat, carrying a different Captain, happened along and stopped within easy haling distance. Our Guide, and the newly arrived on the scene Boat Captain, spoke in familiar tones and terms. I recalled seeing the older, more somber sounding and totally pleasant Captain appearing at Hackberry Lodge's predawn breakfast. The new Captain was Hackberry's most famous senior guide! When Senior Guide spoke, Our Guide listened, and respectfully responded. "As I would have done...had a Marine Colonel or General spoken to me...when I was a mere Captain or Lieutenant?"

Addressing Senior Guide, Our Guide said; "No Sir...Sorry to say...It's NOT a trout. No...I don't know for sure what it is...but it's big and it's not even close to being done. Mr. Pepper is doing a fine job fighting it...he may just land it...given enough time and energy...given a boost by me chasing it with our boat. Yes...I think he might just get it in...land it. We're stayin put until this is done! But NO...it's NOT a trout."

I felt like a four-legged horse winning a three-legged race; a bit of glory gushed from my moment, but there was still excitement to spare. "So what if it isn't a trout! A sparkling revelation that immediately fired up a new question...Then what is it?" Our Guide guessed my fish to be a giant flounder, or grouper that swam into the bay during a strong, overnight, incoming tide; "Possibly even a giant black drum?"

Black drum are common in Calcasieu, but not normally caught while fishing for trout with small lures. Black drum are carp look-alikes. And just like their twin the carp, black drum are strictly bottom feeders. Black drum feed by crushing small crabs and other crustaceans between powerful toothless jaws. Black drum are powerful fighters; like their first cousin red drum. "Red drum...commonly referred to as redfish...are number one or two in popularity among shallow saltwater fisherpersons...big heavy fish ...with distinctive black spots on their tail." Giant Black drum have been caught in the hundred pound range. Anyway; no one on our boat out there in the middle of Calcasieu knew what species my fish was, or was not? No one had seen hide-nor-hair of my big fish. Another forty minutes of zigzagging back and forth across Calcasieu and our Guide calmly informed me that my fish was tiring; that it would soon surface. "Which it did!"

For the last ten-to-fifteen minutes, PRIOR to my fish surfacing, I abandoned my prayers for the God of Fishing to allow me to land the fish, and instead began praying to merely be allowed to simply see it. "I switched prayers when everyone on board decided my fish was a mere drum...NOT a bucket-list-fulfilling trophy trout?"

Another five to ten minutes, we saw a large swirl in the off-color water. Another five; Our Guide confirmed that the tiring fish was indeed a black drum. Our Guide could somehow or another see far enough into the opaque water to determine what no one else aboard could clearly see; "I guess that's why he was Our Guide?" Then Ladd saw the fish. Then even Mr. Budweiser-Buddy-B said HE got a glimpse of my fish. Not me. I had YET to see my own fish. Not that I knew what to expect other than something big, ugly, black, and carp-like. "None of which...except BIG...my fish turned out to be!"

Bordering on an hour since it began, the tired, old, sow-fish breeched; "Some said longer…if we included the time wasted arguing about whether or not our boat was drifting…or if I was snagged…while the fish was merrily swimming away with my lure in its huge mouth!" She was beautiful. It was love a first sight. I had never before caught so wonderful a fish. "And it was my birthday!"

Using a special, rubberized, long-handled, wide-mouthed dip net; Ladd assisting; Our Guide ever-so-gently hoisted the fat-bellied lady drum aboard. Then, with the care one might exhibit handling a wiggling one year old, Our Guide got a solid grip on the giant old sow fish and lifted her high; for a few-seconds-long glance by boaters who had gathered nearby to watch; "for sober witnesses to validate our catch." Then Our Guide instructed his three-lay-fishermen clients to take whatever pictures we wanted, while he prepared to gently weigh my Calcasieu Mistress. Fifty-six pounds heavy! Forty-eight inches long! "Four feet!" Not really a monster for a black drum; "But big for me!" A quick dozen snapshots, a loving pat on her slick, old, boogered-up head, and my big sow drum was gently released back into her shallow, salty domain; allowed to swim free, to cast upon the world's seven seas her belly full of eggs; her pounds of roe it was SO obvious she was carrying. I felt like Noah, or Moses, or Steve Irwin; perhaps even Mother Nature? Aglow from head to toe, breathing again for the first time in an hour, I plopped my overweight ass down on the Igloo beer cooler and accepted a congratulatory cold Bud from beaming Son Ladd. And, as my deceased Daddy up in Missouri would have said; "DAMN Jimmy…You did good!"

"So? How about it? Was I lucky? Or was I good? Some say both…some say neither. I say BOTH…for sure!" There were definite skills involved. We clients were properly outfitted. We were well-guided. We had been placed in the correct spot, at the correct time of day, and were fishing with proper lures, and employing good technique. And. All three of us had made it a point to stay with it; work hard at what we had come there to do; "Catch a trophy fish." Any or all of the aforementioned could be categorized as having contributed to the end result of our day. However! There's also no question that blind luck played a big part; my ten pound-test line somehow or another avoided being razored into pieces by ten billion oyster shells littering the bottom of Calcasieu. My tiny, teeny weenie, witty bitty, insignificant lure somehow or another appeared to be an appealing morsel to the solitary, big bellied, old Momma drum. My layman's knots held. My high-tech, carefully engineered reel, and its sophisticated drag, properly played out what precious little line I was able to retain during the confused stage of my fish fight. The weather held. Our spontaneous audience, which grew into a small but remarkably well-behaved armada, remained clear of and out of the way of our fish fight. Our Guide remained stoically tolerant of my stupidity and rookie ineptitudes; "Remember…during many gnarly minutes of confusion…I insisted that I was snagged on the bottom!" And. No one onboard messed up the critical final minutes of my fish fight; no one spooked the wise old fish into making a line-snapping sudden dash to freedom. "The lucky portion of our day's end result?"

Therefore! Regarding catching my large Calcasieu black drum, from a vast shallow sea, using light line; regarding catching my big striper bass from a roaring river, using a cheap convenience store lure? I conclude; "Fishing involves a handsome dose of BOTH…luck and skill." Same with winning at poker; ditto for winning a tough election; same for buying and selling farm commodities at a profit; no different when talking about marrying the correct partner for life; or choosing the right career; or starting up a new business;

Ladd and **Dad**! A little luck... a little skill... and I landed myself a "Bucket List" trophy... the guide was superb. (2005)

or pulling a slot machine and having a bushel of quarters tumble out; or avoiding sudden death and destruction during combat; or growing old as opposed to dying young; or being confident and knowing oneself as opposed to being unsure or wondering about oneself. I say; all of the aforementioned life-definers, all of the self-defining milestones listed above, are representative of how one of life's oldest quandaries applies to fishing; OR to individual fisherpersons. "I say...we shouldn't vex ourselves worrying about whether it was luck or skill? I say...better to enjoy the benefits of BOTH...as opposed to neither. Experience a healthy dose of BOTH...with BOTH coming at precisely the correct time...as opposed to neither ever happening. I decidedly say BOTH! Look for both. Accept both...whenever either happens...or appears to happen. Sooo...I say...Good Luck My Friends! Learn everything you can...Improve your Skills! While you're out there fishin...hoping like Hell good Luck will save your sorry buttocks from lack of Skill!"

Chris Pepper fishin sun up 'til sun down helped build fishermen from farm boys. (1990)

Chapter Eleven

Big Boy Striper

Likely as not you've heard someone say; "Better lucky than good (skilled)." My entire life I've been forced to endure; "Jimmy...You is one of the luckiest Sons-A-Bitches I ever knowed!" As lead-in to my next fishin story, allow me to offer three, real life, personal examples of skill versus luck. Anecdotal proof illustrating the unanswerable quandary; "Is it better to be lucky...or good (skilled)?"

One: Once upon a time during the late 1970s I was part owner of a small, family owned, tobacco warehouse. Acting as Floor Manager-Buyer for my two partners; Sister Sandy and my Dad; I stood tall and all alone on our tobacco warehouse auction floor and bought the entire day's total offerings. Next morning raw tobacco prices across the entire United States jumped from a dollar-forty, to well over two dollars a pound; "UP nearly fifty percent overnight." The next morning, having worked through the night preparing for the anticipated price rise, our family owned company resold the contents of our warehouse, filled to the brim with the same tobacco I had bought the previous day, for a $500,000 net gain! "A half million bucks...Overnight!" Was I lucky, or good?

Two: In April 1981, divorced from EX Wife Jen-Jen less than one month, down on my luck, feeling like warmed over cow dung, worried sick about my two preschool aged sons sitting at home motherless, standing alone in a crowd in a packed to the ceiling private hunting lodge, marking time in a place I did NOT want to be, greeting people I did NOT want to see; I was confronted with the juxtapositional dilemma of meeting a fare skinned, Young Irish Lass. Met a pretty lady, with whom I immediately struck up a conversation; "small talk...that evolved into a lifetime relationship"; chit chatting with Soul Mate and second wife, Nurse-Wife Peg. Good luck or good timing? Or merely an example of skillfully landing a self-hooked fish?"

Three: In 1992, while walking the dusty streets of Blanco; trying to drum up support for my election to the local school board; "it was a tight...unsavory campaign"; I randomly bumped into one of the crustiest old farts in town.

Who also happened to be Patriarch of one of the largest family clans in all of Blanco County! I stopped Old Fart and I talked to him for thirty minutes. Later, after the election, Old Fart told me that he and his entire Blanco Clan had voted for me. "The result"; I narrowly won my election by a scant twenty-one votes. Twenty-one votes represented half the population of Old Fart's Clan; most of whom went out of their way telling me they voted for me. Was I lucky to have run into Old Fart on the town square; or skilled and courageous to have walked up to him and challenged him and his four-dozen Blanco Kinfolk to have the cahonies to vote for me; versus my opponent? Maybe both? Maybe neither?

"So...To further illustrate my luck versus skill point...Here's a fishin story."

I had recently been ill. Not really sick, or incapacitated; merely recuperating from exhausting, post-event, medical hassles brought on after passing out on a Southwest Airlines flight from Dallas to Austin. "After becoming airborne...the pilot turned our crowded four o'clock flight around and landed back in Dallas...everyone thought I was having heart attack." I was rushed to the hospital where I had a million medical tests performed. Turned out absolutely nothing was wrong; likely suffering from stress. So! I obligingly took off a week to relax. Sons Chris and Ladd were home for spring break and the stars were perfectly aligned for us to enjoy a magic fishin experience.

During the years surrounding this story, the unchallenged Best Fisherman I knew was a small man from Blanco; whose fishin skills were second to few mortals. I have nearly thirty years of Texas fishin experience on which to base my opinion. I have a deep understanding of and appreciation for this particular fisherman's fishin experience and depth of knowledge. The Best Fisherman of which I speak; "Our family dentist...Dr Doug Pautz of Blanco." No question about it. Dr Doug was THE best fisherman I had ever known. "Although subsequently...Perhaps...Replaced atop Blanco's Best Fisherman list by Son Ladd...or Captain Jason Wagenfehr?"

Well, as this story goes, Dr Doug came by our house late one evening and told The Boys and me that big stripers were hitting on large lures in flood stage, white waters being released from Buchanan Dam; "Up near Kingsland Texas." Lake Buchanan is one in a series of Highland Lakes located in what is known as Texas Hill Country; lakes built on the Colorado River to control destructive flooding; including disastrous floods that historically devastated Austin during eras gone by.

Anyway; whenever Lake Buchanan reached "too full", Lower Colorado River Authority people, folks in charge of flood control strategy, predictably released massive amounts of water. The volume of water released and the rate of release were public information monitored by astute fisherman like our dentist, Dr Doug. Good fishermen, really good fishermen, people like Dr Doug, knew that when excess waters were released at a defined rate, for a sustained period of time, small shad and other large baitfish were forced through the dam's infrastructure. Baitfish that were wounded or killed in the process became easy pickings for large stripers feeding below the dam in churning floodwater; "Clear and clean floodwater...coming from the bottom of an enormous lake."

Swimming upstream out of Lake LBJ; "named after America's FIRST President from Texas"; upstream out of Inks Lake; "a much smaller...family oriented campground lake...featuring recreational facilities just downstream from Buchanan"; stripers gathered in large concentrations to feed at the base of Buchanan Dam. Fishermen, hardcore gutsy real fishermen like Dr Doug, congregated downstream from the dam, casting monstrous lures into raging floodwaters exiting the base of the ten-story-high dam; seeking big stripers feeding in broiling whitewater. Restrictions were rigidly enforced regarding how near the dam's base fishermen were allowed to fish; restrictions that changed during different stages of monitored water release. However; boats were never ever allowed near the dam; never nearer than hundreds of yards downstream of the dam; never permitted within casting distance of where the hottest striper fishin took place. "Boats were of no practical use. People fished from the river bank."

The trick to catching stripers was to find a good spot on the river bank and fish; "either side of the flooding river would do...but most fishermen...including Dr Doug... had favorite spots." Toss out giant lures; "heavy ones that you could pitch fifty to sixty yards"; and fish hard for short durations of time. The best technique was to throw your lure so it landed near as possible to the white, frothy water exiting the base of the dam; then allow your lure to be carried downstream by the current's swift, natural flow. Encountering other fishermen on the narrow footpaths of the river bank; and your lure encountering erratically spaced and placed natural terrain features out in the roaring river; precluded fishermen from squatting or allowing their lures to endlessly float downstream. Usually after forty to fifty yards, seventy-five maximum, fishermen were forced to retrieve their empty lure and cast it out again; requiring another long, hard cast high upstream into frothy water. Repeat the process often enough, at the correct time of day, on the correct day, and results could be spectacular. The Boys and I, having been tipped off by Dr Doug, chose to try our luck. A Tuesday morning; which meant popular river bank spots would be less crowded than on weekend mornings.

Having set out early, The Boys and I arrived to discover we enjoyed a rare opportunity to occupy our favorite side of the river and specific location ON the river before other fishermen arrived. Dr Doug told us exactly where to fish. Our general location up or down the river, specific hot holes and riffles in the river, and precisely where to place our lure within the hot spots, were critical to success; "Precise location was the key!" A few yards too far up or downstream, a few feet short of or beyond targeted boulders or rapids; results suffered. "Management of fleeting windows of fishin opportunity...including correct placement of lures...each and every detail meticulously described by Dr Doug...results were predictable...usually spectacular."

The Boys and I benefited for years from Dr Doug's generosity regarding vital fishin information. We learned early on in our relationship with Dr Doug to listen when he spoke regarding Holy Grails of fishin. Mutual acquaintances and fellow fishermen around Blanco sometimes found Dr Doug overbearing or obnoxious; "Mostly having to do with Dr Doug's style of delivery...as opposed to the validity of his information." Potential benefactors were often unwilling to listen long enough or gather in enough details to fully appreciate Dr Doug's effervescent outflow of free fishin information; available, accurate, useful, free information pouring forth from Dr Doug's wellspring of personal experiences and powerful enthusiasm for fishin. Fortuitously; The Boys and I listened; fared better than non-listeners because we were Dr Doug's friend, neighbor, and fellow church member. And, as fishermen, The Boys and I were meek. Dr Doug intuitively realized we appreciated his advice; we solicited Dr Doug's free advice. And. In this striper story, getting up-to-date advice from Dr Doug was paramount to success. "Advice Dr Doug gladly shared with humble fishermen like me and The Boys...because we WERE no threat to Dr Doug's Best Fisherman title.

Anyway! The Boys and I were there ON the river and stripers were there IN the river; six-to-eight-pound stripers running up and down the river in roving wolf packs; feeding in brief, blistering-hot, feeding frenzies; hitting a wide variety of lures tossed into the swiftest current. Within one hour Chris, Ladd, and I had caught a total of six; two apiece. The Boys and I always worked out friendly, communal answers for dictating an internal family "whose turn is it". That day, out there striper fishin, we quickly determined, communally speaking, our best bet was for ONE of us to occupy THE hot spot. One member of our party assume sole domain over one hundred yards of swift river through which our free-floating lures were sure to travel; "THE prime spot!"

The potential for snagging on hidden rocks or sunken logs was great, but fish were plentiful; even though concentrated within a relatively narrow stretch of roaring river. We decided amongst ourselves to rotate frontline access to THE choice hotspot, while two of us alternatively fished less desirable stretches of the tumbling river; typical sharing of the wealth. After an hour or so of hard fishing, the rate at which we were getting strikes slacked off a bit so Son Chris decided to go to a nearby C-Store seeking morning provisions. The store was less than a mile down the road. Assuming he wouldn't miss much, Chris volunteered to step out of rotation and seek hot chow; said he didn't mind missing his turn.

While Chris was gone, Son Ladd and I continued fishing, but were unable to get another hook-up; even though we did have a few strikes. Ladd theorized that it may have been because a large school of lowly white bass moved in and the uppity stripers took leave of the sullied feeding area. Six stripers we had landed were "nice keepers". We were having a good day. Additional fishermen began filtering into the area; a few on the opposite side of the river, three to four on our side. Every fisherman present that morning cooperated; helping one another avoid crossed lines and snagging; stepping out of the way when any fisherman was fighting a striper; "sort of an unwritten rule of the road."

Our first hour fishin had been hot and heavy; lots of long distance casting with heavy rigs, a ton of strikes, several tiring fights to the finish. I was feeling lame. Not ill; not suffering from anything definable. But I HAD recently spent two days in a Dallas hospital undergoing a dozen medical tests. People on the airplane with me the day I passed out told EMS I showed classic symptoms of a heart attack. I remember none of it. One minute I was sitting in my window seat staring at the runway, wondering why our plane's departure had been delayed for an hour. Next minute I was lying flat on my back on a gurney being rolled down the narrow isle of the plane, whisked away in an ambulance; "Sirens blaring…lights flashing!" Someone called Nurse-Wife Peg. She hopped the first plane to Dallas and was at the hospital before I was fully conscious. We never were able to determine source or cause of my mysterious medical episode; "the bottom line?" I spent two additional days in a Dallas hospital. My only lingering side effect was profound exhaustion? After an hour of thrilling exercise, out there fishin, I was weak, exhausted, could barely stand. Fighting and reeling in eight-pound stripers had taxed my withered stamina; "That…and one hundred loooooong casts…thrown with a heavy fishing rig…into and retrieved from swift broiling water."

Chris soon returned with cold drinks and breakfast tacos; provisions meant to revive my sagging strength. But Chris was carrying one thing more; a hideously ugly, large, flat-tailed jig. A behemoth jig that sort of resembled a crappie jig; but with a way too large flat tail, and a way too long minnow body, molded around a jig head. On to which some Korean had amateurishly painted ONE goofy looking green eye on the lure's spooky white face; "I don't know why the cheap lure had one eye…on one side of its ugly face?" The lure's deformed body was the ugliest chartreuse color you ever tried stomaching; with garish silver and gold sparkles sprinkled throughout the lure's soft plastic body. Chris jokingly waved the monstrosity in Ladd's and my faces and swore that he, Chris, intended to catch his next striper on it. Brother Ladd, our family trio's foremost real fisherman, laughed out loud. I laughed too. But only after asking Son Chris if he would allow me to "test fire" his ugly lure; "While he was busy relaxing… waiting to regain his place in rotation…hoping to hook additional stripers." Chris became preoccupied eating his breakfast burrito and watching Ladd hook and land another striper; the first in an hour. "Indicating a feeding frenzy might be at hand?" Idly watching Ladd fight his fish, seriously thinking Chris's ugly lure was a family joke in the making, I tied the C-store special on my medium weight rod. A fine rod, sporting new fourteen pound test line; "I wanted to give Chris' ugly lure ONE ceremonial toss."

After Ladd's fish fight moved sufficiently downstream, out of my way, and before other fishermen happened along to occupy our best spot, I heaved-ho and let go with Chris' flubbery lure. Rearing back and heaving the off-colored jig as far as my "strength sapping mysterious medical condition" would permit. Splash down of Chris' heavy new lure had barely subsided, my line had barely tightened, when an enormous jerk told me all I needed to know; I was hooked up with something? "Something alive…running full throttle upstream." Setting the hook and holding my rod tip up; "just like we've all been taught"; I attempted to begin reeling. "Useless!" I was barely in the initial stage of realizing I had hooked a good sized fish when my suspicion was confirmed, in triplicate; "Confirmed for anyone within hearing distance."

"How?" The drag on my reel began screaming. Set earlier that morning to accommodate the river's swift current; adjusted to the weight of lures we anticipated using; properly correlated to the tensile strength of my line and the average size fish we expected to catch; my expensive reel was screaming; "Loud nonstop screaming!" I knew what I was doing; "Generally speaking of course." I wasn't intimidated by the fact that I had hooked what appeared to be, for that day, for our family trio, and from the very first tug, a bigger than average striper bass. And. It was bigger. WAY bigger!

From the point on the river bank where I was standing, at the precise moment I hooked the big striper, if I gazed across the swift river, I was facing a pickup truck sized boulder rising out of the river half-way across. Dr Doug had advised us to concentrate on placing our lures near as possible to an eddy wallowing to the undulating surface of the river two feet behind that big boulder. My lure landed precisely in that spot, Dr. Doug's prescribed spot, and was immediately jerked upstream.

My line tightened to twangy tight; then it was rapidly carried directly away from me, toward the far shore; carried beyond the far side of the truck-sized boulder. At that critical juncture, my ribbon tight line sort of rounded the bend and headed upstream; became noticeably bent upstream. Within seconds, my stiffening line made solid contact with the downstream side of the gigantic, protruding boulder. "I was helplessly wrapped around the giant boulder...just above the waterline!"

I waited for the universal "thwwwwaaaannng" known to all fisherpersons; waited for my line to snap. But it didn't. Instead; the striper obligingly did a quick about-face and headed south, downstream. Thus an unseen but electrifyingly strong striper voluntarily "cleared" my frozen-stiff line from the first of several obstacles that it, my spanking-new, medium-weight, monofilament line, would reach out and touch during the next forty-five minutes of fish fightin. By the time the big striper headed downstream, I realized it was a WAY bigger than average powerful fish; possibly the biggest fish of the day; possibly bigger than that; possibly the biggest striper I had ever caught?

Fifty yards downstream from the pickup-sized boulder was a treacherous minefield of an entirely different sort. Smaller rocks littered the narrow, swift river's churning surface. Smaller, visible rocks, scattered within a rock-strewn shallow area the size of a football field; smaller rocks that averaged Barko Lounger down to Breadbox in size; raw, jagged rocks, protruding six inches up to six feet in the air above the racing current. The big striper; "evidently well hooked"; began a series of to and fro meanderings around, among, and through the smaller boulders marking the boundaries of the downstream rock field. My line, whining in raw discontent, wailing in protest, caught and momentarily hung on several of the smaller rocks as the big, fast fish passed a tad too near. But! My line never snagged or became overly entangled with any of the dozens of immovable obstacles. The fish continued downstream. "As for ME...have you noticed I am hesitant to YET refer to the big fish...or think of the giant fish...as MY big fish?"

"As the big fish swam south...I kept myself abreast of its dramatic departure from our favorite fishin area...by moving downstream along the river at the same saunter...the identical rate...as the fish's decidedly desperate descending of the river."

Once the fish cleared the second hazard area, the area strewn about here and there with dozens of smallish boulders, I began getting the feeling that there might indeed be a slight, teeny chance of landing the big fish; "Thus...at that point...I began thinking the fish might actually become...my fish." And. I was able to definitively declare, to my astonished two sons, that the fish tugging so desperately hard on the far end of my whistling line WAS indeed big. "Really big!"[1]

"Why stopped at that moment?" At that exact moment the old striper decided to head back upriver; back INTO the minefield of smaller rocks. But! Then it didn't. It instead stopped a few feet downstream from the scattered boulder minefield, reversed its direction, and headed south again with a new vengeance. Perhaps, just at that scary moment in its fish life, realizing that it was a hooked fish?

Another seventy yards downstream, and our moving-downriver-entourage; "me gripping my rod...the tugging fish pulling at my line...my wide-eyed sons tagging along in astonished bewilderment"; encountered our greatest challenge to that point, in our protracted fish fight. We; the fish, my two sons, and me; were a circus on the move. The big fish began ripping extensive amounts of line from my reel, causing my monofilament burdened reel to shudder. Weak, not feeling particularly well when I arrived at the river that morning, I began sweating profusely in the early morning heat. Sons Chris and Ladd rallied on either side of me; stood shoulder to shoulder offering non-stop encouragement. Half-a-dozen standers-by gathered in a loose coalition watching our traveling family trio. Those same strangers also remained respectfully behind and clearly out of the path of our rapidly moving fish fightin folly. Fact; "Respect afforded me and my fish was remarkable ...a big part of the final outcome of this fishin story."

"And then?" Well then; like hearing a far away train whistle in the night, while hopelessly stuck on the tracks; like seeing bright muzzle flashes in the dark, micro seconds before lethal rounds impact underbrush just overhead; like hearing a sickening, cracking sound, an instant after taking three bold steps onto too thin ice; I saw it. "You know...IT...a new...extraordinary obstacle...a REAL barrier to my chances of successfully landing the striper...something that seemed certain to end my quest for calling the fish MINE!"

"So...What WAS IT?" About a quarter mile downriver from where we; "the fish and me"; had begun our fish fight, stretching from one side of the speeding river to the other, secured at either end by garbage can sized,

[1]Footnote: "If there had been anything wrong with my heart...which there wasn't and never has been...then and there at that precise moment...my heart...any weak heart ...would have stopped beating.

permanently planted telephone poles, was a huge, and I do mean HUGE, rusty cable! An old cable, put there long ago by prudent park rangers. A tough cable, its sagging length festooned with no less than a dozen red and white warning signs. A litter of metal signs dangling at precisely spaced intervals the entire length of the old cable; signs demanding "No Boats Allowed Beyond This point"; a temporary barrier never taken down; a formidable barrier intended to preclude overzealous fishermen from going too far upstream; a quick-fix obstacle that over the years had defeated millions of fragile monofilament lines.

Had the gigantic rusty cable been tighter; "like my Mom's clothes line when I was a kid"; had the cable stretched pole-to-pole and up, out, and clear of the water, the problem rising up threatening to put an end to my fish fight would never have arisen. But the old cable wasn't tight; "like Momma's clothesline." The rusty, river-ravaged cable sagged dramatically in its middle. Extra high flood waters, like those we were currently experiencing, grabbed the cable mid-point in the river and dragged it down; dragged it and its useless, festooning warning signs, under; at the swiftest point in the river.

There was a major riffle on the river's surface, twenty yards wide; beginning exactly where the dying cable disappeared beneath the river's surface; ending exactly where the cable reappeared above the river's surface, on the far side of the river; on the opposite side of the river from where I was standing, fighting the still unseen fish. The Boys and I conferred and correctly guessed what might be hidden in the water directly under the rusty cable; causing the wide riffle. "SIGNS!"

My big bass, my striper bass, was heading straight towards the middle of the wide riffle created by the submerged cable and its damned signs! "Shit...No doubt about it!" My fish was barreling downriver with a full head of steam. Meantime; I had yet to retrieve one yard of line. I knew that at the outset of my fish fight, my reel, a Calcutta, Thank God, was full of high quality new line; but guessed my reel was nearing half empty by the time big boy striper headed south towards the festooned, sagging cable. Fortunately my line was new; two big stripers old and spotlessly fresh-fresh at its business end nearest to the fish; "I meticulously retie my lures throughout the day!"

And then; as predictable as the far off death train arriving on the set of tracks holding the stranded motorist; as sure as crippling bullets impacting micro seconds after the Marine seeing ominous muzzle flashes; as likely as too thin ice failing to hold the doomed hunter taking a fatal shortcut across a frozen lake; my big striper hit dead center in the submerged cable's riffle. My line snagged on "something" and took an instant turn to the right; was bent downriver, was turned ninety degrees downstream, at the exact point it encountered the submerged something. Between the two of us, the fish and I, it was me more severely hooked.

I had then and have today no earthly idea why my zinging line didn't snap; but it didn't. Instead; the whopper-striper continued downstream for another hundred feet or so; then went deep. Fortunately for me, unfortunately for the big fish, it found a deep hole and went straight to the bottom; where it seemed to hole up! We; the big fish and I; were at a standstill. The fish was hooked deep by my ugly lure. I was hooked deep on an underwater cable or dangling SIGN, midpoint out in a roaring river. Neither of us; the big fish nor I; could free ourselves from our painful encumbrances. Neither of us; the big fish nor I; could be moved. I did however take advantage of what had essentially become a Mexican Standoff by reeling up approximately one-fourth of my expended line. I reeled in free line "just to the point of" feeling serious pressure from the underwater snag. Then I stopped. I held fast to what I had, contemplating my next move. The big fish held fast to what he had, contemplating God knows what? "Obviously I had no idea what the big fish was contemplating...but he wasn't asleep?"

By that time our crowd of onlookers and well-wishers swelled to something approaching two dozen; every swinging-dick-one-of-them began offering words of encouragement and free advice; "The encouragement was appreciated...the free advice useless." But I understand good intentions when I hear them; what I heard was good. Before too long, a public debate broke out regarding just how big MY unseen fish might be? Not that many onlookers actually believed any of us would ever actually find out.

Son Ladd suggested I give out Major League amounts of slack line, as rapidly as possible; suggesting that my overly slackened line might somehow set itself free from its underwater entanglement out there in the river's swift current. I tried Ladd's suggestion; two to three times. No luck!

Son Chris, the more adventuresome of my two older sons, began stripping down to his tighty whities; declaring that he intended to wade out, swim out, go hand over hand out, to my snagged line making use of the cable; see if he could grasp my line and set it on its way downstream; release my line from the unseen underwater tow bar holding it tight. I immediately forbid Chris his DAI; "Dumb Ass Idea!" The giant cable was there for a reason; "To prevent idiots AND fishermen from entering what were...by anyone's standards...dangerous currents!" No; there would be no wading, no swimming, and no acrobatic retrieval of my snagged line. "Not by either of MY sons!"

Ten to fifteen minutes into our ordeal; into our man-versus-fish standoff; the fish resting in a deep hole, my line hung tight on a submerged cable or sign; someone, I honestly don't know who, everyone seemed to later agree it was Ladd, suggested a novel idea. Regardless of who first suggested it, everyone, onlookers included, seemed to agree that it was a meritorious idea; an idea worthy of trying. Ladd tied on an ordinary lead weight; the old fashioned, bell-shaped kind, with a small metal eye protruding from the weight's top; and went about trying to cast upstream and OVER my snagged line.

Ladd's theory was simple; see if it was possible to throw his weighted line beyond and across my tight line, and then carefully reel in his unencumbered line, thus creating enough downward, gentle tugging action to gently dislodge my snagged line. It sounded feasible. On his third or fourth cast, Ladd was able to reach out far enough; a long, long, looooong cast; and cross my line upstream from where it disappeared below the river's turbid surface. Twice Ladd reeled in, and twice Ladd's weighted line failed to engage my tightened line. Ladd and I couldn't intentionally get our lines tangled while trying, even though dozens of fishermen had accidentally tangled lines that very morning.

Finally, on Ladd's third cross-river cast, his line crossed over and became hooked upon mine; as Ladd retrieved his line. My line tightened. Any previously existing slack between my reel and the point where my line was being held in place by the submerged cable, or sign, was immediately taken up by Ladd retrieving his lightly weighted line. My line was rigidly held downstream beneath the cable and kept entirely void of much slack by the currently sleeping fish. Gentle Ladd reeled gently toward the crowded river bank. "Presto!" "Bingo!" "YES!"

My tightened line "popped" in an ominous water shedding twang and I was suddenly free of the submerged cable; every foot of instant slack gained was immediately carried downstream by the rushing river. But! There was a heart stopping moment involved. The amount of slack line created by freeing my tight line from the depths of its cable-induced doom was dramatic; sickeningly great. At first I was certain my line had broken; had cleared the underwater cable with such sudden totality that it had been rendered into separate halves. I thought my line severed. "But not so!" Reeling like a madman possessed, my slackened line began retightening and all slack between me and the big fish disappeared; the sleeping giant was reawakened, our fish fight was resumed.

The big ole fish on the far end of my line most likely did NOT suffer a mysterious medical event during the previous forty-eight hours; but I did. I was running out of gas; already tired when our fish fight began. When it became obvious that my line had totally cleared the entire, treacherous area near the sagging cable, a mighty roar went up from the hushed, growing crowd. Urged on by the mighty cheering of multitudes, my waning strength returned. Reignited by tightening of my once again rigid line, the slumbering fish regained composure; once again beginning a determined swim downstream. Heave back and reel, heave back and reel, heave back and reel, heave back and…; finally, on the very threshold of being unable to let out more line, I began taking IN line. Making a net gain; reeling in line at a greater rate than I was losing line. Renewed runs of the tiring giant fish were increasingly shorter, noticeably slower. "I was winning!"

Far off in the distance, as far off as anyone could determine by looking, there were no more permanent, or manmade, or unusual obstacles in the roaring river. I began, for the first time, allowing myself to believe that I might indeed land MY big fish. Thirty-some minutes later I did; I landed a large, exhausted striper. But! Not without experiencing one, additional, heart-stopping sub-event. We had no dip net! That's right! The Boys and I had no dip net; none adequate to the task. The pitifully small net we DID bother bringing along was a quarter-mile upstream, lost in poison ivy and weeds. One bystander offered to run fetch a net, which he did; returning, wheezing and out of breath, minutes AFTER The Boys and I dragged the monstrous fish out on to the rock strewn river bank. The tired man exclaiming; "No need for no f—king net NOW!"

But before any of that, the first time my striper; "note the change of pronoun"; surfaced out in the clear river, the heart of every healthy man standing there, skipped a beat! "Literally!" "Briefly!" A cumulative gasp went up from the gathered crowd! "Praise Be to Almighty God of Fishing on High!" Mine was indeed a monstrous striper! But before our family trio could celebrate; before the Good Samaritan could run to his truck and return with a net; our fish fightin family trio faced one final challenge. "How to get the breeching tired fish ashore…how to actually land such a large fish without…the benefit of an adequate net…which we did not have."

EVER so gently, I reeled against the weight of the giant striper; forcing it upstream and into a clear, shallow, confined, eddy; a relatively quiet two-foot-deep pool. In that quiet and still water, at that slightly relaxed but high voltage point, I allowed Ladd to enter the shallow, clear water and help by coaxing the tired fish up and onto a gravel bar. The fish was all in. I was all in. A few more turns of my expensive, and what was by then, according to MasterCard, my priceless reel, and the big striper rolled on its side. Whereupon Ladd gripped it by its gaping lower lip and hoisted it ashore. The fish was now officially mine; "More accurately…OURS!"

An hour later The Boys and I were able to locate a place where we could weigh the fat bellied, bloated fish; we were shocked. My trophy weighed in at just over twenty two pounds! Thirty nine inches! Smashing to smithereens our existing family record!

Giant Stripper caught on the ugliest lure I ever used... fish is bigger than four year old son **John James**. (1995)

Weighed, displayed, and eventually filleted; our family dined on fresh striper for three dinners-running. Years later I took one of the quality photos snapped that day and had the photo turned into a magnificent fiber glass replica; a quality replica like saltwater fishermen helped make popular. "Not cheap plastic shit made in China! My replica was made by Bob Harris...a famous artist located in Houston...and cost a small fortune. Bob is a genuine artist who charges by the inch. Nurse-Wife Peg bitched for months!

"So? Was I lucky...or good (skilled)?" Was it luck that brought The Boys and me to the correct spot, at the correct time, with the correct equipment; "except for the missing net"; or was it skill? Did good luck play a role in my decision to tie on that ugly lure; or good skill? What if I had tied an improper or weak knot? Was it luck that the giant fish turned downstream after first taking me hopelessly upstream, lodging my line against the first truck-sized boulder; or a demonstration of good fishing skills that I had the patience to wait for a favorable turn of events? Was it bad luck that the cable was in my path of fighting the fish; or good luck that my line snagged on a smooth surface? On a surface that not only failed to cut my line, but was also smooth enough a surface to allow my line to be dislodged by tugging son

Ladd's aiding line? Or was it a combination of several people's skills and acumen that allowed us, as a family trio; "with the astute help of public input"; to collectively come up with a strategy that ultimately freed my line and afforded me the opportunity to continue the fish fight? Was it luck or skill that dominated the final half-hour of fish fightin between a weak, tired man, reeling the final required reels, against a weakening, tiring fish? Was it luck or skill that Ladd was not only available and willing, but capable of approaching the tired fish and boating it with OUT the aid of even a small net? And what about Son Chris? Was it luck or skill that Chris bought the strange looking, one-of-a-kind, ugly lure on a whim, and brought it to the scene of our event? Luck or pity, or both, that allowed Chris to be big enough a person to allow ME to cast HIS special lure first? Luck or skill that I tossed the lure properly, landing it precisely in THE spot dictated by the most skillful fisherman I knew; Dr Doug? I say both to all of the above! That's why similar controversies and debates about this type memorable event interminably rage on in the annals of fishin, huntin, and adventure seekin families around the world.

Postscript One: "Son Chris...after all the excitement died down...retied the magic lure on to his line and fished with it for an hour. During which hour Chris hooked and landed five additional, six-to-eight pound stripers...the ONLY additional fish caught by anyone on our side the river the balance of the entire morning...including a growing hoard of wannabe onlookers. When The Boys and I quit fishin...and were preparing to depart the area...several fishermen approached us and brazenly...and I thought shamefully...offered to buy the ONE ugly lure. We weren't selling."

Postscript Two: "The Boys had to carry our fish...including the giant one...and all my gear...including everything except the long forgotten uselessly small net...lost and forgotten forever where it lay in weeds miles upstream from where I finally landed the fish...up the steep eighty foot embankment to our truck...then return and assist lame and lazy me up the same rocky trail to the parking lot. I could barely walk."

Postscript Three: "None of us in our family was ever able to find or buy another lure closely resembling or identical to the all-time ugly lure Chris used to catch his boatload of stripers...I used to catch my giant striper. Just unlucky...I guess?"

Chapter Twelve

Birthday Fish

Mentioned earlier in this book; birthdays in our family have been viewed as a reasonable excuse for goin fishin. "There was my fifth birthday in 1952"; the snowy one my Dad, by his stalwart commitment, turned into a forever-holy memory. "There was the large bass I caught on my nineteenth birthday"; the fish that nearly got my Dad and me shot by an irate neighbor when he thought we were trespassers. "There was the Calcasieu Mistress…a giant fish caught on my fifty-eighth birthday"; the result of work and love exhibited by Son Ladd and his friend Mr. B. Birthdays in our family are historically alive and colorfully strewn-about with fishin stories. Because they are, I would like to group together a few birthday fishin stories; share them here; "experiences enjoyed in commemoration of someone's birthday." Not coincidence I write about my favorites.

There was the 1970 charter trip seeking marlin off the coast of Virginia, with my best buddy, Marine Captain Larry Suciu. There was the 1985 offshore kingfish charter trip on Son Chris' tenth birthday; that ended up being remembered more as a sailing event than a fishin trip. There were speckle trout trips with Captain Fred Wagenfehr; Grandfather of current, world class fishing guide out of Seadrift, Texas; Captain Jason Wagenfehr. Early trout trips taken when The Boys were young and THEIR skills were in the budding stage; later trips enjoyed when The Boys were older and MY skills were in the wilting stage.

During the late 1980s and early 1990s, there were a dozen striper trips taken on nearby Lake Buchanan, with legendary guide Captain Jerry Moore. There were a dozen Lake Fork trips, booked in early spring to celebrate Ladd's January birthdays; one taken in 1987 with eccentric guide Tony, resulting in a trophy lunker bass for Ladd. There was the 2007 red snapper charter; entirely arranged for, paid for, and produced by me; meant to celebrate my Bubba Bob's birthday and triumphant return to Texas under happier circumstances than when he departed a quarter century earlier. And last but not least; there was the poignantly happy-sad final trip I was able to make with my Dad; a guided crappie trip on Canyon Lake with Captain Jerry Moore once again steering the wheel.

When all else has failed us, our combined Pepper Families have gone fishin. When times were hard for our family of five here in Blanco, we went fishin. When an otherwise ordinary day needed commemorating, we went fishin. When life was good or bad, happy or sad, new or old, warm or cold, intense or relaxed, under utilized or over taxed, we went fishin; "Unless of course it was the dead of winter…in the middle of duck season…then we sacrificed mightily…and instead went duck huntin."

Allowing for large blocks of omitted time, let's take a chronological look at a few birthday trips. Allow me to begin in 1970; when I was stationed in Quantico, Virginia.

MIA Marlin[1]

Born and reared in Indianapolis, Indiana; one meaningful reason that Captain Larry Suciu and I became fast, long term friends was that I quickly realized; "no matter what the circumstances…no matter how stiff the challenge…Captain Larry was willing to try and raring to go." Larry and I pulled off a few mighty, and therefore memorable, capers. Our wives were young and in love; "with us"; and were therefore included in 99.9 % of our manly capers. "That oddity alone may partially help explain why neither Larry nor I are still married to our two First Wives…Larry's Karen and my EX Jen-Jen."

Larry Suciu and I tossed down a few cold ones... and cooled down a few hot ones... he was an all-time nice guy. (1970)

Ranging from busting our ass during grueling infantry training at Quantico's Marine Officer Basic School, to killing multiple bottles of expensive wine or champagne, to hunting wild woods morel mushrooms over the long-cold graves of Civil War dead, to digging for ruined artifacts in Virginia's Great Smokey Mountains, to chartering a classy marlin boat at the prohibitive cost of an entire months pay; "If I was IN…Larry was IN!"

And, if First Wife Jen-Jen was IN, Larry's First Wife Karen was IN; we were

---

[1]**Footnote:** For those of you who might be totally uninformed, less than five years old, awakening from a coma, home schooled during the 1980s, or merely typical folks from Flor-a-DUH…MIA is a common military acronym for Missing In Action.

a dynamic, inseparable quartet thrown together by Larry's and my common cause; the minds of all four of us susceptible to being sailed away by the hint of adventure. "And that stuff about forking over a month's pay to go fishin is correct." Capt Larry and I got together and chartered a reasonably nice marlin boat for an entire day. A good looking boat that sailed out of Virginia Beach, Virginia; total cost for the charter…$600!

I enjoy telling my three adult sons, their spouses, and my few surviving friends, that my very first paycheck after graduating college; University of Missouri, Columbia; was handed to me by the United States Marine Corps. As a Second Lieutenant fresh out of college, reporting for eight continuous months of intense training, I was paid precisely $600 per month! Until which time, eighteen months later, I was promoted to First Lieutenant, and my pay skyrocketed to nearly one thousand bucks a month.

"As young carefree officers we felt rich. Captain Larry and I would finish thirty days hard training…then line up for monthly pay call…just like in WW II John Wayne movies…and ask ourselves rhetorically…All this fun…And we actually get PAID?"

Anyway, I handled the booking details and urged good friend Larry to join in; a private charter out of Virginia Beach, Virginia. Splitting the costs helped us enjoy the opportunity to try something neither of us had ever done

Ex Jen-Jen, **Larry** & **Karen Suciu**. (1970)

but had both professed a desire to try. Larry's First Wife Karen could barely wait for the trip. First Wife Jen-Jen ranged between cool and lukewarm about fishing, but WAS game for taking an expensive boat ride on the ocean. She imagined our day like being on Fantasy Island or Love Boat. And First Wife Jen-Jen liked being anywhere there was action. So I promised her there would be plenty of action aboard our all day charter; "and there was."

Our party of four sailed at first light on a Sunday morning in late July; Larry's twenty-fifth birthday; "The birthday part of this story." Training for Larry and me was six to seven days a week; Sundays our only irregular days off. No one in our landlubber foursome knew what to expect, least of all Missouri born me. I just knew that I had read great stories in True and Sports Afield magazines about giant billfish being caught off the Eastern Shore. Being intentionally non-introspective and flip, I told my charter mates that in this one instance I wanted to take a stab at living life to the hilt, without questioning the cause or cost; take life as it came. One of the few things that BOTH my two wives; my current wife, Nurse-Wife Peg, and my ex-wife, EX Jen-Jen; have always agreed upon IS a distinguishing feature of my personality. Both wives agree that I DO attempt to capture the moment, live life to its fullest; often pushing reasonable boundaries of budget and sanity just to lock away a fond memory or two; just to create opportunities to enjoy life. So, that some far off day in the future, I will be able to say; "Yeah...I done been there...Yep...I done tried that shit." Or other catchy words to that effect.

So there we were, the four of us; two newly married couples, both involved to the breaking point in some of this world's toughest military training, both seeking refuge and escape; not to mention a roaring good time. Everyone available to us, within our spheres of influence, warned us to take Dramamine for seasickness; "So we did." By the time our boat cleared giant breakers, encountered as we headed out of Lynnhaven Bay, Capt Larry was zonked; one of the worst side effects of Dramamine.

Two hours of hard bouncing due east, and our boat arrived in the designated fishing area. Our deck crew let down outriggers and we were fishing. There were three professionals on our private charter; our Captain, our First Mate, and one feverish Deck Hand. I haven't the slightest idea what kind of boat it was or how big it was. I knew nothing about saltwater fishing and less about boats. It was a nice boat, and there was a clean and private place for our wives to get in out of the sun and to pee sitting down; or throw up, as turned out to be the case. Had I known a little more about weather conditions; "I would have gone anyway...you can bet your sweet ass on that!"

No one had promised anyone on board a rose garden. Our boat's downriggers trailed four baits; two were giant artificial lures with long colorful streamers attached and two were long skinny natural bait called ribbon fish. Our deckhand was busy; rigging the baits and lures, and poles, and deck chairs, and a place for the ladies to nap and crap. He prepared the food and handed us beer; and more beer, and more beer. No one aboard that day; "except the crew"; failed to get seasick; it was merely a matter of degree.

The first time I puked, I retaliated by eating fifty pounds of saltine crackers; "said to be a surefire cure." Larry puked every time he moved; lurching from one death spot to another, while eating absolutely nothing. First Wife Jen-Jen puked privately; but told everyone on board she never did get sick. "Being seasick during a rough day on the sea is an odd thing to deny...Huh?"

First Wife Karen told First Wife Jen-Jen that her denying she was seasick was a curious way for Jen-Jen to handle what Karen called; "a common human foible."

"Personally...I never thought of seasickness as being a foible?"

Karen told me that she considered her new BFF Jen-Jen's obfuscation a curious flaw. A rather astute observation by Karen I would say; considering our group was awash in our own spewing puke! If Karen puked more than once, I wasn't aware of it? But between the two of us, involuntary vomiting aside, Karen and I DID manage to drink every last beer our party brought on board; something approaching two cases.

Back then, back when we were young and didn't know squat, we thought nothing of buying and drinking a case of beer. We typically shopped for BBQ and cookout beer "by the case"; NOT by the six pack. My favorite was Michelob. No lite beer either; standard heavy stuff, from brown bottles, with lids requiring an opener. I can't remember what all we attempted to eat or failed to keep down that awful day out there marlin fishin; but I do remember standing bent double most of the time, waiting for one of the day's elusive marlin to hook up; "which of course never happened." We DID have one runt sailfish swim by and wink in our direction, and one yellow dolphin fish grab our outmost downrigger. Our sleepy deckhand nearly came unglued with excitement. Ten hours later it was over. Captain Larry and FW Karen, and Lt Me and FW Jen-Jen, were a fried foursome; physically done in by the sun; mentally pounded into submission by our total lack of fishin action; and spiritually assaulted by the flippant attitude of our unsuccessful, heavy drinking Charter Captain.

Marine Captain Larry never complained; "ever." Karen never said one word. I never complained. First Wife Jen-Jen is STILL complaining. Not about the money we spent; not about the seasickness we suffered; not about the boat, or its crew, or the MIA missing marlin. To this day FW Jen-Jen complains that she was unable to sunbathe due to the horribly rough seas.

When she does, I reply; "For God's sake Jen-Jen...we could barely stand! Lying down meant having your body bounced around like a rubber doll." Looking back; referring to EX Jen-Jen as a rubber doll is NOT a bad comparison!

Kingfish *Sailing*

August 16th, 1985 was a good day, oldest Son Chris turned ten; "another birthday spent fishin." Psychological scars marring our transplanted family's outlook on life were healing; scarring suffered during our Border Wars of 1981; which prompted our refugee's flight from Missouri in favor of more peaceful Texas. Within a month of relocating, Nurse-Wife Peg and I were taking advantage of the beckoning call of the Gulf Coast. From our humble home in Blanco it was less than three hours drive; "Even if we stopped to pee." Peg and I officially launched The Boys saltwater fishing careers in 1983, by taking them aboard a half-day bay boat. "Ten bucks per person...free bait...and a six hour opportunity to catch all the piggy perch and hardheads you wanted. But it didn't really matter what we caught...we were fishin...and our uprooted legal immigrant family was enjoying a pleasant distraction."

It had been two summers since our first trip, on that crowded bay boat. The same boat on which our family encountered large Hispanic men catching large black drum; as described in this book in the chapter entitled, 'Growin Up Fishin'. By 1985, our tenuous family situation was more settled. And I was more informed regarding saltwater fishing options and opportunities. I scraped together sufficient funds for a one-day private charter out of Corpus; Son Ladd was eight, Son Chris ten, Nurse-Wife Peg and I were young. Our small, comfortable charter boat was manned by a smiling Captain and one scroungy deckhand named Luke; "Why are charter boat deckhands always named Luke?"

We set sail at seven. Our boat provided everything needed in the way of creature comforts, equipment, and bait. "All that was required of me...money." Nurse-Wife Peg packed too much food, too many drinks, and alarmingly, too little Dramamine. Originally developed as a controlled prescription drug to ward off seasickness, Dramamine in its initial form was crude but effective; I know for a fact it has been available since 1970. However! One of the side effects of old style 1970s Dramamine was instant sleepiness. Modern Dramamine is much improved; I would recommend it, in proper doses, to anyone, anytime, going on any type saltwater fishing trip. "No doubt it works...It saved many a day for members of fishing parties of which I have been a part."

So off we went. I was the only member of our family who had ever caught a decent saltwater fish; The Boys and Nurse-Wife Peg, native

Missourians, had caught zippo-point-zero; "piggy perch and hardheads aside." The Boys snagged a couple of mullet in the surf one day, but mullet are even lower on saltwater fish totem poles than piggies. My experiences were limited; a dysfunctional marlin trip with Captain Larry; one private trip off the coast of Okinawa with my Portuguese Marine First Sergeant; a smattering here and there. But! I knew enough to realize two things. One; if we were fortunate enough to catch a kingfish, ours would qualify as "a good day". And two; comparatively speaking, "kingfish were big". There were size restrictions, but each licensed fisherperson could catch and retain four kingfish per day; provided the fish were over a specified minimum size. "I think the minimum was eighteen inches?" That meant our family could pack home a grand total of sixteen keeper kingfish; IF we were so lucky. "I was feeling optimistic...The Boys were feeling pure joy...Nurse-Wife Peg was feeling our family's pulses...and recommending more Dramamine!"

From the outset, ours was a nice day. The sun rose bright and clear as we headed out to sea between monstrous jetties; on out through mild breakers; then southeast towards the open gulf. I can NOT tell you where we were or where we went; "even if I had a map of it tattooed on my ass?" The only thing I was able to determine, for certain, was that we were heading east. "How?" I was forced to pull my battered old cap down to protect my eyes from the sun. There was ZERO danger of me returning to any of the fishing hotspots our Captain was taking his rookie saltwater fishermen to exploit. "Besides...I wasn't paying attention?" We've all heard stories about other fishermen, cheap scoundrels, who actually do it, but I couldn't have stolen our guide's secret spots on a tall bet. I didn't know up from down, shallow from deep, when it came to saltwater fishing; "One reason to hire a guide!" After two hours of wide-open running, our boat was pulled to a motor-roaring, side-slipping, stop; "Why do guides and Charter Captains always roar their big motors JUST prior to stopping...There's gotta be a reason?"

The deckhand baited four heavy rods and placed them in four widely dispersed rod holders located near the rear of our bobbing boat; "some folks prefer stern." Rods attached to the outside of the boat were placed in outrigger devices that kept our baited lines and trailing lures following the boat on trails parallel to, but different from, the two rods mounted directly ON the stern of the boat a half foot either side of two, huge, silver and black Yamaha outboard motors. I was impressed that all four lines, trailing four separate baits, remained perfectly spaced throughout the day; including maintaining proper spacing during large, looping turns; back into the direction from whence we had just come? Returned IF we were successful in getting a strike within a given area; "The Captain negotiated the broad sweeping U-turns…and all four lines…attached to all four rods…would follow…as our Captain smiled and strutted his stuff."

Friendly deckhand Luke recommended we set up a family rotation, which would allow each and every person, Nurse-Wife Peg included, to participate in what Luke called an orderly procession. Luke said it was highly unlikely we would "hook up" more than one kingfish at a time. And that by rotating individual "hook ups" within our family, each individual would stand an equal chance of catching a fish; or catching multiple fish in equal numbers, when it was his or her turn. As opposed to one person randomly grabbing a rod when different rods randomly "went off"; thereby avoiding "hogging" and lessening the potential for "family disputes"; all that complex structuring designed to deliver us from the evils of chaos.

"And when we DID get a strike…I mean a hook up… there was NO doubt about two things! We WERE getting a strike! And it WAS somebody's turn!"

Our Captain or deckhand Luke or both men simultaneously, would yell loud enough for all southeast Texas to hear; "FISH ON!" There was never any deviation, always; "FISH ON"; as if we clients couldn't tell. When a kingfish struck one of our lures at the far end of one of our lines, all Hell broke loose. The heavy duty rods would bend double and gargantuan monofilament line would scream, and I do mean scream, off the reel; monstrous black and silver reels of an unrecognizable brand name. Whatever brand the reels were, they worked well; not one of the reels ever malfunctioned.

Our internally organized family trick was to have ONE designated fisherperson standing ready, near the railing of the back deck, near-as-possible to the four rod holders; ready to pounce on any given "FISH ON" rod. When action came, it was explosive; "train wreck exciting." We allowed Son Chris to go first since it was his birthday. Since Son Ladd was a mere child of eight, he was second up to bat. Nurse-Wife Peg was third; and as any gentleman would have insisted, I was dead last; "happy merely to be alive and participating in such glorious fun created by me…FOR my family." Our wee family of four didn't have long to enjoy the sweetness of anticipation; heightened here and there along the way by staring down through deep, clear water at our trolling lures; "BOOM!"

Our first rod of the day bent double and lurched far to port. Was bent downward and tugged to one side in such an awkward way, in such a dramatic way; was jerked about in such a forceful way; I was certain the rod would break or be torn from its holder. "Not so!" The rod tip was tugged, re-tugged, and began bouncing in quick, rhythmic, repeat tugs; all that tugging occurring before previously-coached ten year old Chris assumed the predesignated position, hoisted the heavy rig, and began reeling. Hoping to accomplish a boyhood first; successfully land a kingfish, the first of his entire life; "a life predestined to include much saltwater fishing…that up to that point had included none."

Holding his breath, his eyes wide open and bigger than two shiny quarters, eight year old skinny Son Ladd crowded nearer the remaining three twitching rods. Where moments before, deckhand Luke had inadvertently committed an understandable, natural faux pas; asking me, loud enough so that Ladd overheard, if I thought Ladd was strong enough to handle reeling in one of the big kingfish. My wordless glance of total incredulousness was answer enough. Ladd didn't smile, but I could hear the wheels turning, thinking; "I'll show Luke who is strong enough."

On his 30th birthday... **Chris** hoists aloft this beauty. (2005)

"FISH ON!" Kingfish number two, first for Ladd, was a shutdown monstrous whopper. By day's end it turned out to be bigger, by ten inches, than any other fish caught the entire day! "Well…Except for one OTHER fish…which we as a family are reticent to bring up…determined to never again mention…are strictly forbidden to mention…or dwell on…FOREVER!"

Within minutes of the tenacity of "skinny Son Ladd" being rewarded with the biggest kingfish of our day, we heard it again; "FISH ON!" We were off to a good start. And just like the nursery rhyme character Mary, who owned that persistent little lamb; "Wherever The Boys went…Nurse-Wife Peg and I were sure to follow." Within thirty minutes, no more than an hour; including time spent stopping, starting, and putting out trailing lures and downriggers; our wee family of landlubber, interloping Missourians had won our saltwater wings. "Four kingfish in the (ice) chest…all four well over twenty inches long…identical in color and configuration…identical in excitement generated. The clamoring for MORE onboard our boat would have awakened the dead."

No one in our family had been even slightly seasick. The sea was calm and bright, blue and clear. "How can sea water…deep sea water far out to sea…be both clear AND blue…at the same time?" Seafarers, men of the sea, might know; but for that day it remained an unsolved puzzle for two excited MO boys. It didn't matter. Large darting kingfish had gathered near our boat in an invisible school; which our Captain could somehow or another miraculously see. An order or two, and we were quickly off chasing after more kings. The Captain revved up his giant motors and our boat scooted a quarter mile to the left; or was it to the right; doesn't matter; we moved. "And the results?"

Good and noteworthy things occur in fours. Four seasons in a year, four years between Presidential elections; four quarters in a football game, four years in high school to play football; four legs on a table, corners on a house, directions on a map, legs on a mammal (except homo sapiens); four disciples leading off the New Testaments, Mathew, Mark, Luke, and John; four kids in my family when I was a kid. Like I said; good things, memorable things, landmark things, things we all point to and remember, occur in fours. Our day out there kingfishin was like that; divided neatly into fours. We were four members in one family; we had a family goal of catching and keeping four kingfish each; we would require four complete cycles of our self-imposed family rotation to reach our goal. "AND…We were fishin four light years from shore"; at least Nurse-Wife Peg said so. She never got over her queasy, uneasy feeling about being in water over her pretty head. She's five-ten; "NOT quite tall enough to wade ashore from where we were."

It seemed mere minutes passed before our twelfth kingfish was gaffed aboard and order restored to our family rotation. At which time our Captain made a suggestion that since our time to head into port was drawing nigh, he would like to fire up the motor and try one final hot-spot nearer shore; see if he could put us in touch with our last four kings; "our final four…in a series of sixteen."

We faced a long haul west, back to the mainland; "West would be towards Texas for you Folks from Flor-a-DUH!" Captain said he would like to make the two hour run, then stop and fish near an offshore oil well. Said he had been having success nearer shore in late afternoon; fishing in close proximity to oil well platforms. We landlocked Blanco Countians could not have agreed quicker; "Sounds Great!"

Our sea legs were holding up OK; "Not great…just OK!" Our stomachs battling a bit to contain our day's onboard rations; most of it still only partially digested. But! In spite of general-uneasiness and gastro-queasiness, we were having one of our best fishing days ever. However! We WERE getting weary. Heading to shore sounded good. And. It was a frightfully looooooong haul back to dry land. We weren't quitting. We were merely repositioning ourselves for final victory; "FOUR LIMITS!"

Finally, within clear sight of land, Our Captain cut the engine and yelled at deckhand Luke to rig the downriggers; "Let's FISH Luke!" And fish we did! And forevermore; the next hour of fishing, shall live in infamy in family fishing lore.

Just prior to our Captain hauling up downriggers and commencing our long run back towards Texas, I caught my third kingfish; a fat twenty pounder. Therefore; when we stopped fishing, to make our move, it was Birthday Boy's turn to next answer the call; "FISH ON"! Our previously established order of march remained intact; mildly nauseous Son Chris, hard fishing Son Ladd, sleepy Nurse-Wife Peg, tired but determined Dad; "four kingfish to go?" New spot! All four lines in the water, trolling speed resumed, it was mere minutes until; "FISH ON"!

Awakened from a deep nap by the agitated cries of "FISH ON", blurry-eyed Son Chris took control of the wildly bucking, bent-double rod. Sweating profusely, grabbing the rod with sweaty, trembling hands; Chris suddenly began spewing a gallon of rancid, undigested food across the boat's otherwise pristine deck. Bearing ten thousand gritty effusions of vomit, over-shone by one dazzling smile; Birthday Boy Chris landed himself a prized, twenty-two pound kingfish! "Just like Our Captain said Chris would."

When Our Captain first called "FISH ON", Nurse-Wife Peg and Chris had been sound asleep; Son Ladd and I ever vigilant. Our family's two overdosed druggies nearly required a dousing with cold seawater to revive them; to physically rekindle their mental awareness and sensibilities to fish. But! Awakened from a deep nap, forced back to the bending rod and screaming reel, Son Chris had quickly responded. Mere minutes into THE fish fight of his young life, and here comes breakfast, lunch, and a small keg of soft drinks. But Son Chris never stopped reeling. While busy upchucking lunch, Son Chris came close to losing control of the frantically bucking rod; a high dollar rod, with a hard fighting, healthy kingfish attached at its far end. And as Chris' whistling line tightened, but then held; it was both a wonderful and awful moment. It was a proud moment for us two, very happy, willing parents. "Our Boys were having a GOOOOD day!"

It was fascinating watching deckhand Luke masterfully gaff and land Chris' big fish. With each excitement-induced grin, a bit more color returned to Chris' chalky face. I was also keeping a sharp eye on Nurse-Wife Peg; watching for renewed signs of her Irish-Caucasian-Greater-Female-Seasickness. "Truth is...Peg looked like hammered feces. Apparently Chris and Peg's below deck naps were NOT in their best interest?"

Chris' kingfish was thrown in the bulging ice chest, the boat's sloppy deck was swabbed stem-to-stern, reels were checked, lures returned to downriggers, order was restored aboard our bobbing boat; things returned to normal. We waited. Ladd waited hardest. Enduring the "boring as Hell normal" every fisherperson is forced to endure between strikes. Then it came, another; "FISH ON!" Momentum was building. The moment, the hour, the day, our entire trip out there on the deep blue sea, was electric; you could feel FISH ON excitement racing through the crew, the boat, the air, the known universe. Our boat had barely resumed normal when a second and harder striking king signaled Son Ladd's turn at the podium; marked Son Ladd's imminent fish fight with a loud zzzzzzzzzzinging kingfish racing to the deep; a gigantic lure and mile of heavy line in tow. A gallant fish fight, a flashing gaff, and Son Ladd's fourth of four kings was safely aboard and packed on ice. "I was The Gulf's most elated Dad."

Smiling broadly, I was standing near Nurse-Wife Peg; idly watching, feeling content. Having witnessed the swiftness of the two preceding strikes, anticipating her own, Nurse-Wife Peg was ready; already seated in the boat's lone fighting chair; "which The Boys and I would have died before using." I had persuaded Peg to suck it up and mentally prepare herself for fighting her final king of the day by convincing her to sit down and relax and take advantage of the chair and its harness. I was preparing to lecture Nurse-Wife Peg on the subject of setting a good example for The Boys, when I caught a glimpse of something big flash directly under our boat; "Then all Hell broke loose." The biggest, stiffest, most frequently hit-upon of our four rods doubled over; the tip of the rod actually plunging into the bright, sparkling sea. Something big; really big, had happened. Everyone sensed it. The voice of Our Captain and Luke rose as one; "FISH ON!"

Our Captain, showing unfettered, uninhibited emotion for the first time, shouted; "LUKE...Grab the f—king rod...I think it's a big Sail!"

"As in Sailfish!" It was Nurse-Wife Peg's turn; HER fish to land or lose. But! Unlike Chris, Nurse-Wife Peg showed little confidence; appeared NOT up to the task; seemed a reluctant participant. Peg saw the bucking rod, heard the screaming crew, and immediately wanted OUT of the fighting chair. Suddenly wished she could get far away from the wild, bucking rod and scorching reel.

Peg and I had argued the night before; it had been all I could do to coerce her into coming. She was frightfully paranoid of being so far out to sea; out of sight of land. There's no telling how many hours of that day Nurse-Wife passed wishing she were safely ashore, sitting on a solid rock, reading a book or relaxing by the hotel pool. But such was not her reality, not that day;

that day and in that special moment, there she sat. It was only after much consternation and soul searching that Peg had finally agreed to go out with us and give it a try. But willingly there; or not; Nurse-Wife Peg was now being forced into REALLY giving it a try. "One of Peg's great attributes as a wife...mother... and friend...is that she...Nurse-Wife Peg...was nearly always willing to give it a try. Nearly anything...as long as it was moral...legal...or ethical."

As if suddenly touched by the cold hand of determination, Nurse-Wife Peg placed both hands firmly on the vibrating rod, both feet in the stirrups of the fighting chair, and inexplicably screamed. "I've noticed women tend to scream at the oddest times?" Peg sat straight up in the fighting chair. Once she made up her distractible ADHD mind to give it a try, I was amazed at how swiftly she reacted; how proficiently she performed.

"Me?" I was standing there in awe; feeling, among other things, a wild case of raw jealousy. I couldn't stop myself from wishing out loud that it had instead been MY turn! And! Before you jump in to condemn me; to any husband who pretentiously or piously says he would have reacted differently; "I say BS...kiss my butt ...because I simply don't believe you." I also quickly point out; "actually I insist"; had it been either of our two SONS sitting in that fighting chair, then it would have been a biscuit of an entirely different baking. It was my reluctant wife; brow beaten by ME to attend the event! And. "There was only ONE lifetime...huge sailfish! I couldn't help wishing I were THE PERSON sitting in the fighting chair! The reel was smoking!"

About two minutes into the reel emptying, rod bending, gut wrenching fight; with thick line screeching off the giant Penn reel like a bullet leaving a gun barrel; Nurse-Wife Peg appeared ready to collapse; "All in...Her lovely drawers near-to-droppin on the wet deck." She began emitting a barely audible, almost soundless scream; sort of a half-ass plea for help, while not really expecting help. But! There was no help coming. Either Nurse-Wife Peg would; or Nurse-Wife Peg would NOT; land the big sailfish? And in one sense of the word, that was too bad. "Why?"

To me it was clear. Having been Peg's devoted husband for years, it was crystal clear; "Peg was NOT psychologically prepared for the battle she was facing." Deckhand Luke gave me a discernable nod and a wink; the meaning of his signal also crystal clear; no room for misinterpretation. Luke then said it out loud. Suggesting, in rather definitive but deferent deckhand terms, that I should take Nurse-Wife Peg's place in the fighting chair! "There!" A welcome suggestion to which I instantly and loudly agreed; a polite suggestion to which used-up Nurse-Wife Peg instantly and quietly agreed. And. After it was perfectly clear to everyone involved that all the perplexing pieces of our intra-family puzzle had been rapidly and peacefully put in place; knowing there was zero chance of offending his clients; our Captain made a loud "command decision". Announced that the switch should be made; "Mr. Pepper…Take the chair…Your wife appears beat (tired)!"

But making the decision about which Pepper would occupy the fighting chair, and actually carrying out the required strategic switch, was a classic "easier said than done" challenge. Nurse-Wife Peg was already engaged up to her well-plucked eyebrows in a one-on-one, no-one-dares-blink, tough, fish fight; a fierce squabble yet to show the slightest sign of diminishing in intensity. Meanwhile; I was quietly being instructed by Luke exactly how I should grab the rod and take over; "without losing the big sailfish."

Without uttering a word, deckhand Luke helped me into a backup fighting belt. Then, working as gently as a groom with his virgin bride on their wedding night, Luke silently freed Nurse-Wife Peg from the fighting chair. Out of the stiff, bulky, leathery, belty, harnessy chair; that suddenly appeared way too big and far too heavy for Peg's thinly-built, female frame. A cumbersome contraption; into which deckhand Luke had moments earlier just finished securing our sizzling boat's lone female occupant.

"But Nurse-Wife Peg is no quitter. She'll stay in any fight to its bitter end. She was merely being relieved OFF the battle line…being allowed to step down from front line duty…being allowed to return to the rear for a little well deserved R&R."

But! There's a sadder truth here; a confession awaiting disclosure. "While I was exceedingly proud of Peg…happy for her in the moment…I was also silently GLAD that she had grown too weary to fight the fish. GLAD Nurse-Wife Peg WAS intimidated by her chance circumstances…GLAD she felt TOO on-the-spot and seasick to realistically continue. GLAD Nurse-Wife Peg readily agreed to Luke's suggestion…that I…not she …fight the trophy sailfish tormenting the far end of our screaming line. GLAD to suddenly be the center of so much hysterical boater attention. GLAD that………!"

"All good things must come to an end." "A bird in hand is worth two in the bush." "Don't count your chicks before they hatch." And, "No good deed shall go unpunished!" Take your pick, they all apply. Once a firm decision had been reached that I should replace Nurse-Wife Peg in our family rotation; "Tragedy!" Within seconds of ME assuming domain of the fighting chair, being put in a proper position to fight the big sailfish; "The big sailfish was gone…In Mere Seconds!" Some say ten, some say five, I say fewer; in a heartbeat, our family's gorgeous sailfish made one, quick, spectacular run directly at our bobbing boat; leaped ten feet into the crystal clear, salty air; arched its mighty sailfish back in a death-defying plunge into the depths of the blue Gulf; "And in the blink of an eye. . . spit OUT my lure...Peg's lure. . . OUR lure!"

It was over. Our day was over.

When the line went slack, I blinked; and the length of my life was cut short by a year. "No. . . make that two years!"

One's gut cannot ache more; one's stomach cannot be more tightly tied into a grizzled knot. Nor can feelings of embarrassment, shame, and agony come upon one any quicker or in greater doses. There have been few times in my adult life when I have wished harder for a dark hole into which to step. Wanted more for a high bridge from which to leap. No one knows why, nor how, Nurse-Wife Peg's sailfish got away?

"But really. . . Does it make any difference?" The big sailfish shook Nurse-Wife Peg's hook from its beaky, sailfish mouth and roared off to be caught on another day in another way. Perhaps by a better husband; a man not quite so selfish as I; perhaps a husband who didn't wish so hard that it be HIM instead of his deserving WIFE chosen to sit in the fighting chair. A better man, allowed by God Himself on High, to actually HOOK; "when it was his turn"; the big sailfish, the really big sailfish, that GOT AWAY!

Snappy Snapper

By January 1983, newly wed Nurse-Wife Peg's and my lives were exiting the unstable house of turmoil, entering the promising home of transition. Man and Wife barely a year, Peg and I were forced to pack our court-acquired sons in a spanking new GM conversion van and essentially flee the fine state of Missouri; war refugees from our hotly contested custody battle with EX Jen-Jen. Ours a brutal and gutting conflict; one from which Nurse-Wife Peg and I emerged victorious, but bent; bruised and in dire need of repair. During the months immediately following our marathon struggle, Peg and I became desperate for mental refuge and financial renewal; craved a new start for our reconstituted family of four. As a result, we decided to relocate our new family eight hundred miles south; move from northwest Missouri to the glorious state of mind; Texas! "It was my destiny to become a Texan. Not born here. . . I arrived as soon as possible."

By February 1983, I had landed a dream job; Executive VP of my Loving Uncle's booming real estate company located in Texas; "A new career in a new environment." Within weeks of arriving in Texas, members of our extended families back up in Missouri had cumulatively put together a sizable amount of private $cash$; which was then invested in Loving Uncle's booming land development and RV park business. Arriving with a bucket full of new Missouri money, Peg and I instantaneously put ourselves on Loving Uncle's business map. Everyone involved soon became emotionally involved, a me too band wagon effect broke out, and dozens of additional Fine Missouri Folks practically insisted on investing in Loving Uncle's land development projects. "While it was occurring...WHILE it was happening...we were...ALL of us were... blindly optimistic...HELL BENT on succeeding...careless and carefree! And everyone knows what happens when we get careless."

The sun had barely set on Peg's and my tough decision to relocate to Texas; "an earnest effort to improve our conflict altered lives"; before some of our Missouri family members began hankering to join us in Texas. Join us in what was perceived to be, by people present and paying attention, a legitimate family gold rush. "The end result?"

MY longtime friend, Bubba Bob Coffer; "who just happened to be Nurse-Wife Peg's brother-in-law"; and Bubba Bob's lovely wife Christie; and Bob and Christie's two teenage children, Dina and Greg; sold their home and property in Missouri and moved to Texas. "That's right!" Bubba Bob and his lovely wife Christie and their family joined Peg and me in Blanco, Texas; which at the time, served as World Headquarters for Loving Uncle's private real estate company.

Back during the 1970s, a precarious although undeniably exciting time in our lives, Bubba Bob was counted FIRST among ALL friends! Bubba Bob and I lived through the barbaric 1970s; sequestered up there in my original hometown of Weston, Missouri. A he-man wonderland for two studly young husbands living in Suburbia, USA; Bubba Bob and I were faced with a million golden opportunities we participated in but never revealed. Dubiously tawdry, borderline, behavior-ly unbelievable opportunities or excursions; "Bob and I were...unquestionably...Running Mates of The First Order!"

Bubba Bob Coffer was THE person responsible for FIRST introducing me to Nurse-Wife Peg; during a steaming hot BBQ hosted on Bubba Bob's back deck up in Weston. "Whoa!"

And so it came to pass; Friend Bob, later down the road Brother-In-Law Bob, and Bob's extra lovely Wife Christie; Nurse-Wife Peg's older, wiser, and far-far more demanding sister; uprooted their ho-hum lives and rushed down to Texas to participate in the roaring 1980s land rush. "Those two sisters...Christie and Peg...are so much alike... it scares the livin shit out of me"; Bubba Bob was oft heard to say.

"Well?" Not everything in life ends as we wish it would; not all stories have a happy ending; especially stories where The End is prematurely written. Nurse-Wife Peg's and my extended families investment $$$$$ in Loving Uncle's land development business didn't pan out. Everyone lost nearly all their money. Partly due to the savings and loan debacle and real estate crash experienced throughout greater Texas during the mid 1980s. Partly due to ineptitude, greed, and sleaziness that permeated the entire land development industry into which we Missourians invested our hard earned money. It was no one's fault; things just didn't pan out; similar in many ways to financial waywardness defining the era JUST prior to America's 2008 financial crash. "Too much greed and corruption...like with Bernie Madoff!"

In the end, the sad end, our families' giant financial misstep into Loving Uncle's land development business would have likely "died quietly away", with little erosion and few ripples, had it not been for one important factor; "Bubba Bob uprooted his family and moved to Texas to participate." Moved

Christie (L) was her baby sister's friend and identical twin/clone... a few years older, but decades meaner! (2007)

to Texas hot on the heels of Peg's and my move; a precipitous, scary move Peg and I were forced to make out of necessity; "We really were fleeing Missouri...seeking refuge as far from EX Jen-Jen as the law would allow." But when Bubba For Life Bob heard glamorous details describing the investment opportunities in Texas; heard thrilling stories about the amount of money that potentially might be earned from investments in Newest Favorite Uncle's real estate company; nothing short of a bullet to Bubba Bob's big soft heart would have prevented Bob from selling out up in Missouri and joining Peg and me in Texas. So...it came to pass; Bubba Bob DID move to Texas. And as they say; "The rest is (unpleasant family) history."

So what does all that upheaved family planning have to do with my book of fishing short stories? "Well My Reader...a lot...a whole lot!"

"Bob and I weren't merely friends...we were Bubbas. Soul Mates. Long before the term was popular. Running Mates. Conquering...killing...cleaning and consuming live critters to feed our hungry tribes. Bubba Bob and I drank good whiskey...played cheap poker...told tall tales...exploited wild life...dealt heads-up and head-on with friend and foe alike...until our (mine and Bob's) non-stop ass kickins caused the hair of less fortunate bastards all around us to turn green and hurt with jealousy!"

First off; Bubba Bob and I worked like dogs; shared millions of hours working as indentured servants in Missouri's tobacco industry; that, and much more, before Bubba Bob plunged headfirst into joining me in Texas. So; when things didn't pan out, I felt responsible. Felt guilty. Felt a strong, overpowering sense of owing Bubba Bob payback. Even though Bob's Wife Christie, Bob's Sister-In-Law Peg, and a hundred other Fine Missouri Folks purportedly tried to dissuade Bob from making his precipitous move to Texas; "None of that mattered." Bob came to Texas. We failed. Our land developments failed. Bob and I, all of us, failed. We lost millions. Every one of us lost our money! And sitting squarely atop the list of individuals hurt MOST by what happened to us in the land development business here in Texas; "Peg and me." We lost all our money TOO!

"But then?" Well then; following a crushing The End to our Texas misadventure; a strange and wonderful thing happened. Adjustments were made. Twenty years went by. Life went on. Time ticked by. Changes occurred.

"The End?" In 1985, barely twenty-four months after moving to Texas, Bubba Bob and his family returned to Missouri; chagrinned and subdued;

Bob and I rode life hard and enjoyed the hands we were dealt. (2007)

The End. Bob took a job with a big time liquor distributor in Kansas City and began rebuilding his financially crippled life. Later, in 1987, also chagrinned and subdued, I too started over; as a struggling, rookie business broker attempting to rebuild my financially wrecked life. Time ticked by. In 1991 Nurse-Wife Peg gave birth to our only biological child, John James. More time slipped by. Less than a year after John James was born, Nurse-Wife Peg's nephew, Greg, was killed in a head-on car crash on the busy streets of Kansas City. Greg was the only son and oldest child of Bubba Bob and Lovely Wife Christie; only son of Nurse-Wife Peg's sister Christie; oldest child of MY soul mate Bubba Bob. More time went by. Within a year; Wife Christie and Nurse-Wife Peg's seventysix year old, whiskey drinking, Irish Bulldog Union Boss, lifetime resident of North Kansas City, Dad, Big Jake, died of cancer. Meanwhile; EX Wife Jen-Jen got remarried; divorced; remarried; divorced; and remarried again...sort of? For most of us involved IN or impacted BY Peg's and my Missouri Border Wars of 1981; "a viciously fought custody battle"; life continued marching forward. Changes; large and small, significant and trivial; continued occurring for all of us involved. Those of us who suffered most, battled hardest; to restore normalcy to our scattered but not shattered lives. And in the real The End; "Ever body got over it...focused on good stuff...and got on with life!"

During the twenty-five tumultuous years from 1981 to 2006, an important pre-existing relationship between two bonded sisters was first strained, then nearly ruined, then stabilized, then restored, then nurtured, then allowed to grow and flourish. Strained by Peg's and my protracted custody battle from Hell. Strained by Bubba Bob and his lovely Wife Christie's disastrous move to Texas. All but ruined by our financial dream-turned-nightmare of NOT succeeding in Loving Uncle's land development business. Stabilized by two estranged sisters sharing the dualities of joy and tragedy. Stabilized by two sisters; one bearing, the other sharing; in the birth of a newborn child and nephew, John James. Stabilized by two families losing our bigger than life Dad, Big Jake. Stabilized by sharing the tragedy, bearing the grief, of losing nephew and son Greg in a fatal car crash. Restored by the persistent effort put forth by two maturing sisters; both sisters demonstrating mutual love for one another's kids, husbands, and families. Nurtured by increasing wisdom and greater insight; granted to everyone involved with the passing of time. And finally! After all of us were born again, like new Christians, allowing our prior good feelings for one another to grow back and flourish. Surviving children, grandchildren, new careers and challenges; rushed in to fill the painful void left by loved ones departed and opportunities lost. New professions and powerful personal interests swooped in and packed full our adult lives. And a previously warm and cozy quadrangle; two wives, two husbands; four good friends; was restored.

And through it all; through the passing of twenty-five YEARS; through tuff times and terrible tragedies; here and there, scattered through the years like flavoring grains of salt, viewed by those of us involved as mere oddities or aberrations to seemingly greater events in our lives occurring during the same time frame; fishin stepped in to have a hand. "Yes!" "Fishin." Fact is; fishin is why this particular story was deemed worthy of being included in my first book about fishin. "Oh…Huntin had a hand in restoring our fractured relationships TOO! But for now…I'll stick to fishin. Catchin fish…catchin big fish…catchin lotsa fish…catchin some of the best damned eatin fish in the whole world! AND! On a special birthday fishin trip planned just for him…Bubba Bob Coffer catchin a humongous red snapper…the size of a frickin wash tub!"

Bubba Bob grew up in a family of modest means in North Kansas City. Modest means is my politically correct euphemism for dirt poor; "Which included about ninety percent of ever body I knew…nearly all of us north of the river. BUT! None of us knew we were poor…so we didn't give a rat's ass! We were…as my Dad used to say…fat, dumb and happy!"

When Bubba Bob and I first fell in together as friends, he and his lovely Wife Christie were living and working in my former hometown of Weston. Bubba Bob was making a handsome living working as Chief Financial Officer of McCormick Distillery located in Weston; "America's oldest continuously operated distillery." Within weeks of first meeting Bubba Bob, he became one of my best buddies; after a year or two, my constant companion. But Bob was ever body's buddy. Bob was a great cook, hosted the best parties, and was always able to come up with a few bottles of McCormick's Gold Label whiskey; "The old Weston distillery's top drawer label back during the 1970s and early 1980s." By the bottle or by the case, if any of us Bubbas needed whiskey or gin or vodka our Bubba Bob could get it; seemingly in unlimited supplies? "Bob never turned me down…never said NO to any of his good buddies."

Bubba Bob and I spent ten of the best years of our lives doing a lot of wild things, exciting things; crazy shit for married men with children. Looking back, Bubba Bob and I agree that many man-activities enjoined and enjoyed in our youth are MOST reasonably portrayed in an old and accurate Marine Corps brag. Bob and I claimed then, and claim now, that he and I could; "Ride…Fight…Fart…F—k…Shoot the Shit…and Drive a Truck …better than any man around!" Could heave-ho at the grist mill of life with the best of men; certainly better than many of our herbivorous, grass eating peers holed up behind their wives skirts up there in Platte County Missouri!

Ride? Bob and I rode every back road for forty miles round Weston; killing every critter we deemed deserving of execution; bad critters like coyotes or skunks. Also creatures we considered good fare for eating; like rabbits, squirrels, ducks, and doves. Not to mention frogs, raccoons, opossums, deer, turkeys, quail, pheasant, geese, and a few unidentified flying objects Bubba Bob and I boiled whole or ate raw; while drinking.

Fight? Bubba Bob and I took on, fairly and unfairly; it didn't matter to Bob and me; any man or wimpy team of half-assed, mellow-fellow men who ever felt the urge or up to the challenge. Took on all comers; whipped every friendly adversary; usually at sports no more dangerous or rowdy than fighting over who was the best poker player, best shot with a shotgun, best fisherman or fundraiser; or best man to have on your team during any sort of community effort meant to enrich the lives of poor souls less fortunate than ourselves. Bubba Bob and I trounced all competitors at every undertaking; things like busting our asses on Weston's Volunteer Fire Department, leading our Jay-Cees Club, raising money for the local Lions Club, funding and producing our hometown's Fourth of July Celebration, financially backing and supplying whiskey for Weston's annual Homes Tour; and a thousand other minor venues where a dash of brains, a bucket of balls, and a stiff neck were the primary requirements for getting the job done right. "Bob and I were affectionately called "animals" by our other Bubbas. Bob and I didn't mind. Fact was; Bob and I LOVED animals...We ate damned near ever frickin animal we killed!"

Fart? Bubba Bob and I passed along, both orally and anally, enough metric tons of hot air and natural gas to power a naval armada; gas created from constantly imbibing free whiskey and gorging good food. Bob and I spent life impaired, overstuffed. Bob's well-known culinary expertise and endless supply of quality whiskey were a near lethal combination; worn out to excess by Bob and all his friends; ME included.

F—k? Bubba Bob and I indulged in plenty of intercourse alright; literally and figuratively. Literally with our lovely spouses, "99.99% of the time with our spouses"; figuratively with hapless victims who mistakenly stumbled into our cross hairs; IF and WHEN the situation required a good F—king? But only figuratively, and ONLY if it was the kind of situation where some bad ass deserved a good F—king. However! Writing about F—king can be a dainty subject; one I refuse to go further into at this time. Some stories are best left untold or left to the imagination of poor wretches who have nothing better to do. "To Numb Nuts who...for inexplicable reasons...remotely give a shit?"

Historically speaking, nearly all, if not ALL, F—k stories about Bubba Bob and me were third-hand versions of someone else's interpretation of the figurative meaning of the F-word. Tall tales, laced with wild speculation, referencing someone else's liberal interpretation of the F-word; enormously careless stories, more conjecture and myth than reality. Most F-stories about Bubba Bob and me were little more than skimmed tidbits of truth, mixed with prolific illusion. Highlighted here and there by Bob's glamorous reputation as a connoisseur of all things fine; and the high profile, public figure role I held there in my former Missouri life; "My family just happened to own the largest business in town...a tiny town...where we employed over one hundred freezing souls... during the dead of winter...in a highly seasonal...agriculture based...dirty business. Where we kept body and soul together for the masses...from cold November...through freezing February...people were bound to talk about somebody...sometimes me."

Shoot the shit? Hell! That was nothing. Shooting the shit was Bubba Bob's and my euphemism for shooting the breeze, for talking a lot, about a lot of things. Shooting the shit, usually about nothing in particular, was characteristic of both Bubba Bob and me. Exercising our common gift of gab, which both Bob and I have long been accused of too frequently displaying, was fabric to our way of life.

Drive a truck? That's just another euphemism, for working. Bubba Bob and I worked; every day, all day long. Work was something Bob and I knew plenty about and usually enjoyed. "Bring it on...the more the better!"

So! Looking back, thirty-plus years! I guess The Marine Corp's half-century old jingle about Riding...Fighting...Farting...F—king...Shooting the Shit...and Driving a Truck was reasonably applicable to Bubba Bob's and my 1970s run up the mountain.

Eventually, Bubba Bob was able to get his post-move-to-Texas life straightened out; and likewise, me too. We both got our lives back on track; our luck and good fortune in life improved; good times rolled again. By turn of the Twenty-First Century our two wives; "sisters by birth...identical twins born seven years apart by deed"; lovely wives; still hanging in there AS our wives by only the slimmest of margins; were fat dumb and happy to have their personal prosperity restored; delighted to once again have an unlimited supply of high dollar fine wine on hand, ready to be swilled. While Bubba Bob and I were once again; "doing just about any damned thing we pleased!"

"That's right! So long as Bubba Bob and I made sure there was plenty of good wine to drink...expensive cheese to eat...steak to grill...hotels to frequent...trips to be taken...our two maturing but still very elegant rejoined at the hip sisters...Wife Christie and Nurse-Wife Peg...were easily pacified. But...Don't EVER tell our wives I said they were...fat dumb and happy!"

In an attempt to make up for some of the horrible parts of our shared family history; to assuage lingering feelings of guilt; to offer a modicum of real-time restitution in such a way that I could forever feel better about Bubba Bob enjoying his long overdue paycheck from Texas; I set up a fishing extravaganza for Bob and me here in Texas; a three-days-running fishin trip of the first order. Part of my effort was overtly directed at Bob's big heart; an out in the open attempt on my part to sweeten the bitter almond taste left in Bubba Bob's mouth two decades earlier when he and I watched our hard earned Missouri money evaporate in the sizzling Texas sun. So! After having had a near record year in my new career as a business broker selling small Texas businesses; feeling flush and on my feet for the first time in years; I invited Bubba Bob to come on down and stay awhile and celebrate life by; "Goin fishin til we can't stand it no longer!" Our fishin expedition was great; good food and good times rolled better than before; "And Bubba Bob…fat ass landlubber that he was…caught one of the biggest red snapper I've ever seen. And ever body who knew Bob said…It couldn't have happened to a finer person."

For our snapper trip, Bubba Bob's and my red snapper trip, I booked us a full day charter out of Port Mansfield, Texas; a small but never sleepy coastal town about three fourths of the way down the Texas Gulf Coast towards Mexico. There's one narrow straight road leading into Port Mansfield, one road coming out. Guides for any type fishing are available upon demand; by the day, week, or month. Two prior days running, Bob and I had fished for speckle trout. I planned our snapper trip as third and final day; "Meant to be the climax of Bob's trip…which it proved to be…in more ways than one."

Having checked in briefly with our Charter Captain the night before, Bubba Bob and I were at the dock by seven next morning; chomping at the bit for a full day of offshore fishin. Seven was late as charter departures go, but that was the time our Captain insisted on as the "correct time" for Bob and I to meet, greet, and get going. Bubba Bob's and my first real surprise, of our already electrified, super-energized, three day fishin extravaganza, came when we first met our jovial Captain's decidedly handsome First Mate.

"Allow me to point out something very important…right here. Strong proper emphasis needs to be placed on the mate part of First Mate; "you'll soon see why." Our spry and perpetually grinning Charter Captain had just that week celebrated his seventieth birthday. "That's correct…seventy!" After retiring from NASA down in Houston…our Captain had been running snapper charters out of Port Mansfield for twenty years. He was crusty…feisty…and fun as any Charter Captain or fishin guide I ever hired. I was glad of it…happy for any tidbit of joy that added to Bubba Bob's big day saltwater fishin. And…obvious to any observer…our charter boat's First Mate was our

Captain's FIRST mate...if you know what I mean?"

Bubba Bob had never before been saltwater fishing; never, not once! That and the fact that he and I were celebrating Bob's birthday were cornerstones for my generous fishin trip reasoning; the story behind the story of me lining up, paying for, and producing three consecutive days of guided fishin trips for me and Bubba Bob. I intended to put Bob on more good fishin in three days than he had seen in three decades back home in Freshwater, Missouri. I made the effort and Bob appreciated what I was doing, solely on his behalf; "I merely went along to watch...but stoically managed to suffer through it."

Our Captain, his name withheld out of professional courtesy and respect, was quick to point out that our First Mate was an experienced salty hand. A knowledgeable deckhand capable of any and all chores that might befall HER that day! "Once again... proper emphasis needs to be placed on gender...I did say HER!"

I realize that HERS come in all sizes, shapes, constitutions, and moods; "I've known a few hers in my day." But during my many years of hiring guides and charter boat Captains I had never before encountered a HER. And! Well! There was more to this HER than merely her gender being opposite mine and Bubbas. Our First Mate, her name also withheld out of respect and professional courtesy, fit every overly-endowed female stereotype you may have ever seen, read about, or heard about. But our First Mate also just happened to carry herself well, and repeatedly performed her long list of arduous First Mate chores beyond the call of duty.

So there it was; Bubba Bob's and my first anomaly, of many anomalies, during a long and interesting day out there fishin. Not only was our First Mate a near dead ringer for Jane Mansfield; she was at least, "bare minimum", thirty years younger than our Captain. "Normally...I would have written bare ass minimum...but don't wish to unnecessarily lead anyone's thinking down any unseemly trail." I was pleased at the sight of our HER; pleased at the thought of having a female First Mate around all day tending to our boat borne personal needs; pleased that our Captain was open minded and forward thinking enough to include a proficient HER in our day's planned activities. "But I was also skeptical." Skeptical that she, any HER, could hold up to the rigorous duties I had seen other lone deckhands and/or First Mates asked to perform on similar sized boats on similar, daylong, offshore charters. Later, according to Bubba Bob; "You (me) shoulda had your (my) skepticism shoved up your (my) chauvinistic butt!"

However! Although Bubba Bob refused to admit it, he was initially skeptical too; perhaps less so than me, but skeptical just the same. In my case there was good reason for skepticism. I knew how much difficult work lay ahead for our deeply tanned, buxom, lone deckhand. Bob was merely being a male chauvinist. And even though I had a good idea what was coming during our rough day out there fishin, and WAS skeptical; I should not have been. And even though chauvinist Bubba Bob didn't think any woman could do a man's job, and WAS skeptical; he should not have been. Nope! Bob and I should have relaxed, while we still had the opportunity; and enjoyed our boat's more-than-ordinary all hands on deck internal scenery; "if you know what I mean?" Later on when Bob and I and our two slightly curious wives, Wife Christie and Nurse-Wife Peg, were discussing Bob's and my wonderful day out there snapper fishin; I just happened to mention that our First Mate was female. According to Bubba Bob; "Oh she (First Mate) was f—kin female alright…that's a sure fire fact…to which I will most assuredly attest!"

So! With both primary Homo sapien gender groups fairly represented; all hearty souls aboard who were coming aboard; Bob's and my grimy Missourian gimme caps turned round backward for proper aerodynamics; and our charter boat's two giant motors roaring to life; away we four seafarers went looking for big snapper. "DAMN it was exciting!"

However! Instead of a customary two to three hour boat run out to deep offshore snapper beds in bottomless water, our Captain cut the motor after no more than thirty minutes. Accomplishing one of those ignominious side-sliding, engine revving, sudden stops for which all fishin guides are notorious, our boat seemed to pirouette on a dime. Our Good Captain told Bob and me later that we were never fishin more than nine miles from shore. The clear and blue Gulf water was filled with wonderful aquatic wildlife, ranging from oversized green sea turtles to dozens of shiny bottle nosed black porpoise; "The kind like Flipper…remember Flipper?" We saw ten million jellyfish and a smattering of other fishin boats; no sharks, no stingrays, no billfish.

Supposedly, according to our Captain, we were fishing in a rare aberration on the gulf floor, in approximately sixty feet of water, near an old submerged shipwreck and two old sunken oil rigs. Generally speaking, The Gulf isn't very deep; but contains more than its fair share of underwater fish habitat or structure. Good structure provides breeding and feeding grounds for tiny sea creatures and baitfish; which feed predator fish; which feed bigger predator fish; which feed biggest predator fish. The Gulf of Mexico is a fertile and diverse fishing ground; "If you haven't tried it…you should…I promise you won't be disappointed. But hire a good guide and be prepared to have fun."

There was however one minor drawback; one cold wet blanket thrown on our otherwise wonderful opportunity to go to sea and catch red snapper; a statutory restriction imposed on our day that has gotten worse since Bubba

Bob and I set out to catch Bob a Birthday Boy red snapper. Bob and I were allowed to catch and keep only FIVE red snapper each; all five of which were required to be beyond a minimum size. Texas Gulf Coast fishermen are accustomed to dealing with and adhering to size minimums and size slots. Fishing within a slot means that your fish must be of a designated minimum length, but cannot exceed a designated maximum length; "must fit within a defined slot." If not, the fish can NOT be retained! That's right! The fish must be released. Or, as is the case with red drum; not to be confused with red snapper; only two red drum beyond the designated maximum may be retained per fishing license, per fishing season; not to be confused with the designated minimum for red drum.

The aforementioned are good rules; set in place to protect the species and allow older breeding sow fish the opportunity to effectively regenerate their species. State wildlife and fisheries people, acting in conjunction with private sportsmen's and professional guide associations, exert political control and practical management over Texas Gulf Waters; promulgate rules and regulations meant to protect sport fish species and assure a continued quality fishing opportunity. The collective efforts of those involved; from fisherpersons to politicians; is considered a Major League success story throughout The Gulf, much of it spearheaded here in Texas. Other coastal areas of the US, of the World for that matter, should be so smart. "Adhering to complex but prudent rules and regulations is reason enough alone to hire a good and proficient guide…it's NOT the only way to go…it's the BEST way to go."

Anyway; Bubba Bob and I set out, that day, to catch five red snappers each. Each snapper was required to be larger than a certain minimum size, with NO upper maximum. And. We were allowed to catch any unlucky mackerel that just happened to swim by. Our crew had mentioned zero plans about trying for a kingfish or billfish; "Such prolific sport fish were not considered catchable so close to shore. Our boat's focus that day, all day long, was directed at catching keepable red snapper. And, not to worry, our Good Captain seemed to know his stuff.

Nearly anyone; "there MAY be a few possible exceptions"; who visits our beautiful Texas Gulf Coast; "America's Third Coast"; who also happens to be a fisherperson, or who has kids crying out to fish, or who wants to catch an exceptionally good eating fresh fish, or catch a popular local species of fish; should take the golden opportunity to go out for a day, or half-day, snapper run. Snapper party boats are tug-like boats with waist high railed sides and one hundred fishin stations per boat, logistically supported by huge bait boxes and mammoth public ice chests. Snapper party boats are BIG boats that routinely accommodate twenty to fifty fishermen per day, per trip, on long voyages that usually involve one-to-three-hour boats rides getting OUT to and returning IN from prolific public snapper beds. Such day-trips are a popular, inexpensive venue for bachelor parties, church retreats, business and client gratuities, and other small group special getaways down here in Texas. On the other hand; the availability of all-day small private charter craft to pursue red snapper are fewer and farther between and are comparatively expensive. But! I wanted Bubba Bob to catch what most experts believe to be one of the best eating fish in the world. Even if; "Snapper aren't considered among the world's best fighting…OR most spectacular appearing…fish." But as things turned out, Bob and I got lucky and caught all three; good eating fish, great fighting fish, AND one of the most spectacular looking fish I've ever seen hauled aboard a boat. "We also nearly drowned our seasick…saltwater soaked…overweight…tired asses."

"The first step at our boat's first stop?" Instead of rigging our lines with heavy weights and round circle hooks and fishing deep and dead on the bottom, our First Mate double-timed her pretty bottom round the poop deck of our bobbing boat; tying on medium sized hooks for Bubba Bob and me. First Mate then baited up two medium-weight rods with small but whole sardines, one fresh dead sardine per hook. Then First Mate tossed the quarter-pound sardines overboard in sort of an off-hand easy rolling cast, allowing the baitfish to splash down about twenty feet out and be sunk by its own weight. Then F.M. let out another twenty or so feet of heavy mono-line. F.M.'s hook baiting and line tossing was directed at the exact midpoint of a spreading pool of bloody chum hustling she had minutes before quietly ladled over the side. When our bait sardines settled in at the far, tethered end of Bubba Bob's and my slack lines; "about fifty feet straight down"; Bob and I could see the dead sardines shimmering in the gin colored water; "It was a bright sunny morning." "And then?"

Well then; a broad, flashing blur of reddish-gold zipped by and Bubba Bob's rod bent double in his wet hands. And before I could say shit, both our rods went down; the one I was holding, AND the one Bubba Bob almost allowed to be jerked overboard by the suddenness and ferocity of the big game fish's initial impact. A dozen minutes of joyous Bubba shouting and wild explicative deleted yells later, and two nice, six-to-seven pound red snappers were hoisted aboard; but only after the fish had put up a largemouth bass-like solid fight. Fighting hefty snappers on free floating baits, without cumbersome six ounce weights dragging our baits down, without our fish being bloated or sometimes even popping from being reeled one hundred feet straight UP, was someone's gem of an idea. For Bubba Bob and me it was like hooking giant, twenty pound carp back home in Missouri; only this time

Bob and I were watching the entire zigzagging fight in 3-D Technicolor through crystal clear sea water. Big snapper can fight; WILL fight! Those of us who have caught red snapper the old fashioned weighted down way, KNOW that snapper can fight; but also know we are rarely rewarded with such a delightful experience due to the two big inhibitors I just described; "caught deep...slowed by weight."

Eight separate baits delicately placed in the water by our indelicate First Mate, and Bubba Bob had four keeper-snapper aboard and iced down; ditto, four for me. As a team, cumulatively, Bob and I were a highly respectable eight-for-eight using the whole, fresh dead, expensive sardine baits; "I knew our sardine baits were expensive...because our Captain told me so...workin me early on for the good tip he rightfully hoped to earn."

The key to Bubba Bob's and my extra pleasurable fishin technique was the direct result of our Captain's bright thinking; "Using bloody chum to bring the snapper UP to us ...especially bigger and quicker snapper...as opposed to slumming around on the bottom where nothin but little snapper hang out!" Working his guidely wisdom, practiced and spoken according to our Captain; once again, subtly reminding me of his professional expertise. Our Captain said he had been using his secret free-line chumming method for years. But; only when and IF he had on board his charter boat experienced fishermen, capable of fighting powerful snapper, on medium weight rods and lines. Our Captain had previously asked Bubba Bob and me if we had ever fished for freshwater carp, or caught saltwater red drum. Now I understood why. Big snapper are similarly heavy-bodied, and pull like runaway calves. It was barely mid-morning and Bob and I were 80% finished; "I was just sorry our fun and excitement was so swiftly passing."

Clearly, obviously, so was our Good Captain. But; he was The Captain! Bubba Bob and I were merely humble clients, along for the ride. "So!" For several important reasons; "reasons not the least of which was that our Captain had the talent and plenty of time to spare...and was experienced enough to spot capable fishermen when he encountered them...and knew that longer and fuller days generally equated to bigger and fatter tips"; our Captain volunteered that he had more fishin of a different variety in mind for Bubba Bob and me. Our Captain confessed he had been harboring a special auxiliary plan for Bob and me; a well kept secret our Captain had yet to disclose to his grinning clients? Said The Captain; "We're gonna do some more fishin...entirely different...for another awesome sport fish...if you want we can.........!"

Having either secretly suggested there might be, or outright promised there would be, a healthy tip paid by Bubba Bob; "which...if you knew

Bob...would have been 100% typical of Bob"; or having merely observed Bob jumping around like a joyfully drunken schoolboy at a FREE fireworks stand? Either way; smelling a giant tip in the making; our Captain upped the ante by ordering First Mate to up the anchor. Whereupon our able bodied First Mate upped the anchor; "Oooops...Did I just say...able-bodied?"

Our Captain fired up his boat's two giant outboards and tore off in the opposite direction; away from the bright morning sun, back west, back towards land; "like lightening had struck his tail." But before our boat went any where, our Captain announced in a dramatic voice; "Men...You need to hold on to your asses...THIS boat load of highly skilled...extra privileged fishermen...is goin after kingfish!"

I was thrilled. Fishin for kingfish was NOT part of our day's original agreed-to agenda. But! IF we could hook and land a kingfish, it would be an incredible bonus for my Missouri-born and city-reared Bubba-In-Law, Bob! Our Captain said he knew where to find a few big kings; "So...By God...We were gonna go have a quick look see."

As a bonus, just prior to upping our anchor and switching rods to pursue kingfish, Bubba Bob caught a gigantic sheep head. Catching any sort of additional species, even a mongrel species like a sheep head, is a thrill to saltwater fishermen; part of the overall lure and mystic of a sport many of us enjoy. When our Good Captain told Bob that sheep head were ornery to clean but great eating, bottom feeder Bubba Bob asked that his weird looking, bony, but white-fleshed, fish be retained for cleaning; which of course it was. "Sheep head ARE wonderful to deep fry...if you have fillets from large fish...and a good friend to clean them...sheep head are VERY tough to clean!"

Nimble First Mate iced down Bob's flopping sheep head and confiscated Bubba Bob's medium weight snapper rod. Then First Mate patiently rearmed both of her spellbound client-students with different rods. All her admirable First Mate work done while our boat was speeding across The Gulf at forty knots, bouncing across humpback rolling waves like a sled scoots over drifts of hard packed snow. First Mate rearmed Bob and I with entirely different, much heavier rods; loaded with much heavier line; to which she attached, at the line's terminal end, tying a perfect sailor's knot, a much bigger set of much uglier hooks. First Mate actually tied on four-to-five medium sized hooks; which, when baited, were mostly hidden by a totally different kind of longer, skinnier-bodied, fresh dead, baitfish called a ribbon fish; "Imagine a long...slithery...very skinny fish... with four to six hooks strategically staged along its pencil thin body."

First Mate next checked the drag on each reel, set the rods in holders on either side of the boat's giant motors, and then hand-fed out approximately one hundred yards of heavy line; all of that adroitly accomplished while our similarly adroit Captain was slowing our wave skimming boat to a steadier, much slower, trolling speed.

"ZING!" Off went the rod on Bob's right; Bubba Bob was in business. Minutes later, Bubba Bob, from landlocked Missouri, had landed our day's first kingfish; a giant.

Just prior to letting out the fastidiously baited kingfish lines, ambidextrous First Mate urgently insisted that Bubba Bob be outfitted with an ungainly fish fighting belt. A heavy harness designed to be worn around the fisherman's waist. Engineered to carry away and dissipate the tiring weight of the rod and energy of the fish during what F. M. anticipated would be a lengthy fight. Carry the fish fight away from the fisherperson's arms, which tended to more easily tire, down to the legs and body, where most people have greater endurance. Trouble was; Bubba Bob weighed three hundred pounds! First Mate had great difficulty adjusting the fishin harness to accommodate Bob's great girth.

During "harness fixin time", Bubba Bob seemed to have great difficulty keeping his swarthy mind on special fishin instructions being told him by First Mate; as First Mate wrapped her long, tanned, muscular arms, and other strategic parts of her tight and nimble body, into twisted formations near-to and near-round Bubba Bob's mountainous body, in her diligent, exhausting effort to properly fix Bubba Bob in the fishin harness; a mighty feat that First Mate eventually accomplished. "Good Thing too!" The tired, old, obviously well-used, fishin harness made a huge difference when Bubba Bob hooked and landed, what was for Bubba, a personal record kingfish! "It was a personal record alright…it was the FIRST damned kingfish Bubba Bob had EVER caught!"

No question about it. Bubba Bob's first kingfish was a true whopper by anyone's standards, and easily won Best Fish of The Day; weighed in back at the dock at nearly thirty pounds! For perspective, realize that Bob's first ever kingfish was nearly twice the size of average keeper kingfish iced down and brought in by the ten-dozens on a million ubiquitous kingfish boats plying the same busy gulf; that day or any other; twice the size of THREE additional average keepers Bubba Bob and I landed and iced down that same afternoon. "And speaking of other boats?"

We had seen fewer than a couple dozen boats since leaving sight of land; none in over an hour. There was a good reason why charter boat traffic had all but disappeared from The Gulf. A big northerner was due to hit the area any time, certainly before sunset. Many small boats; "boats like the one on which Bob and I were stumbling around"; boats that had begun their day out there fishin with us, had disappeared; had headed to harbor. But our boat had not headed anywhere; except to another hot spot for catching kingfish. "Head in?" No way! By that point in a happy day, our expertly Captained boat was officially fishin for greater kingfish; even though our boat still lacked one red snapper per fisherman. But! "If Bob and I WERE lucky enough to fill our daily limit of kingfish... our day's second species of game fish...fish we were earnestly seeking by that point... and IF we...Bob especially...limited out on TWO big time big game fish species...then our big day out there fishin would most assuredly be a day to remember!"

Even though clouds had gathered and the wind had been rising, our Captain remained calm, saying; "Don't worry Men...This is nothin! Jim...Now that we've caught four kings (two was the limit)...I want your Brother-In-Law to get his final snapper! Maybe even a big one? I know a spot where we've seen a few giants...a secret spot nearer shore. Let's get your kings iced down and head that direction." Our Captain's really-REALLY secret snapper reef was within a mile or two of shore.

First Mate finished her kingfish icing duties. Then served Bubba Bob and me cold fried chicken, scrumptious ham sandwiches, three kinds of fresh fruit, crisp potato chips, homemade brownies loaded with black walnuts, pecan clusters the size of German Shepard dog turds; all washed down with blistering cold beer. Bob asked; "Jim...I was wonderin how First Mate keeps the potato chips so crisp out here on the friggin ocean."

Bubba Bob and I hadn't realized it, but we were ravenously hungry. Both of us began blubbering...yes...yes...yes...to anything and everything First Mate suggested. Affirming our desire to consume whatever foodstuff First Mate offered loooooong before realizing the amount offered and eaten was simply WAY too much food and too much drink to belly-down under deteriorating weather conditions; seas were building.

"Realistically...Neither Bob nor I could have said NO to anything pretty First Mate offered. Some people are hard to deny. Pardon me digressing."

"Mysteriously...worst during the harness fixing episode...it seemed difficult for Bob or I to concentrate on fishin? Maybe it was the beer we quaffed down during our too big lunch? We were swilling Buds like there was no tomorrow! Whatever? It became a chore to concentrate...even to eat...while also attempting to speak coherently to First Mate? Eating...talking...even thinking clearly...seemed especially difficult whenever First Mate's sun bathed svelte body...clad in only a bikini...happened to occupy space TOO close to the rear section of the boat...where Bubba Bob and I were attempting to relax and enjoy our lunch? Anything approaching a reasonable rate of beer quaffing or sandwich gobbling became next to impossible...there were too many distractions. It became a chore for Bob and me to keep focused. When either Bubba Bob or I required any sort of official help...First Mate's performance of her duties...her demeanor at all times professional and stoic...under tough and deteriorating conditions...was nothing less than superb...throughout our entire day spent together bobbing around The Gulf!"

Through it all, First Mate remained on deck serving her clients; tending her failing-flailing client's every bump, bruise, and seasick gag. Looking back; I would say Bubba Bob's and my sudden lack of ability to focus was NOT entirely the result of severe weather or seasickness. Nope! More likely it was merely the distraction posed by constant close proximity to First Mate. But! I'm declaring, ON the record, that any delusional figments buried deep in the mush in Bubba Bob's and my thick skulls had nothing to do with First Mate's perfectly aboveboard and straight as an arrow forward demeanor. However! "Does thou thinkest perhaps I protest too greatly...that maybe I declare Bubba Bob's and my innocence too loudly? It doesn't matter! Lovely First Mate is way down there in South Texas...and Bubba Bob is way up there in North Missouri...and I'm standin guard down here between them!"

Anyway! As our already insanely successful day wore on, as our quest to hook just one more big snapper for Bubba Bob continued; The Gulf's troubled waters began rising, became more difficult to ignore. Our bobber-sized boat was being tossed stem for stern. It seemed that at any minute we might be swallowed whole by fifteen-to-twenty foot rolling swells. "I kept having visions of George Clooney in "The Perfect Storm".

By the time our boat traveled another thirty minutes landward, and our Captain reestablished proper anchor over his REALLY secret snapper bed, our Captain began expressing his first notable reservations regarding his own recently modified plan to seek one final snapper for Bob. Speaking softly, our Captain simply said; "Gentlemen! Perhaps we should fish here a few minutes...no more than half an hour...then we better get on in (to harbor)...there's a big blow comin...and truthfully...our little boat might not be big enough to handle this kind of sea."

The Captain's self-commiserating objurgation sounded ominous as Hell to me; but then I wasn't in charge of this fire fight. Someone I had thus far instinctively trusted WAS in charge; "Our Captain...and he remained... large and in charge."

Bob and I smiled, shrugged, and went back to fishin; "Harder and Faster!"

In The End, Bubba Bob and I never caught MY final snapper. There was a good reason why not. Bob caught HIS final snapper, first! And it took Bob nearly thirty minutes to land his huge fish. An important half hour; during which time black storm clouds exploded on the horizon wrapping The Gulf's frothy surface in white capped knots that threatened to drown our little boat. All the while bolt lightening and cracking thunder rumbling closer by the crack.

But our Captain refused to give up; refused to cut the line on Bubba Bob's beautiful big fish; kept countermanding his own quasi-muttered suggestion for Bob to abort the prolonged effort at landing what was obviously an enormous fish. Instead; our Captain opted to allow Bob to land the trophy we had come seeking; THEN make a mad dash for harbor to save Bubba Bob's and my landlocked, saltwater soaked, sun bruised hides! "I woulda cut and run an hour earlier…but then…like I said…I wasn't in charge."

Bob's tortured, throbbing rod had nearly gone overboard when the whopper snapper tagged Bob's free floating sardine bait! Thank GOD Bubba Bob was still wearing the ungainly fishin harness; which had accidentally remained hooked to Bob and hooked to his much heavier kingfish rod. "First Mate hadn't had time…or inclination… to switch out Bob's rod…switch back to medium weight snapper rods." Had she done so, I'm certain Bob and I would have returned home with no story to tell about any giant snapper. Except maybe a story about how Bubba Bob lost his unattached rod overboard to a big fish; or how Bob now owed our Captain for a new rod, to replace the one jerked overboard. A yearling bull on a Hereford ranch in Clyde, Texas could not have pulled more strongly or longly on the heavy line attached to Bob's screaming reel. Bob's eyes became bulging tennis balls; fixed globes, reflecting half shock and half terror. I seriously thought Bob might suffer cardiac arrest; I nearly did just watching!

"Ziiiiiiiiinnnnnnnnnnnnng!" More line out; no let up in sight. When it seemed Bubba Bob's smoking reel was in danger of igniting, or locking up and quitting; our dainty, nimble First Mate stepped in closer to Bob. Forced her smaller hands onto Bob's larger hands, and managed to reset the much too-free-wheeling drag. "Again…I nearly had cardiac arrest merely watching…the extreme fishin action…NOT the dancing duo of Bubba Bob and First Mate…both dancers putting mutual and increasing pressure on the big fish from the pitching rear deck of our suddenly too small sport fishing boat."

"Ziiiiiiiiiiiiiiiinnnnnnnnnnnng!" More line lost; more frantic counter-reeling by astonished Bubba Bob. And once again First Mate was forced to intervene on behalf of Bob. Later, First Mate confessed to Bob that during her second drag tightening go round with the stubborn fish, she had set Bob's drag at its maximum; screwed the drag down all the way to XL tight; "firm as possible." All-the-while gritting her pearly white First Mate teeth in anticipation of a line severing, loud thwwwwaaaannng she knew was sure to come. First Mate confessed that she expected Bob's line to snap. Said she was NOT the least bit hopeful that Bob's line would NOT snap! Said she genuinely feared Bob would, after risking all our lives to hook it, lose his special fish. All-the-while, suffering the mixed emotion of not wishing or wanting to shorten Bob's day, OR lessen her First Mate duties or work load. Just wanting to get Bob's fish aboard and head home; increase the odds of our tiny boat surviving the brewing storm. First Mate admitted she almost made a different, on-the-spot, command decision; one she believed might have been in the best interest of all aboard; her own sweet self included. Glancing up from Bob's toil, eyeing the building whitecaps and rolling storm, First Mate admitted thinking; "God…You better bring this fish tussle to a quick close…one way or another? We need to land that big fish NOW…or lose it NOW…Right God?"

God may have intervened? "Who knows?" First Mate's second drag tightening held; did the trick. Bob's line was strong enough. The fish tired out soon enough. The seas were building fast, but held off long enough. All of the aforementioned coming together in one joyous swirl of heart beating excitement. We got Bubba Bob's damned fish in and safely on board. At the last moment, none too soon to suit every living soul aboard, Captain included; Bubba Bob's fish more or less gave up and rolled over on the choppy surface of the storm prodded Gulf of Mexico. "At first glance I thought my EX Jen-Jen's long forgotten 1974 gold colored Volkswagen Beetle had somehow inflated with air and popped to the surface of The Gulf! Wrong!"

It was instead Bubba Bob's exhausted snapper, a giant among coastal waters red snapper; later weighed in at the dock at just over sixteen pounds. Neither a record, nor anything like a record; "Unless of course you're a whisky sellin wanna be tobacco farmer from Platte County Missouri!"

OBTW! Just minutes after Bob's big red snapper was hoisted aboard, having finally ceased my transfixed stare at the fight occurring before my eyes, I vomited my precious ten gallon lunch overboard in one, huge, gut-emptying, high, arcing, spew. That indignity, my most untimely embarrassing moment of the day, occurring just as Bob's heart rate returned to something under four hundred beats per minute. Both personal health issues taking place while First Mate was securing Bob's trophy red snapper in its own private ice chest. All three predictable events having occurred while our Captain was prophetically and eerily announcing; "Folks…Even though we don't have far to go …I think we're in for a rough run to harbor…I hope we make it?"

As God is my witness, our Captain actually said…I hope we make it; with just enough genuine misgiving in his salty voice to "piss the scare" out of us Missourians. When Bubba Bob flopped down beside me on the tightly secured ice chest, he too finally realized that he was exhausted; wrung out. "Sick too!" Over the side went Bob's eight gallon lunch. The Texas Gulf was two-for-two on weak-livered Missouri Farm Boys! "So much for Riding and Fighting parts of my old-time Marine brag...and...we'll never know about other unmentionable parts of that old jingle!"

First Mate had been everywhere, all at once, all day long. When our Captain told First Mate to secure everything for a rough ride, he meant "rough". And First Mate knew her Captain meant it. Only Landlubber Bob and I were left in the dark; preoccupied gagging up ham sandwiches; too seasick, too astounded, by our day's unbelievable catch to worry about trivia like drowning.

Later on, Bob and I learned that several small charter boats did founder that day. Unfortunately, two fishermen were lost at sea in the deadly squall line that blew through. The weather was never a laughing matter; merely a matter that mostly passed over Bob and I unseen; glanced over the heads of two tobacco grubbing happy snapper fishermen; "so we lived to laugh about it later." Fish weighed, fish cleaned, beer toasts made and returned, we four surviving sojourners of a rough day at sea sat down to enjoy a fancy restaurant prepared meal; fresh red snapper prepared to order.

"Tipped...zipped...and certainly well equipped...First Mate and Our Captain... sailed out of our lives...likely forever...likely the last red snapper

First Mate, **Bob**, and **Captain**. The only thing bigger than his red snapper was the smile on Bob's face. (2007)

Bubba Bob will ever catch. But then...who would even think of attempting to match the wonder of such a matchless day? From red snapper pulled from the deep...to red snapper endured on the deck...it had been a perfect day."

Boyhood home of **Brother Ben** and author **Jim Pepper**, Weston, Mo. (2010)

Chapter Thirteen

Ladd's Jack

The answer is; "Ladd Ashley Pepper". The question is; "For years...who has been the best fisherman in the Jim Pepper Family of Blanco Texas?" After gaining notoriety by winning his first official tournament in 1980 at the ripe old age of three and a half, Son Ladd swiftly became our family's unchallenged best fisherman. Most, first, biggest, last, most different species; Ladd seemed to win, hands down, every internal cash pot contest our family set in place. "After a while we discontinued our farcical effort to determine a Family Champ due to lack of meaningful competition."

Somewhere along life's winding path, I once upon a time said of Second Son Ladd; "Ladd could catch fish on a gravel road...OR...catch fish in a parking lot on a hot day." I had two slightly different versions, both implying the same truth. I got a few laughs for my original quip describing Ladd's prowess as a fisherman and carried it forward in life. Now I want to validate that notion; provide an anecdotal example of why I have said such things about Son Ladd.

There's no question Ladd has evolved into an all-round good fisherman;

Ladd and Chris. (1979)

Ladd 30 years later. (2009)

Note: Dr Pepper Shirts!

one of the best I've personally ever known. And while Ladd's reputation as Best Fisherman is strictly unofficial, it is also quite real here in Blanco County, Texas. Round these parts Ladd's skills are, perhaps, surpassed only by Blanco's Doug Pautz DDS. The same Dr. Pautz described elsewhere in this book. Early on in Ladd's life, in addition to being our family dentist, Dr. Doug was our friendly neighbor. Dr. Doug willingly took Ladd under his more knowledgeable fishing wing and taught Boy Ladd a few critical things about hardcore fishing; offered Boy Ladd free but also entirely sound advice about some of the finer points of fishing.

And. "Who would EVER have guessed it?" After the passing of many years, polarity of the coveted Best Fisherman title reversed itself. "Fact or opinion?" Both! These days, I would willingly bet the ranch that former mentor Dr. Doug could pick up a dip net full of useful pointers from Former Student Ladd; could gather a full stringer of practical information from Ladd. Hot tips Ladd uses to consistently catch a wide variety of fresh and saltwater fish. "IF...Dr. Doug's ego would allow him to relax and learn from someone much younger than himself? Not easy for hardheaded former mentor types like Doug and me. But! Give Ladd ten years and he'll be where Dr. Doug has sought to go. "And Ladd should thank Dr. Doug for helping him (Ladd) get there!"

Ladd caught these catfish while we were duck hunting on Falcon Lake! (2009)

Meanwhile, let's look at Ladd's Best Fisherman reputation; do a quick review of Ladd's fishing history. Ladd caught a four pound channel cat to win a private fishing tournament at age three; caught a four pound smallmouth bass to get in Minnesota's official book of Junior Anglers at age five; caught a Texas Size ten pound Lake Fork largemouth to get in the Lone Star State's "Share A Lunker" program at age ten;

caught an official Somerville Lake Record at age nineteen; "such a record smashing enormous fish it brought Preacher and I scurrying northeast to Somerville to photograph the fish"; caught a million redfish in the Inter Coastal Canal near Winnie, Texas by age twenty-five. Caught the biggest trout, most white bass, most crappie, most catfish, most and biggest fish in a single day of family fishing on the Blanco River, most bluegill from any water we fished, most speckle trout on every family trip, first-most-biggest red snapper on every family snapper trip, biggest kingfish, most Falcon Lake channel cat put on our family stringer, most Lake LBJ crappie and bluegill from one dock, most trout in a single night aboard Louisiana's Hackberry Rod and Gun Club's Night Stalker, biggest largemouth from the Blanco River for our family; most, most, most, most! "Yadda… Yadda…Yadda! Gag me with a spoon! It makes me ill remembering even HALF the times Ladd whipped his Brother Chris' and my highly competitive family asses!"

From child prodigy to top captain in twenty five years... **Captain Jason**. (2006)

Ladd's loooooong list of fishing victories; both large and small, both meaningful and meaningless; have written Ladd's epitaph, have carved Ladd's legacy, some eighty years before the end of Ladd's natural life expectancy. Long before passing from this humble earth up to God Almighty's glorious Fishing Heaven, Ladd has truly become a living fishing legend.

But! Back here on earth, it was late October, 2006. I had booked a two day fishing trip for Ladd and me. Unintentionally; the date conflicted with Nurse-Wife Peg's and my Twenty Fifth Anniversary. But! Peg appreciated it when I managed to be gone fishing or hunting on our anniversary; "Cut down on demands on her time." Ladd and I were to be guided by rookie guide, Captain Jason Wagenfehr, fishing out of Bay Flats Lodge near Seadrift, Texas. Back in 2006, Bay Flats Lodge was relatively new. But! It was then, and is today, a superb hunting and fishing establishment. Featuring fine fishing, finer duck hunting, and some of the finest home style expertly prepared meals this tired old planet earth ever offered up to hungry mankind. Captain

---

Footnote: "Fishing Heaven is where mortal fisherpersons know for CERTAIN we will have the opportunity to fish nonstop for really big ones…hoping like HELL we get Up There…in spite of horrific boldface fishing lies told while mortals here on earth!"

Wagenfehr; "I call him Jason…because that's what I called him for twenty-five years while he and our two older sons were growing up together here in Blanco"; is one of the nicest humans I know. Growing up as legitimate Country Boys, our older two sons and Jason were inseparable fishing chums. "Wantta know the REAL reason the Blanco River never achieved state or national notoriety as a fishing venue? During the late 1980s and early 1990s our three boys…Ladd…Chris…and Jason…kept long stretches of our rocky-bottomed little river fished empty…fished void of catchable fish!"

Anyway; Jason, Ladd, and I were fishing south and east out of Seadrift; far out in San Antonio Bay, up towards Grass Island, even as far out as Steamboat Island; tiny islands not typically indicated on anything other than a high quality boater's Atlas. All three of us; Jason, Ladd, and me; were alternating between wade fishing and drift fishing. We were using small lures, fishing for speckle trout or redfish. Fishing Jason's favorite hot spots; crisscrossing back and forth in shallow bay water; more or less following ubiquitous cuts that run in and out and through shallow water in that area. Because it was getting on towards the end of the day and because all three of us were tired, we had removed our wading gear and were fishing from the deck of Jason's fancy new boat; leisurely drifting, sometimes coming very near to and drifting parallel to the sixty foot deep Inter Coastal Canal.

The Inter Coastal is a utilitarian water feature. A shipping channel used by ocean going vessels, coastal traffic, tankers, and hoards of oilfield workboats. Clearly marked in that area of the bay by a thousand buoys and distinguishable as a major water feature to passing boaters; depicted on every maritime map in the civilized world. "Folks from Iraq or Afghanistan may NOT have heard of America's Inter Coastal Canal? But then! What the Hell HAVE they heard of over there in that God forsaken part of the world?

"F—'em! And F— the spotted red pony they rode over here on to blow

---

Footnote: "To this day and probably for always…I have a difficult time referring to Jason as Captain Wagenfehr. Not that Jason expects me to call him Captain…or cares one flipped shad body WHAT I call him. I think my hesitancy to switch nomenclatures for Jason is similar…perhaps identical…to my one of my Dad's proclivities back in 1973? Back when I first returned to my boyhood hometown and became my Dad's adult business partner. After me being gone for eight years…four years college and four years active duty in The Marines…including one year in Viet Nam serving as Company Commander in charge of two hundred combat Marines…the most meaningful assignment my Dad could think of for ME…think of on his own…without me helping him…was for me to go uptown and pick up our company's mail at the post office four blocks up the street. Calling me Jimmy when he hollered across our crowded warehouse floor…my Dad would yell for ME to run do it! Mindsets or images we grow up owning or sharing with those who either love or hate us…are difficult to alter or divest."

up our Twin Towers! Sorry! But I get carried away and emotional when it comes to national or international politics! I hate the useless war America has been dragged into fighting! I fought in one just like it...We called it Viet F—ing Nam."

"But forget the shit...that's why we go fishing...to get away from shit like TV... politics...war...our sour economy!" We weren't thinking about crap back home. We were having a good time. Ours had been a long and superb day out there fishin. Each of us; Jason, Ladd, and I; had caught a lot of small trout. And each of us had caught at least one semi-trophy. "For me, trophy trout officially begins at twenty-eight inches."

Our trio had landed a couple of twenty-five inchers and a four-pack of twenty-one inchers. We had carefully released every trout in the semi-trophy size range. We had also nearly finished catching our legal limit of keepers; sixteen to nineteen-inch keepers; nice sized trout for filleting and deep frying. We were just woodpeckering around, piddling, seeking another trout or two, winding down after a good day; meandering towards home. "We were far beyond the point (in our day) of trying a new area. Enjoying the waning day...reflecting on our personal prowess as capable fishermen... congratulating Jason on becoming a recently licensed guide...a magnificent professional achievement for him. We were kickin back...fixin to sip a cold one...fishin...but not really givin a rat's ass if we caught anything. It was Miller Time!"

Meanwhile; the wind had picked up and our boat began bobbing about a bit in the choppy shallow waters of the bay. We began drifting; getting a tad too close for comfort to the turbid deeper waters of the Inter Coastal. Aware of our boat's drift, aware of the time of day, aware of the satisfied countenance of his clients, Captain Wagenfehr said; "Men...I think we better head on in!" But we didn't. We didn't head on in because we instead headed on OUT! And we headed on OUT because something happened that caused us to head on OUT! Immediately after Captain Wagenfehr issued his directive about heading on in; hoping for another Calcasieu-like miracle; hoping for more final cast black magic; I was finishing an intentionally s-l-o-w retrieve of my favorite lure; "After having loudly announced and made a formal...final cast." But not this time! Not this trip! And not for me! Nope! My futile final retrieve finished; the meaning of Jason's head on in directive clear and understood; our boat did NOT head on in! It instead headed on OUT; because Son Ladd, Ladd The Fisherman, Ladd The Extreme Catcher of All Things Catchable, Ladd The Patient, Ladd The Persistent, had at the precise moment I completed my final s-l-o-w retrieve; hooked something? Something big! Something REALLY big!

And how did we three Fishing Mates instinctively know Son Ladd's fish was big? Well! There are ways! First off; Ladd had gotten a glimpse of the fish as it tore passed at the speed of sound, striking hard at Ladd's small white trout jig. Second; Ladd's expensive line was zipping off his medium weight Calcutta reel in smoking swirls; singing THE Gospel to us Three Fishermen. Little ordinary fish don't zing out line the way big horse-sized fish zing out line. Ladd's fish was a horse; "FOR SURE!" We Boat Mates could tell, in an instant. The music pouring from Ladd's reel was sweet serenity to hardcore fishermen. Sojourners in a bobbing boat, drifting in an endless sea, we could just tell, we just knew; without waiting for Ladd's self-effacing half-assed description of a fast-assed big fish. Ladd The Fisherman, sitting in the front of our boat, yelled to Jason The Captain, sitting in the back of our boat, that he had seen a dark blur swallow his tiny trout jig; an underwater inhalation of Ladd's bait by a fish of the first magnitude; a large fish moving at mind boggling speed; "Both younger fishermen ignoring Payer For The Trip Me...sitting in the middle of our boat!"

Fishing mates for three decades... what **Ladd** didn't know... **Captain Jason** did! (2007)

Ladd's reel was a good one. One of the best bait casting reels a fisherperson can possibly own; "A genuine Calcutta." Calcutta reels have been around for years; are second to none when it comes to dependability and durability. Two important features to ardent fishermen like Son Ladd; important features to professionals like Captain Wagenfehr; important features to anyone who wants to properly outfit themselves for hanging and LANDING a really tough game fish under challenging conditions. Ladd's line was top drawer too. Ten pound test Spyder Net ™ rigged for wade fishing by tying a heavier shock leader on at the line's terminal end. Ladd used about eighteen inches of heavy leader to increase the durability of his line when fishing in oyster and rock beds; "Expensive lures tend to remain attached to our lines longer if we don't break off on every fourth cast." Ladd's lure was an ordinary quarter ounce lead-headed single hook jig, baited with a white Twister Tail fished on or near the bottom; "the only ordinary part of Ladd's fish story." Ladd's skills were Superb with a capital 'S'; as in Superman! Ladd's talent was up to the challenge; which was, "Landing a twenty pound fish on a light trout rig...loaded with lightweight but high quality line."

But the suddenness of Ladd's big fish hitting and the dramatic unexpected zinging off of Ladd's line caught our boat totally off guard. Essentially we had been on autopilot; unusual for our trio of seasoned fishermen. The three of us; Ladd, Jason, and me; had fished together many times, under a wide variety of interesting conditions. Assessed as a trio, our likelihood for fishing success was considerably better than average. "Whatever the Hell average means? Ask any fisherman and everyone will always say...We did better than average...OR...I did better than average. Someday I'd like to meet the poor blokes who go around doing...worse than average. That would be half of us you know!"

Doesn't matter! At the particular moment the big, unidentified fish decided to strike Ladd's lure, the three of us; Jason, Ladd, and I; were more relaxed than usual. We were, after all, coming to the end of our fine day. We were preoccupied with post event pleasantries and acknowledgements. We were busy describing the good time we had just finished. We were absorbed in the process of reflecting on our day. "We were debriefing...like we used to do after combat missions...fixing memories of the day in our addled brains so we wouldn't forget important stuff...telling our stories to each other to test their believability...testing important details...like total number caught... different species caught...and most important of all...SIZE caught...reiterating and yakking about already exaggerated successes...doing what fishermen tend to do when we suddenly realize our precious time together is nearing an end." Each of us in our own private way was mentally and mechanically preparing to depart the choppy waters of San Antonio Bay, in favor of the more soothing atmosphere of Bay Flats Lodge. In favor of quenching our thirst with cold beer and satiating our hunger with inch thick steaks smothered in rich Bay Flats fixins. And even though totally true, merely saying; 'nearing the end of our day...Ladd made a sloppy half-hearted cast and hooked a giant fish'; it wouldn't be entirely descriptive. It wouldn't be fair to the moment. It wouldn't paint an accurate picture of the amazing moment that was about to forever be suspended in Three Fishermen's shared memory. Also! It's vital to posterity to point out that Ladd was NOT officially making a pre-announced final cast when his big fish struck. There's a critical distinction between what happened to Ladd, and what happened to me, when I caught my giant black drum described in 'Calcasieu Mistress'.

Nope! Final cast magic is NOT what happened to Ladd; not at all. Ladd was loafing. Klutzing around near the front of our boat; half-heartedly, randomly, tossing out his tiny trout lure. When Captain Wagenfehr coincidentally mentioned it was nearing time to head on in; "Believe me...No one said nothin about no final cast!" For the sake of your grandchildren, be certain you understand that there IS a vital difference! There's an almost supernatural difference between making a final cast of the day and merely quitting fishing for the day. A final cast, made when the cast is recognized in advance to be THE last cast of the day, is a fisherman's time honored way of solemnly showing respect to the Fishing Gods. It's a sacred thing. And because final casts ARE sacred, final casts are quite often "God Blessed"! Final casts are, without question, one source from which living legends spring. Final cast of the day; final cast of the trip; or most Holy of all, final cast of the season; are supernatural moments fondly held in reverence by fisherpersons or outdoorsmen. And if something really big just happens-to-happen on a genuine final cast; "like me catching my huge Calcasieu black drum"; then you got yourself a natural born legend. "And if you've ever experienced one…a magic final cast resulting in a big catch or kill…or been present when someone in your family…or a good friend experienced one…you're already hooked on the concept…usually hooked for life…and my explanation is unnecessary."

We've all heard the stories; seen the uncanny results of authentic final casts. The trophy bass caught on last cast of the day; the banded Mallard drake called into range and dropped from the last flock of the day; the Boone & Crockett last buck of the morning that froze in place and was taken at the last minute of the day; the twenty inch bearded gobbler killed on last gobble of the morning, during the last possible moment of hunting; last worm of the day, attached to our grandchild's last bobber in the tackle box, pulled outta sight by the biggest bluegill ever seen, on the last day of fishing, during the LAST minute of fishing, on the LAST day of a two week family vacation! Final cast is a real and actual phenomenon; an unexplainable reality of fishing and hunting. Final cast magic is genuine, special, universally recognized; one of the extraterrestrial, supernatural things that makes hunting and fishing the wonderful mystery it remains. Nope! Final cast magic is NOT what happened to Son Ladd that day while fishing San Antonio Bay with Captain Jason Wagenfehr and me!

"More accurately…Son Ladd was just plain old lucky that his lure was aimlessly dangling in the water." And to his credit, Ladd would be the first to admit it; would enjoy pointing out the difference. If Ladd's trophy fish would have struck Ladd's lure and would have been caught as the result of a recognized Holy-of-Holies TRUE final cast, then the legend of Ladd's fish would be different. "Not necessarily better…but certainly different…with more emphasis on style…less on substance and skill." The ultimate stature of Ladd's accomplishment, the brilliant sheen of his prize, only slightly diminished by the fact that Ladd's big fish just happened to come near the end of our day versus more legendary final cast of our day. Ladd's skill as a fisherman was what really mattered; not his ability to have had a premonition and formally announce a final cast of the day. "And...If all this parsing of the English language and word minutia sounds like just so much idle sportsman's gibberish to you...then Baby...YOU ain't been there and done that! And! You fisher-MEN among us who don't get it...better run out and have your fisherman scrotum checked for proper content! And! You fisherpersons among us...of either gender...who don't get it...better go to the nearest local authority and have your "True Passion For The Sport of Fishing" ID card checked for authenticity." Final cast magic IS real; final cast magic IS an acknowledged, spiritual phenomenon common to fishing and other outdoor adventure and achievement.

Anyway! Lightweight line was disappearing off Ladd's reel faster than the value of our stock portfolios during fall 2008. A realist; I readied myself for the inevitable; mentally prepared myself for issuing politically correct, audible big sighs meant to properly acknowledge Ladd's accomplishment. Prepared myself to grant Ladd the respect he deserved for momentarily having hooked what was obviously a large fish. And. Even though mentally prepared for uttering customary big sighs; having mentally sorted through my "Awkward Fishing Situations Dictionary" for just the correct words for expressing to Ladd how sorry I was that his unidentified, giant fish had just spooled him and gone back to the farthest corner of the Gulf; "That isn't what happened!"

The day Second Son Ladd hooked his San Antonio Bay trophy fish, Captain Jason Wagenfehr was thirty-three years old. Thirty-three is young for a licensed charter boat Captain; "So let's take a look at our Captain." Jason is quiet and serious minded. The kind of young man any parent would automatically adore and proudly call 'My Son'. Sentiments Nurse-Wife Peg and I have often expressed to anyone who would listen. But my point; it is fortuitous Jason was young. Jason needed to be young, and skilled, and patient, and kind, and wise; in order to successfully negotiate the next ninety, adrenalin stoked minutes. An hour and a half, during which time our boat did NOT head on in; during which time Client Ladd, Friend Ladd, Long Time Childhood Fishin Buddy Ladd, landed what would eventually become another of Ladd's beautifully and perfectly mounted trophy fish; "All of which currently hang in MY office!"

Out went more of Ladd's lightweight line. "How long does it take to empty an eight ounce drinking glass? I'll tell Ya! Not long!" Approximately the same amount of time it was going to take Ladd's big fish to empty Ladd's expensive but virtually helpless reel. To those of us with experience, "the future", as it applied to Ladd's fish, was totally predictable; "Jason and I were VERY experienced...we knew what was coming." There would be a sharp thwwwwaaaannng and we three Shipmates would know Ladd's line had given up the ghost and snapped. Then We Three would issue our collective, audible, perfunctory, big sighs and be on our collective way; get back to doing whatever we had individually been doing when the large and intrusive fish so abruptly interrupted our otherwise peaceful process of standing down for the day. "But that didn't happen."

What instead took place next was part miracle, part skilled seamanship, part superb guidemanship, part exemplary fishing skill, and a whole boat load of plain old Irish luck. "In this case Irish luck made sense...if you think about it. Yep! Ladd's ancestors were Irish. According to Ladd's Grandma Bojie...my ninety year old Mom up in Missouri...Ladd is descended from "Irish Kings". It's a long standing family joke; a real oxymoron. Personally...I always thought there weren't any Irish Kings? I thought that's what Mel Gibson was fighting about in Brave Heart? But Ladd and I...and Ladd's older brother Chris...all three of us...DO enjoy tipping our mugs of Irish beer...soaking down our fair share of cold Irish brew in warm Irish settings. Maybe that's what my Mom was referring to? Doesn't matter...Ladd DID have the luck of the Irish with him that day...and he sure as Hell was going to need it!"

Because Jason WAS skilled and young, he was able to move with the swiftness and decisiveness of a high school quarterback; which fifteen years earlier Jason had been. Within sixty seconds; "at most"; Jason was able to regain our small canvas sea anchor, fire up our boat's giant motor, and chug off over the horizon towards Ladd's concurrently fleeing fish...full speed ahead. All of the above accomplished by Captain Jason before Friend Ladd's precious last few spins of dainty monofilament line ran dry from his shiny new gold Calcutta. Later, after it was all over,Ladd told Jason and me that at the very moment Jason managed to get our boat underway, Ladd had glanced down and could clearly see the shiny black inner spool of his gleaming gold Calcutta: and guessed he had maybe five SECONDS of line remaining before hearing that God awful and expected thwwwwaaaannng!

Our motor started and boat underway; our boat freed of protruding encumbrances like me s-l-o-w-l-y retrieving my lure, and our canvas drift anchor dragging us down; our boat steered in the exact proper direction by Captain Jason; Son Ladd maintaining his death grip on his overheating, expensive reel; and miraculously, within seconds, Son Ladd began retrieving desperately needed yards of way too dainty monofilament line. Son Ladd began rewinding and restoring to his warm reel a modicum of lightweight line; made available to Ladd and suddenly retrievable by Ladd NOT because

Ladd's fish had been turned, nor because Ladd had gotten the giant fish under even the slightest bit of control. "No! Neither! Far from either! Not that fish! Not that day! Not under those extreme circumstances!" Ladd was able to gain a little line ONLY because Captain Jason was steadily motoring our sleek boat directly towards Ladd's escaping fish, at a greater rate of speed than Ladd's fish was fleeing Ladd's rod tip. As our boat gained ground on Ladd's fish, Ladd was able to retrieve smidgeons of lost line; so long as Captain Jason advanced our boat in the direction of Ladd's racing fish, at a rate of speed GREATER than Ladd's fish was fleeing our boat! "Simple fisherman math."

However! Jason approaching Ladd's fish too close with the boat, or Son Ladd putting slightly too much pressure on his dancing rod tip, and the wily, unseen fish could and would go on a supercharged run; which it DID… on a dozen separate occasions. Too much resistance by our boat, or Ladd, and the fish could and would go deep and hug the snag-littered bottom of the bay; "Which it DID…on ten separate dives." Undue or erratic boat maneuvering or reeling by our boat's Client-Captain Duo and the terrified fish could and would easily snap Ladd's fragile line; "Which it easily COULD have done …but DID NOT do!"

A powerful fish; that could easily have cleaved the final few precious yards of fragile straining line remaining on Ladd's pitifully depleted shiny new reel; ending Ladd's stalemate standoff with a frenetically fleeing juiced up brute of a fish. It was a cat and mouse game. Madly reel in; retrieve all the line available to be retrieved; cautiously approach the spooky fish; frighten the mulish fish off another vaunted rip across the open shallow bay, or into making another soundless dive into or across the deepest, darkest crevasses of the murky shipping channel; then begin the entire process anew on the far side of the bay or channel. Back and forth across San Antonio Bay, back and forth across the deeper shipping channel, our towed boat of three at ease sojourners fished. One roundtrip out and back; two roundtrips out and back; three roundtrips; four; by our fifth roundtrip up and down and all around an unremarkable saltwater bay somewhere east of dry land, all three of us Fishermen began wondering aloud; "Can it be done?"

Ladd, being the gentle and genteel son that he has always been, repeatedly offered to cut his line and allow the gallant, giant fish to swim free. Neither Captain Jason NOR Captain Dad would have any of that! We, Jason and I, wanted to see the confounding damned fish; which by that point, we were fairly certain was a rough species or nuisance fish; "NOT a trout…or redfish…or black drum!"

Within seconds of hooking it, Ladd had told us that he was almost certain; "but not entirely certain"; that it was a large Jack Cravelle. A bony, tuna-looking, heavy bodied, odd-looking fish; with a distinctively thin blunt face, topped by a dome-shaped head, and further defined by its spectacularly shaped, almost too delicate, tail; a fighting fish capable of outracing a jet ski. A strong swimmer not typically sought by sport fishermen because it is virtually inedible. Fun to catch, fun to hook, but also NOT routinely fished for because it occurs in hit and miss patches and unexpected places. A speedy fish found here and there in twos and threes but never in predictable concentrations like redfish; a loner fish whose feeding patterns, movements, and habits are highly unpredictable and therefore unfishable. And. In most cases, Jacks are absolutely too fast and too strong to be landed by an average angler. Next to impossible to land on lightweight tackle from shore or while wading. "But for that fish…on that day…things was different!"

Ladd's fish was indeed a Jack Cravelle. And. It would succumb. It would be landed. Ladd's middle-aged, medium-sized Jack had met its match. Two longtime good friends, both young relative to the age of their query fish, Friend Ladd and Captain Jason, were engaged in a real street brawl, with a worthy adversary. And in the end, the Two Fishermen would prevail. But first! Near disaster! Disaster that struck first in our minds before NEARLY striking in reality; in the midst of Ladd's protracted fight with his tuff fish; "A near miss with a not realized destiny…a bullet dodged…a fate not lived."

With each roundtrip across San Antonio Bay, our boat, its highly skilled young Master at the helm, was being inexorably drawn back and forth across the bottomless Inter Coastal Canal shipping channel. I sat watching, and listening, in awe; "a mere dumbfounded spectator"; as Jason and Son Ladd conferred and agreed that Ladd's sage, old fish seemed wise enough to be attempting to regain the much swifter, and in places, far more treacherous current of the deeper shipping channel; use the deep, swift channel to facilitate its escape back to The Gulf. Had I not known better than to challenge the two younger men's fishing judgment; "when the subject had anything to do with fish or fishing those two young men were it"; I would have thought their youthful explanation a bit ludicrous. But! Into and UP the fathoms-deep Inter Coastal shipping channel our towed boat did go.

"The problem…the bullet we needed to dodge?" Prior to Ladd's deep running Jack deciding to make its final all-out, all-in mad dash for freedom, our towed boat had been located on the landward side of the Inter Coastal Canal, facing seaward. On this, its final run, Ladd's fleeing fish didn't head back directly across the channel; making what would have been its fifth or sixth cross channel excursion; the Great Fish instead turned north and swam, at top Jack speed, directly UP the middle of the swift shipping channel. "So?"

"SO!" That shipping channel is there for a reason. A giant, rusty, tramp steamer bound for the shores of Tripoli was at that very inopportune moment heading directly towards our tiny fishing boat! Keep in mind; it was the ugly tramp steamer's shipping channel to ply, not our bay flats sport fishing boat's shipping channel to ply. Little ships defer right-of-way to big ships; big ships give way to bigger ships; bigger ships get the Hell out of the path of biggest ships. Our tiny fishing boat was a gnat on a mule's ass; we weren't even a little ship. Our sport fishing boat had NO right-of-way on the shipping channel and we three fishermen knew it. "I think Ladd's salty old Jack knew it too?"

Anyway! Ladd's big fish towed our wee boat UP the narrow, swift channel in the general direction of Grass Island; Captain Wagenfehr nervously following. Helmsman or Captain of the smelly tramp steamer saw our tiny spec of a fishing boat in his path and began tooting its gloriously loud fog horn. But! The rusting hulk of slow moving WW II era scrap steel, disguised as a tramp steamer, also continued steaming IN our pitifully exposed witty-bitty boat's direction. However! Our tiny boat's showdown with a steel tramp steamer ten million times the size and weight of our boat was NEVER gonna happen; we were NOT gonna play "high school chicken" with the mule on whose big ass our gnat sized boat sat. Captain Jason was too cool for that; too professional; too cautious. Jason said; "I'll hold steady…until it's no longer safe…and then abandon trailing Ladd's fish…in favor of safety." OUR safety!

At the last possible moment, just as Son Ladd seemed to relax a bit and begin to accept that which appeared inevitable; "anticipating the infamous thwwwwaaaannng all experienced fisherpersons deplore"; a minor fishing miracle occurred. Old high-finned bony-backed Mr. Jack Cravelle did an unexpected "about face" and headed straight as the flight of an arrow back towards shore; back towards Seadrift, Texas; back towards Bay Flats Lodge; back towards our personal reserve of cold beer and thick steaks! Someone; "perhaps Zeus himself"; must have informed Old Jack that the sun was blood red and goin down 'in Georgia' and it was near quittin time?

Successfully negotiating our way into and UP many treacherous miles of clearly marked shipping channel; finding ourselves staring death in the eye at the hands of a creaking old ship's rusting underbelly; finally emerging on the landward side of the shipping channel, SAFELY heading back towards Bay Flats Lodge and cold beer; had taken an additional forty minutes. "I was official timekeeper."

Having not been ground into bloody chum by the tramp steamers loudly clanking, badly out of balance propeller; glad to simply be alive forty minutes later; I found myself preparing to net Ladd's still rambunctious fish. Net the fish with a tiny, short-handled net Jason used for wade fishing; a flimsy net, way-WAY too small for Ladd's dome-headed skinny-tailed Jack. "Provided we ever got to a point in our three-man fishing process that required a net… wherein any sort of netting device would be of any actual use!"

After the tough old Jack's final turn out of and away from the Inter Coastal Canal, out of and away from the shipping channel, inexplicably abandoning its best potential for salvation; "which contributed mightily to the likelihood of we three fishermen's salvation"; Ladd's Old Jack was ours for the netting. Ladd allowed the fish to play itself out as Captain Wagenfehr; exhibiting the patience of a Dad teaching his child to ride a bicycle; inched closer and closer to the gasping Jack. The fish came up. Jason and I saw the fish. Ladd once again offered to cut his line and release the fish. Jason and I once again told Ladd to "kiss off" and land the fish. And finally! I plunged Jason's half-pint, way too small trout net just inches below and slightly in front of the slow moving, barely wiggling, tired Old Jack. The fish was ours. Was Ladd's! Was Jason's! Was Mine! Was OUR'S!

A few quick pictures; six hundred dollars[1]; ninety days; Ladd's slick looking, fine specimen of an Old Jack Cravelle was hanging on the wall in Ladd's home in Schulenburg, Texas. "GOD! Ain't life grand? Really! I mean it! Ain't it grand?"

One large Jackfish... one big smile... **Ladd** could catch fish on a dirt toad! (2006)

Footnote: Six hundred dollars was for a mounted fiberglass replica…which I gladly paid for…and Nurse-Wife Peg and I presented to Ladd on his birthday. Ladd's exquisite EXACT replica of his Jack Cravelle was produced by legendary saltwater taxidermist and artist, Bob Harris; in Bob's Saltwater Taxidermy Studio in Houston, TX. After pictures…after all had been said and done…that was ever gonna get said and done…while out there fishin on San Antonio Bay…Son Ladd kneeled down on one knee…bent over…and literally kissed his gallant Old Jack Goodbye…then snipped the tired lightweight line…allowing the exhausted tough old fish to swim away to freedom. It was a proud moment for everyone.

Chapter Fourteen

Rachel's Fish

In this story there are three important components; the deal, the girl, and the fish. The specific nature of each corner of that triangle becomes clear as introduced. Watch for the three pieces; look for the three legs; in a trilogy that took years to unfold. Each tri was an independent leg of a bigger story; each tri folded into the next; and then the next; eventually completing. . . the whole damned story. The confluence of many complexities, resulting in one simplicity; "a big fish"; provides insight into how life really works. How it all came together and actually happened IS the story! The critical elements; deal, girl, and fish; are described in chronological order. Deal first, girl second, fish last. Got it? Two of the three; OR each of the three; could have occurred independently; could have come into being without ever combining, without becoming a triumphant trio. But that's NOT what happened! There WAS a triangle; which in turn became a real fishin story.

The Deal

This story was years in the making; therefore I will use a simple format to lay out a few historical details; "tell the beginning parts as simply as I can."

First; in February, 1987 I hired on with a business brokerage company in Austin, Texas; working fulltime as a licensed business broker; selling small, privately held businesses. "Setting."

Second; our company was licensed to do business in seven states, including Oklahoma. This fishin story actually began in Oklahoma. . . sort of. "Setting."

Third; because I was "the son of a tobacco farmer. . . with a college degree in Ag Econ"; my boss assigned me a juicy feed mill deal located in Oklahoma. Walked down the hall, plopped the file on my desk, and said; "Sell it Jim!" "Plot."

Fourth; a colleague had been working with a buyer prospect from Winters, Texas; a nice man, an interesting man, who already owned a feed mill." "Plot Thickens."

Fifth; since I was just beginning my search for a buyer for my newly assigned feed mill, I thought; "WHO on earth would make a better buyer for a feed mill…than a man who already owns a feed mill…in Winters TX?" "More Plot."

Sixth; my colleague offered to trade his broker rights to the good prospect from Winters…for ten future draft choices to be named later. "More Plotting."

Seventh; by virtue of an inner-company memo, the "nice man" from Winters was reassigned; became MY buyer prospect!

Eighth; I immediately contacted 'Mr. Winters' regarding our company's recently listed feed mill. He was interested. So…He and I traveled to Oklahoma to meet the current owners of the feed mill. Thereafter; everything moved forward in typical business brokerage fashion.

For a variety of unrelated but legitimate reasons, no deal was ever made. "None!" However! There WAS a lengthy, twelve to eighteen month negotiation process; during which time it appeared there WOULD be a deal made; a tedious process that included several offers and counteroffers and private meetings with the feed mill owners; each and every meeting requiring a repeat trip to Shawnee, Oklahoma. After many meetings and many months, Mr. Winters finally DID break down and buy me ONE inexpensive lunch; a BBQ sandwich from Shawnee's "premier lunch hot spot", The Roasted Pig. From that humble beginning Mr. Winters and I began forging a real and lasting broker-buyer bond.

Months went by. Deals came and went. Mr. Winters and I developed a "new friendship"; mostly based on mutual respect for one another's working knowledge of business transactions and the difficulty of life in general. At the time he and I met, Mr. Winters had three grammar-school-aged children; one daughter and two sons. I had two middle-school-aged sons.

Years went by. Nurse-Wife Peg and I were blessed with a third son. Mr. Winters and I met in Big Springs, Texas to look at another deal. Nurse-Wife Peg and Mr. Winters were introduced for the first time in the dining room of the Drury Inn, in Big Springs. Nurse-Wife Peg was carrying our infant son John James in a bassinette when she arrived at the breakfast table.

Somewhere along the line Mr. Winters and I began calling one another or meeting somewhere out there in the business world for lunch, happy hour, or dinner. Ours was a warm and blossoming relationship; based on mutual politics, reverence for our families, and common interests in buying and selling small businesses. When I had a tough deal, I called Mr. Winters to get his learned opinion. When he had a tough deal, he called me to get an independent, third party, objective opinion.

Our relationship grew by the year, and by 1995 or 1996 Mr. Winters and I had become "solid friends". Our wives met somewhere along the way. On several occasions, while traveling in their part of the world, I stayed overnight with Mr. and Mrs. Winter's; in Winters, Texas! Oddly enough I had never met Mr. Winter's three children; nor had he met my older sons; only our infant son JJ.

"Not until one day in Menard Texas." Mr. Winters had recently bought a small getaway ranch in Menard and wanted me to meet him at his new ranch and give him my honest opinion of his latest acquisition; which I did. But not before inquiring into the propriety of bringing along both my older sons; both currently attending college; both home for the summer. Since both older boys loved fishin, they jumped at the chance to travel with me to Menard and try their luck fishin in the San Saba River that passed through Mr. Winter's new ranch. Once there, both boys were politely introduced to my business associate and friend, Mr. Winters. The four of us had a casual lunch at a local BBQ. During lunch Mr. Winters asked my sons; one a junior, the other a freshman at Texas A&M; if they would mind "keeping an eye out for" and "looking after" Mr. Winter's daughter; who was planning to attend A&M that fall as a freshman. Mr. Winters' fatherly request resulted in one perfunctory and "unimpressive" phone call by diligent son Chris; "end of obligation."

More years went by. Oldest Son Chris graduated from A&M and headed to law school at Texas Tech, in Lubbock. "Tic Toc!" Second Son Ladd headed to Lubbock to join Older Brother Chris; ostensibly to attend grad school. "Tic Toc!" Third Son John James moved up the scholastic ladder within Blanco's 2-A school system. Mr. Winters' three children graduated high school and enrolled in A & M. "Tic Toc!" My aging Dad died. Mr. Winter's aging Dad died. I prospered. Mr. Winters prospered. Mr. Winter's and my "long distance friendship" continued as a "pleasant aside" to our independent careers. "Tic Toc!" Our business meetings continued. And even though Mr. Winters and I worked hard at "closing" the sale of several deals; "at least half-a-dozen"; for one reason or another; usually good reasons; Mr. Winters and I, seemed destined to close NO deals. "Tic Toc!"

More years went by. Mr. Winters and I expanded our relationship to occasionally include his wife or mine; enjoying rare but pleasant outings as a trio. Both sets of Texas parents; "Blanco and Winters"; were devoted to our kids, involved in good careers, active in our communities, and enjoying our Texas life style. Life was good. Mr. Winter's daughter and two sons were continuing along their successful trails of life. Our children were one item Mr. Winters and I faithfully brought up at every business meeting. He and I shared many laughs and minor worries relating to our six children, but life was generally progressing nicely for all younger members of both families.

By 2000, Mr. Winters and I had endured twelve years of intermittently working together; attempting, in vain, to close on the sale of several small businesses; sometimes coming close to closing the deal; sometimes not. Life moved forward. When Mr. Winters and I met for our routine lunches, we seemed to talk more and more about our six kids, and less and less about our potential for doing a big deal.

Eventually it came to pass that Mr. Winters contacted me and told me he was contemplating buying one or two reasonably priced businesses for one or more of his college educated, grown children. The exact type of business was left open to my abilities to search. I searched my heart out based on instructions given me by my trusted friend Mr. Winters. As a result of his stated intentions, and my diligent work, I disclosed to Mr. Winters, met with him about, toured and showed to Mr. Winters, a dozen reasonable candidate businesses. But NONE met his rigid criteria; none fit precisely enough to bring about a "closing". I continued looking; basing my efforts on the premise I was helping someone I cared for on a personal basis.

The Girl

Indeed; several years HAD gone by! It was late fall 2001! Thirteen years since Mr. Winters and I first met up in Shawnee, Oklahoma; "to show him the feed mill." Recent efforts on Mr. Winter's behalf had focused on finding "a nice little business" for his daughter, as he put it; "Something to gainfully occupy her bright mind." I dutifully showed Mr. Winters every last and lonely business I thought might suit his needs, but alas none would do; "same old NONE results." Meanwhile; Mr. Winters and his lovely wife, Mrs. Winters, built a spacious new ranch home on their family ranch near Clyde, Texas and moved back to their childhood hometown. Mr. Winters briefly ceased his active search for any type business; even one for his grown daughter. Consumed with the rigors of building his new ranch home, frequency of our business meetings diminished; as did the volume of our direct phone contact. But! We kept in touch; "both of us were just busy…perhaps even a little distracted." Here and there and yon; in a variety of subtle ways; a couple of our grown kids were going through a tough time.

"Tough time?" Oldest Son Chris had graduated from law school and become engaged. Son Chris's fiancée of eighteen months suddenly got cold feet and returned his engagement ring; told Chris she didn't want to marry him. Son Ladd was forced to move back to Blanco for a few months; prior to attempting a "Re-Launch"!

Having recently been abandoned by a young male friend who "parted her company in favor of seeking HIS fortune in California"; Mr. Winters' daughter had moved to Austin "in search of HER future…and happiness"?

Life trekked forward. One morning in late January 2002, just as I returned to my truck following duck hunting, my cell phone rang. It was my friend, Mr. Winters. He surprised me by inviting me to join him for lunch in Fredericksburg; "about an hour west of my duck lease." Mr. Winters insisted that I hurry; but DID encourage me to clean up a bit and change clothes. Said he had "important people" with him he wanted me to meet; "new people" I had never met. I agreed to hurry.

When I first walked in the trendy new brew pub on Main Street, Fredericksburg, I spotted Mr. Winters at a front table; seated with an attractive young lady and a middle-aged man. After a brief "Hello", I focused politely on the important new people Mr. Winters wanted me to meet; Mr. Winters CPA-Friend and Mr. Winters' oldest child, Rachel. As the four of us exchanged cordial words of inquiry; a lovely young lady, an engaging and gorgeous young lady of twenty-four, emerged before my eyes; "Where moments before…had sat a total stranger." Our large, wooden, brew pub table was adorned with fresh pitchers of cold beer and a festive mood set in; "Jim…This is my oldest child…Rachel. Rachel…this is my good friend…the man I've told you about …the Austin business broker…Jim." With that succinct introduction, for those of us involved, life began taking a new turn; a new race in life to run; put there by altered circumstances.

After introductions and pleasant small talk, Mr. Winters told me he had purchased a business in Fredericksburg; and that he and his daughter Rachel and his CPA-Friend had closed on the sale that very morning. Mr. Winters further explained that he didn't feel comfortable buying a business located so near my home; "thirty-five miles in rural Texas was considered practically in my back yard"; with his daughter Rachel and CPA-Friend being so deeply involved, without giving me a proper heads up; even though the business was NOT one of my 'For Sale' businesses.

Lunch went forward. More cold beer was consumed. Mr. Winters' Lovely Daughter Rachel; "did I mention she was gorgeous… highly intelligent… incredibly capable… a budding young businesswoman… enormously energetic… captivatingly conversational… AND recent honor graduate of Texas A&M"?; excused herself to go to the lady's room. Mr. Winters CPA-Friend departed for another meeting. Alone; Mr. Winters and I began reminiscing about good old brokering days gone by.

While the two of us, Mr. Winters and I, were waltzing down Memory Lane, it became apparent that Mr. Winters was, among other things, relieved that his daughter Rachel had a new business; "to take up slack…in her evolving life." Glad his daughter Rachel would have; "limited time for pining over recent changes in her life." Unsolicited comments by Mr. Winters that seemed to reflect a smidgeon of worry? Semi gregarious and somewhat an extrovert, I felt compelled to mention that I TOO had similarly been relieved as a worried parent. Updating and informing Mr. Winters that our wonderful number one son Chris had recently become UN engaged; an unlikely turn of events that had been weighing heavily on Chris' mind.

My relieved parental comments were followed by relieved parental comments by Mr. Winters; then another exchange of relieved parental comments; then more. Fatherly relief poured out like carelessly spilled beer; of which, by then, there may have been one too many pitchers; beer daintily consumed from frosty cold mugs by Me, Mr. Winters, Lovely Daughter Rachel, and CPA-Friend. BUT! "Hear me and hear me WELL!" Beer goggles had NO part in my first, or my second, or my longer lasting permanent opinions of Mr. Winters' Lovely Daughter, Rachel. "First impressions and opinions OFTEN prove accurate…ever read Malcolm Gladwell's book 'Blink'?" And exactly WHY am I so adamant about my first impression of Daughter Rachel being an accurate one? Because today I have more than one beer sodden luncheon on which to base my lasting opinion. "That's right Bubba…MUCH more!"

It was six months before I next SAW Mr. Winters' Lovely Daughter Rachel; meantime I was hearing bits and pieces, a word here and there, about "progress she was making with her new business". Then; lo and behold, as if by magic, On Fourth of July Weekend, 2002, she was standing on MY rock patio in Blanco, Texas! Lovely Daughter Rachel had been brought to our Blanco home by Oldest Son Chris. To participate in what was, for Son Chris and Mr. Winters' Daughter Rachel, their "official meet the parents date"! "HOW SO…inquiring minds want to know?"

"WELL! It's simple. Mr. Winters and I HAD…at long last…finally set about "closing" ONE deal…a masterful piece of fatherly brokering-match making! It all began right there in Fredericksburg at that big wooden table littered with wet beer mugs. While Rachel was gone to the bathroom…after CPA-Friend left for parts unknown…while Mr. Winters and I were pouring out our feelings of relief regarding our adult children…Chris and Rachel, innocent and idle chin chat had set in…filling a void…mere musings…that suddenly took an awesome turn. One idle comment led to another. Questions were asked. An innocent idea was mentioned. Nods were exchanged. Smiles were exhibited. Rachel returned. History was altered."

"Yes! Both doting Moms immediately got involved…TOO!"

"Yes! We four parents…acting in concert…DID see to it that Son Chris was given Daughter Rachel's private phone number. Yes! Yes! Yes! The wheels of romance were intentionally set in motion."

And what happened after that, according to Paul Harvey's "rest of the story", was then, and is now, up to God Almighty! One year later; Fourth of

July, 2003; on our same Blanco rock patio, Son Chris proposed marriage to Lovely Daughter Rachel; only daughter of rancher and entrepreneur Mr. Winters; oldest son of school nurse Peg and business broker Me! And on December 13th, 2003; in Abilene, Texas; nearly seventeen YEARS after the Oklahoma feed mill, the deal; Lovely Daughter Rachel and Sir Lancelot Son Christopher were joined in Holy Matrimony. "The girl…Hopefully…Forever!"

Mr. Winters, whose first name is actually Murray, and I stood before no less than five hundred spellbound guests and raised a glass of fine Champagne to our fatherly brokered couple; his daughter, my son; the ONLY deal Friend Murray and I ever worked on together that EVER closed! "Also the BEST deal either of us EVER closed"; or so Murray and I claimed during our rambunctious wedding reception Champagne toast. An important concept Friend Murray and I continue to believe deep in our happy-go-lucky Grandfathers-In-Common hearts. Pause. Give it a bit of thought. Murray's daughter. My son. Murray's grandsons are my grandsons. Forever! "Bubba! That's a deal…and a girl…worth tellin about!" So what about the fish?

The Fish

The wedding was in Abilene; "a fine wedding." Nurse-Wife Peg and I chartered a Greyhound bus to carry guests from Blanco up to Abilene and back. Peg and I hosted a rehearsal dinner at the Texas Land and Cattle Company Restaurant in Abilene. We decorated the private party room with hunting and fishing paraphernalia. On THE morning of Groom Chris and Bride Rachel's wedding, thirteen of us men folk from the wedding party, dressed in full blown camo and battle gear, gathered in the hotel lobby, then drove twenty miles to Murray's family ranch to go duck hunting on a large private lake. Everyone in the wedding party killed ducks; some of us killed many ducks; "Check out pictures of the hotel marquee!" Four days later Bride Rachel and Groom Chris were honeymooning in Cabo San Lucas, Mexico! And while I am NOT privileged to everything our happy young couple may have done on their honeymoon; I AM told their activities included two euphoric days of chartered fishing. So! For the purpose of completing my fish story, I will disclose pertinent details shared with ME by Groom Chris; "under strict client-lawyer privilege."

As a Lovely Lass growing up in Winters; Rachel learned her three Rs, studied music, was a cheerleader, got a good, small-town education in public schools, and played basketball WELL! "God only knows what else Rachel learned as a young girl…I never raised a girl…I don't know?"

Rachel is tall and pretty; also very athletic. In high school she was an All State basketball player; as were both her parents; "Good gene pool from which to start a herd of grandkids…Huh?" Friend Murray, whose ancestors were Texas cattle breeders; and I, whose ancestors were Missouri mule traders; were inclined to openly consider the gene pool qualification thing during our match making pre-planning. Daughter Rachel comes from an educated family; a spiritual and Christian family; has a million good attributes and character traits that easily qualify her as a prime candidate for becoming anyone's daughter-in-law. Son Chris, ditto; as to qualifying for and becoming anyone's son-in-law! "ANYONE'S!" "Either way!" "They were a perfect match!"

However! And this WAS a big thing! On the day Bride Rachel married our son, she DID possess one tiny but glaring flaw; an incongruity in her otherwise perfectness which Bridegroom Chris quickly set about rectifying. Incredibly, Rachel was stigmatized by one, huge, painfully sad, shortcoming; a vital personal experience sadly lacking from her otherwise cosmopolitan and diverse background. Prenuptially speaking; there existed one awful omission from Lovely Bride Rachel's resume of lifetime experiences, from which she had been too long allowed to suffer. And because Son Chris was the person HE was; as 'Groom Chris' he felt compelled to immediately set in motion events that would provide healing salve, to be applied to new Bride Rachel's sad situation; to provide the soothing balm Rachel required to finally make her whole. And exactly "WHAT" you may ask was the critical experience missing from perfect Bride Rachel's persona? Easy! She had never been FISHING! That's right! "Hard to imagine...Huh?"

Some families play and sing music; as a family. Some families enjoy theatre, or art museums, or tour famous landmarks; attending as a family. Other families enjoy taking communal European vacations or exotic trips to far off lands like Africa or Asia or Japan; as a family. Many families here in Texas enjoy simple hunting and fishing, or camping; as a family; "on any available venue." Not so Bride Rachel's Winters-Clyde family; not so regarding hunting and fishing on ANY venue! I realize how difficult it may be for readers to fathom; but there ARE lost souls here on earth that have never known the pleasures of fishing. God help me for disclosing such a sad truth; but there really ARE! Lovely Rachel came to us here in Blanco, SO sorely deprived; SO severely inhibited; such a lost soul, regarding fishing. We righteously feared for her completeness.

"But pray for Rachel no more!"

"That which was missing was found!"

"That which needed changing was changed!"

"That which needed fixin was fixed!"

"And like Eve and the apple...that which had never before been tasted...was tasted and enjoyed!"

"Enjoyed...Along with other things about which Lovely Bride Rachel may not have had prior knowledge…other things she may have ALSO refrained from previously enjoying…that is…refrained from previously enjoying…in her entirely Christian and wholesome life…until she went on her honeymoon with Groom Chris!"

"STOP IT JIM!"

"OK Peg!"

So! Son Chris, as Son Chris has had a lifelong tendency to do, soon fixed ever thang for his Bride Rachel! And! "Just as I…for ONE…maintained it most certainly SHOULD have been…fishing WAS immediately…WAY prior to the lovely couple's wedding day…placed ON the Honeymooner's honeymoon agenda!" And here, a brief summary, precisely where The Fish came into our fishin story; "A true story…about the big one that did NOT get away!"

On December 17th 2003, four days after their big Abilene wedding, at eight in the morning, sharp; Groom Chris and Lovely Bride Rachel boarded a private charter fishing boat, Minerva II; a large, big game, sport fishing charter, home ported out of Cabo San Lucas. Aboard were; The Captain, First Mate Pime, and Deckhand Jose; all three 100% attentive and accommodating to their star-struck client couple; Groom Chris and Bride Rachel. In route to the nearest fishing grounds, a hot spot fishing grounds VERY near to shore; "compared to most places in Continental USA"; the charter boat's early morning cruise took the perpetually smiling Honeymooners near the "still standin in the middle of nowhere" movie set used in filming Brad Pitt's movie "Troy". The movie set could be clearly seen from a few hundred yards offshore by Groom Chris and Bride Rachel. Movie set details far ashore that were observed, in all their glory and splendor, as the Texas Honeymooners sat comfortably aboard the pristine decks of the Minerva. Chris was ecstatic. So much so he called me the night before their charter trip to share the excitement of his fishing plans; "Chris knew I would be green with envy."

Within one mile of shore, the indigo Pacific was measured by the boat's depth finder and discovered to be in excess of eleven hundred (1100) feet; "That's deep Bubba!" Following an announcement to the Client Couple Honeymooners that the two lovebirds could expect to catch a variety of large game fish, Chris said the crew immediately tied on extremely large Rattle Trap ™ lures as bait; "To go seeking Rachel's first fish EVER!"

"That's Right…First fish EVER! NOT…First Fish of the Day! First Fish EVER! In her entire lovely life! Really…CAN you imagine…A married woman seeking her first fish? NO…You CANNOT imagine! You're thinking; What the Hell DID they do out there in Winters…besides play basketball and raise good kids?"

Rattle Trap ™ lures you and I are accustomed to using might be the size of your thumb; the honeymooner's lures were eight inches long, with finger-sized bronze hooks. The Minerva's motors were set at trolling speed, and their huge lures were fished forty feet straight down; held in place by downriggers masterfully placed out either side of the trolling boat; rigged just so by highly skilled Deckhand Jose and First Mate Pime. "Big baits running deep!" "Texas Honeymooners happy!" "Deckhand and First Mate attentive!" "The couple's day nearing perfect...then...Zzzzzzzzzzzzziiiiinnnnnng!"

The biggest and newest looking of the charter boat's huge reels screamed bloody murder. *"El Pescado A! El Pescado A! Pesca! Senora Pimiento (most recently Senora, no longer Senorita)! Senora Pimiento (Pepper)! Senora Pimiento! Grande Pesca La Liana! Es El Caleinta! Undelea Senora! Undelea! Presto Senora!"*

A huge, and at that point unknown, species of fish was robbing Bride Rachel's, "Senora Pimiento's", monster-sized Penn reel of its treasure of heavy monofilament line! A thousand words and loving hugs of encouragement from Groom Chris, a bit of sweet sweat lost forever at sea by Bride Rachel, a swift slash of a long gaff in the hands of skilled Deckhand Jose, and the grande el pescado was dragged aboard. Before their day was done; before the sun set on the greatest fishing day of their "Just Married" lives; the first day EVER fishing for Bride Rachel; Groom Chris and Bride Rachel had a sport cruiser icebox full of pescado; two large tuna, two medium Wahoo, and seven extra large mahi mahi (dorado). But! There was only one HUGE pescado; only ONE monstrous gigantes el pescado; only one FIRST FISH in Bride Rachel's lovely life! That's correct! Non-fishing, "but game for anything moral...or not TOO unhealthy"; Bride Rachel, "willing to try anything at least once to please her new Groom"; had just landed her VERY FIRST fish of her otherwise entirely normal life! "No ordinary fish either!"

Nope! No way! Instead of a puny bluegill, or catfish, or bass, or crappie, or perch; like most of us experience catching as a "First Fish"; Bride Rachel caught a real trophy. An enormous Wahoo that was weighed a few times, tape measured twice, and photographed a million times. The results were staggering! A lifetime fish; that was an incredible sixty-eight (68) inches long, nose to tippy tail; seventy-eight (78) pounds, flesh and bone inclusive. The entire village of Cabo San Lucas, ALL the Native People, dined well that night; including our bright-eyed and wonderstruck Bride and Groom.[1]

---

[1]Footnote; two years later, Nurse-Wife Peg and I presented the happy young couple a perfect fiberglass replica of Rachel's Fish.

Bride Rachel's first fish...a Wahoo... Cabo San Lucas, Mexico... Honeymoon with Chris! (2003)

One first fish... many to come... **Bride Rachel** and **Groom Chris** went to Costs Rica for their fifth anniversary. Both young marrieds were having a go at cathin' the big ones!!

Chapter Fifteen

What Glenny's Caught "Fishin"

July 1977. One of the pleasures inherent to the concept of fishin is anticipation; "NOT knowing ahead of time what we might catch!" That concept; "the experience of catchin the unexpected"; came into play when a good buddy and I and both our wives went trout fishin. My good buddy's name was David. We caught a trophy trout but there was more to it than that; "David's wife Glennys caught somethin big none of us were expectin to catch." Since my buddy David will be telling this story, allow me to provide a little background.

David and I first met way back in 1953 in first grade. Eight kids from our high school graduating class of 1965 began first grade together and

David & his dog **Soloman**, **Jim**, and **Chris**, goose hunting at Iatan Power Plant, Weston, MO. (1985)

attended all twelve years together! During our school years, Buddy David and I occasionally stayed overnight at one another's house; a convenience during the "one car per family" 1960s. By the time high school rolled around David and I weren't best friends, but did play varsity football together on our 1964 championship team; we were good buddies. David was a track star, competing for ribbons and medals all the way to State. By our senior year David's circle of friends had grown to include Danny; another track star from nearby small town, Platte City. Two young men from small rival schools who just happened to become friends during boring hours spent together waiting between track events. "There was no such thing as girls track back in those days…or David and Danny might have found something more interesting to occupy their time."

Track Stars David and Danny loved bragging about the year they both went to State and competed against one another head-to-head. In May, 1965 ever body from both small schools graduated and scattered; in pursuit of life, liberty, and happiness.

My Buddy David and his Buddy Danny reestablished their friendship a few years later when Danny returned to Platte County and bought a home out in the countryside near Weston. But! Former track star buddies, David and Danny, encountered each other MOST often when both men happened to be invited to social events at my house!

David and his lovely bride Glennys were married in June 1965; "one week out of high school." David went to work as a sheet metal specialist for Trans World Airlines. David eventually rose to the rank of Supervisor at TWA's overhaul and maintenance facility near Platte City; where KCI Airport is located today. I was gone from Platte County for eight years. As a result of our diverse trials, travails and travels, David and I saw little-to-nothing of one another. About the time First Wife Jen-Jen and I arrived back in Weston in 1973, David and his bride Glennys departed on a three-year, overseas assignment sent there voluntarily by TWA.

David's specialized job skills were in demand in Saudi Arabia. In Saudi, David received incredible pay, bonuses, and tax benefits. He was able to salt away enough savings to return and buy a twenty acre tract of land and build his sweet wife Glennys a contemporary home in rural Platte County. "David was living his dream."

Buddy David was extremely proud of his accomplishment of buying land and building a house. Growing up with me in Weston as a wild and wooly youth, David never dreamed he could manage such a feat. David was usually first among us to point out that he carried a mild chip on his nice guy shoulder. David was often heard to say; "I haven't done too bad for a sharecropper's son...Huh? Whadaya think Jimmy? I got it made don't I...My shit don't stink no more?"

Comments such as those were David's way of expressing genuine pride in his middleclass status. David enjoyed drawing attention to himself and the subject. David's parents were indeed sharecroppers. But! They were also kind, loving, decent, honest and hardworking people who raised a family of five; four sons and one daughter. David was an all around nice guy. He always fit in. Nearly everyone in our graduating class of 1965 liked David; most of our classmates considered themselves David's friend. "Why?"

Bull Shoals, MO. White River Dam in background. (1977)

David was a hard worker, had a good sense of humor, was above average in intelligence, knew "a little bit" about everything, and knew "quite a lot" about a few things. David was interesting to know and share time with, IF you could tolerate his hardheadedness and contentious teasing. If David himself had not gone around telling anyone who would listen, no one would have guessed or cared either way that he was in fact; "The son of a tobacco tenant." But because David WAS, he enjoyed reminding people of it; so he could point out the contrast.

David loved telling people; "Me and Jimmy are good friends...have been since first grade"; which of course was true. During the late sixties David told people; "My Buddy Jim...is a student down at that university in Columbia!" By the early seventies David could be heard telling people; "My Buddy Jim...is an officer in the Marines serving in Nam!" And by 1977 David loved telling people; "My BEST Buddy Jim... owns Game Hill (a hunting preserve and sportsman's country club)." David loved my new business, Game Hill, and everything it represented.

One day while David and I were out hunting together, enjoying Game Hill, a bit of irony popped up. Both of us suddenly focused on the realization that during the time David's parents had "once upon a time" toiled as tobacco tenants for First Wife Jen-Jen's Grandfather, back in 1957, I had spent the night with Buddy David in what was then his parent's sharecropper house. A humble, white-frame farmhouse, which twenty years later was occupied by MY sharecropper Leroy; on First Wife Jen-Jen's and my tobacco farm. A farm Jen-Jen and I inherited from her grandfather; a farm my new business partner and I renamed Game Hill. Mere yards from the old but still serviceable farmhouse, set Game Hill's newly remodeled, fancy clubhouse; that David's Mom, Jackie, had once-upon-a-time used as her henhouse; in which to keep safe her precious four-dozen laying hens; from which she gathered eggs to feed me and my ten year buddy David breakfast! David LOVED telling people that particular "twenty-year connection" story! David especially enjoyed sharing his former son-of-a-tenant-tales with Game Hill's well-heeled, big city, celebrity clients; out and about seeking "a quiet day in the country" at Game Hill.

David told people; "Jim's the ONLY person in this whole town...that ALWAYS treated me with respect. Jim don't give a peach pit WHERE I come from (heritage)!"

There were plenty of others who respected David, and treated him well, but he focused on me. When David returned from Saudi Arabia in 1976, our initial re-contact occurred at Game Hill. Good Buddy David drove up, stepped out of his spanking new four wheel drive pickup; "with lockout hubs"; brandished a shiny, new, double barrel shotgun, for effect and high drama, and within easy hearing distance of no less than two dozen shocked Game Hill patrons announced his Good Buddy hunting intentions. "I'm gonna shoot the Dog Ass who owns this mother lover (Game Hill)!" From that moment of "genuine male bonding" forward, there occurred a rapid rebuilding of good old times. Male camaraderie, marked by bellicose bragging and boisterous teasing, were the trademark of David's and my broader, genuine relationship. Both of us, David and I, loved telling our stories. I would tell David my Viet Nam stories; David would tell me his Saudi Arabia stories. According to David; "From our stories...it was hard to tell which country was the most messed up!"

Immediately upon returning to Missouri, David bought a full-blown, expensive membership to Game Hill. That same year David and his Dad, Owen, moonlighted by growing a small crop of tobacco. Naturally David and his Dad became patrons of my family's tobacco warehouse. That's an important tidbit of trivia! During the mid-1970s, no matter how badly First Wife Jen-Jen may have wanted to squelch David's and my reconstituted 1960s friendship, she didn't dare. "Why?"

I would never have allowed First Wife Jen-Jen to interfere with, or cut me off from, ANY customer or client of either of my thriving businesses. First Wife Jen-Jen was aware of my clearly stated and formidable ground rule. As a result, she eventually ceased her shallow effort to "DIS" Buddy David. First Wife Jen-Jen instead continued musing, carping, and generally discouraging what she considered; "Poor (unfortunate) Jim's out of place friendship with such unattractive people (David and Glennys)." First Wife Jen-Jen's exact words; NEVER my words NOR my opinion!

In July 1977, twenty years after I spent the night with David as his fourth grade buddy, twelve years after track stars David and Danny competed at State, David and his sweet wife Glennys; "and three hundred other fine folks"; attended an extra sad funeral in Platte County, MO. A heartbreaking funeral; for the deceased wife of a man, who, by 1977, had become David's and my mutual friend; Danny. Following the "total downer" funeral services, David and Glennys joined a host of other friends gathered at Danny's home. A tiny home located one mile down a gravel road from First Wife Jen-Jen's and my rural home, just north of Weston. And thus it came to pass, our trio of high school buddies; David, Danny, and Me; were thrown back together. And through sharing Danny's great tragedy, grew closer than ever before. Reunited by the triangulation of our personal histories, our special interests, and our lives' random meanderings; we three young men, sharing routine contact within the community, were regrettably catapulted into a much closer relationship by horrific events surrounding Danny's deceased wife's gruesome death. We three "young married men with kids" experienced a renewed, strengthened, three-way relationship; culminating and reaching its natural peak immediately after deceased wife Suzy's funeral. "Did I say gruesome death? Danny's dead wife Suzy drank a can of Drano! She lingered for months before repeating her particularly horrific act of self-destruction a second time and killing herself! Can you imagine the pain...the gore...the suffering? I had never seen anything quite like it."

Definitely a terrible event, dead wife Suzy's bloody suicide became THE bonding tie for our renewed three-man, he-man trio; David, Danny, and Me. As a direct result of close contact and shared tragedy, it came to pass that Danny was invited to join David and me on a trout fishing expedition David and I had previously been planning with our wives down to White River, MO. The decision to extend an invitation to Danny was intended to help cheer up our sad mutual friend. "David and I were bending over backwards trying to make things better for Danny...doing anything we could to help. Danny was hurting. BAD! His two Momma-less children broke our he-man hearts."

Following here is a narrative description of our three-man, two-woman fishin trip; an epic story, recorded from memory by David; told from his point of view. Minor parts of David's rendition are repetitive. Some of David's language is explicit and dark; some a tad vulgar. But! David's account IS an accurate account; a truthful description of real life events that occurred on our trout fishin trip to the Ozarks. Two sojourners; on a male bonding, brotherhood building, "simple fishin trip"; that just happened to include a benevolent, mercy bestowing, compassionate, and last minute invitation for Widower Danny to join David and me and our wives. And, as David said when asked to retell his version of this story; "The shit Jimmy wrote down IS verbatim! You know...ex-ackly what I said. You know...ver-bait-him! Oh Hell...You know what I mean!" Buddy David IS, in fact, quoted here...VERBATIM! SERIOUS WARNING! There is significant BLUE LANGUAGE beyond this point! Proceed at your own risk. "For Open Minded Adults...ONLY...OR...Closely Supervised Minors...ONLY! The faint of heart should stick with Alice In Wonderland or Pinocchio!"

****

David's Fishin Story[1] ...About MY Fish!

SO! You've been forewarned. GO! The words from here on are David's."

"Danny and Jim was acquainted from back in high school days. Danny was a star football player...the Pirates (Platte City) fullback...Jim was our (Weston's) quarterback. Them two was hard dicked (staunch) rivals even back then...but we were all friends too. Danny and Jim had real respect for each other...even back in high school. They knew each other purty damned well. Jim and Danny BOTH dated Jenny during high school... although...I never understood why either of them two studs would ask Jenny out?"

"When Jim got home from the Marines...Danny lived just up the road...bout a mile outta town. So Danny and Jim become friends all over again. Them two took to fishin...huntin frogs and mushrooms...playin poker...gettin drunk on beer...did all kinds of good shit together. Jim liked Danny...and Jenny liked Danny's first wife Suzy. Them FOUR...Danny and Suzy...Jim and Jenny...took to doin all kinds of shit together too... cookin out...goin to fancy restaurants and parties...all kinds of shit. Then Suzy up and kilt her self! Jim was one of Suzy's paul-bury-ers. Meantime...me and Jim was plannin a big fishin trip down to the Ozarks...with our two wenches (wives). But us two...me and Jim...we decided to invite Danny along...totally sperm of the moment (spontaneous). After that awful funeral and all...we

---

[1]Footnote; Telling this story "after the fact", David used dozens of colloquial terms, euphemisms, and "uniquely David" figures of speech to describe (on audio tape) what happened on our simple fishin trip. Many of David's colorful quotes have been shown in italics; (with parenthesis following); "to help define David's meaning." All grammar and phonetic spellings are David's. What is written here is precisely as it was spoken; with the notable exception of omitting, by substitution, in EVERY instance, David's proclivity for using the 'F' word. "I HAD to do something?"

We kicked back... caught a million trout... "and seen some real sights!" (1997)

figgered it would help cheer Danny's sad ass up!"

"We drove down to The Ozarks in Jenny's[2] big new Olds 98. It was the nicest car in our group. It easy held (comfortably accommodated) all five of us...Jim and Jenny... Glennys and Me...and Danny. We went to Gaston's White River Resort...just below Bull Shoals Dam. We reserved ourselves three cabins in a row at Gaston's. It was a great lodge...right on the river. You could watch trout feedin and jumpin from the dinin room window...while you ate! We stopped ever thirty minutes drivin down...so Jenny could pee. GOD! That woman peed a lot! We drank a lot of beer on the way...ceptin fer Jim...he was drivin. At first...ever body was havin a great time. Danny even got to laughin. I think Danny was relieved the shit was over. You know...the shit...Suzy's sufferin...her death...the funeral...all of it...the shit...was over."

"The first day fishin...me and Glennys went out with a guide in one boat...Jim and Jenny went with a guide in another boat...Danny went by his self and a guide. Them guides would take three fishermen per boat...but Danny said he wanted to be by his self. All of us...in three separate boats...caught our limit the first day. More than our limit really! Jim caught THREE limits and iced em down. Jim's guide didn't give a rat's ass (wasn't concerned) bout no damned limits. The second day we did exactly the same thing. You Know...Used three boats and all. We was havin a great time...catchin more damned trout than any of us EVER seen! Them guides really knew their shit (experts)."

"At night...after fishin...all five of us got together for fancy dinners over

---

[2]Footnote; Anyone who has read any of my books, knows that I intermittently and interchangeably refer to my first wife as; "First Wife Jen-Jen" or "EX Jen-Jen". There were reasons why "First Wife Jen-Jen" became "EX Jen-Jen". Reading this simple fishin story; "which IS a good fishin story"; might, in addition to making you laugh, shed a little light on the experience of my "First" becoming my "EX"!

at the lodge dinin room. We drank...ate big steaks...kicked back...let our hair down...had us a frickin ball mind you (a 'copulating-ly' good time)! None of us WASN'T havin a good time (WERE)! The food was great! The fishin was great! We was throwin down stiff martinis (drinking) like there was no tomorrow...talkin bout the good ole days back in high school. Danny come outta his shell...he was smilin and laughin...talkin and carryin on like in the old days...definitely feelin better."

"After dinner the second night...when we all started walkin back to our cabins... Jenny started draggin ass...hangin back. She was out of it (tipsy) on gin and yakkin with Danny...just them two...one on one. Jim and me...we was walkin out front...way ahead ...busy plannin our last day of fishin. Glennys was walkin alone...not far behind Jim and me. Jenny and Danny was walkin slow...like runny shit oozin down the cracka yer ass (moseying). Them two...Jenny and Danny...fell further behind...still followin...but gettin farther back."

"Me and Jim...we decided that come mornin...we would go out with the best guide. We wanted to go after a trophy. Jim and me planned on skinnin back the crap (cutting to the chase) by takin OFF our piss ant (small & typical) lures...and tyin ON ball bustin (large & atypical) lures! Fishin strictly for trophies! No more ice chest fillers (small trout) for me and Jim...we done had our selfs a belly full of that cheesy crap (were tiring of the mundane). We wanted to catch a gut strainin wall hanger (heavy trophy). Me and Jim decided...the women should go with Danny...three in a boat... and catch more eatin size trout...little shits bout this long (gesturing 8-12 inches)."

"When we got back to our cabins...me and Jim told the three stragglers our plan. Glennys announced she was tired of fishin! Two days in a row...gonna be three...was a lot for a woman...even a fishin woman like Glennys. She wanted to spend her last day loungin by the pool...restin...doin idle shit. Quicker 'en a bitin gnat (fast)...Jenny chimed in...Me Too! Danny surprised ever body by chimin in...Me Too! Said he had zippo interest in doin more fishin (none). Wasn't hankerin (wanting) to spend his day floatin round in a crowded boat with me and Jim...probably catchin nothin! Me and Jim was full blowed aware (cognizant) our odds was slim...different methods...different lures...different fishin spots and all. Danny said a day sunnin by the pool...just relaxin... sounded good to his pale ass."

"Danny was fallin backwards happy (incapacitated with joy). Me and Jim didn't give a flimsy flyin fart (one iota) what our women did! Ever body was happy...doin what they wanted. And me and Jim knowed for sure what WE was gonna do! Our plans was simple. Tie on big lures...go for lunkers!

What time our guide was leavin was the only thing me and Jim cared about…and THAT time was five sharp…first light…the crack of dawn. When daylight come…we was there…me and Jim was there…out of our funky smellin cabins…stumblin around in greasy fog (thick)…our women still sleepin…Danny still sleepin. Sleepin and eatin…or eatin and sleepin…take yer pick…that was the only damned thang Danny and our wenches (wives) wanted to do…and that ain't much."

"Me and Jim's routine was set too…fish all mornin then have lunch. Then fish again til five. Usually we pulled up to a burger stand in the boat…or packed lunch and ate on a dry sandbar. We made the most of our time on the river. We fished til five…or later…IF we could talk our guide into doin such. Our wives didn't expect to see nothin of our fat asses until five. No way was no body quittin early THAT day…it was our LAST day! There weren't no way me and Jim would come in early…not without a trophy! We told ever swingin dick in the bunch (our group) to sleep in…and don't bother lookin for us til dinner! It was our routine…You Know!"

"Right after lunch…bout one…me and Jim's guide made a long run ALL the way up to the dam. We still didn't have one stinkin trout! But we wasn't discouraged. We knowed we was in for a looooong day…usin big lures. Me and Jim wanted a trophy…or nothin. On his first cast after lunch…his VERY first…Jim hooked a HUGE mother lover (good fish). Jim was usin a whole giant night crawler…a real one…a live one…hooked on a lead headed jig. Jim cast the whole damn mess…the worm AND heavy jig…as far as humanly possible…up into boilin white water comin out the bottom of the dam. There was a big DANGER sign up there. Boats wasn't allowed no closer than a hundred yards! But when our boat slowed down…Jim stood up…looked at me…gimme that shit eatin grin of his…and cast his giant glob of shit (bait) near about to the dam (a long way)!"

"There was a big splash…then…ZZZZZZZZZZZIIIING! Out went Jim's line. He done hooked a trophy alright! A huge mother! A big ole sow! Jim played her like a drum…fer twenty minutes! He was frothin at the mouth. I never seen Jim so damn excited! He didn't know whether to shit green or go stone blind…or both! He was smilin and yellin. I've NEVER seen Jimmy so frickin worked up! NO SHIT! When he finally got his fish in the boat, he just collapsed. Flopped down like a beached whale…yellin and laughin. Our guide put Jim's trout in the live well…VERY carefully…and told us Jim's frickin trout (substantial) would go five pounds! In Missouri…or Arkansas…or anywhere else on the White River…IF you caught a five pounder…you was put in a special club…was automatically a stud. State wildlife people gave out little gold trout pins…to trophy trout fishermen…you know …to wear on their fishin caps and all. IF Jim's fish WAS a five pounder…and sure as shit stinks we all knowed it WAS…then Jim got his self one of them fancy gold trout pins! I saw some lucky bastard walkin round Gaston's wearin nine or ten of them damned pins! Some candy assed rich fart who probably didn't know dick from wad (up from down) about REAL fishin…Not like me and Jim. SHIT! Let's face it. Me and Jim knowed ever thang there was to know bout fishin!"

"I looked at Jim…Jim looked at me…We both knew…That's it mother lover! Jim was D-O-N-E…and I didn't give one shit neither. We would head in…call it a day! What the Hell? What could we do to top THAT shit (great feat). Huh? We got what we come for…a mother lovin trophy! Weren't nothin else gonna happen THAT day! Nothin of no real importance. Right? You can bet your sweet ass on that! Me and Jim…We was done…ALL in!"

"All three of our ice chests was full up with eatin size trout…Why catch more? Jim got his big one. Now we could drink whisky and REALLY howl at the moon (party)! But we WAS tired! We caught…I mean JIM caught…a dream fish…a real life-timer! Rich fart handles from the city (other patrons)…fish all their boar hog tit lives (useless)…and don't catch a five pounder in the White River. I told Jim…Let's go in …See what our wenches (women) are up to. I couldn't wait for Danny to see our frickin fish! I told Jim…Danny's gonna wet his pants (be excited) and squat to pee (act like a girl)! Said…Wait til Jenny sees our fish…She'll shit her fancy pants twice over (be excited too)!"

"By the time our guide got me and Jim back to Gaston's…and we got all our fishin shit (gear) outta his boat…it was three o'clock. We left our trout…I mean JIM'S trout…in the boat…and told our guide to hold his dick (wait). We wanted Danny and the wives to see Jim's fish…alive and well! We wanted to weigh it live. I ran up to the cabins to get Glennys and Danny…and grab a camera. Jim ran to his cabin to get Jenny. Glennys was takin a nap…but it didn't take ME long to roust HER ass! Glennys told me Danny was takin a nap. I seen Jim runnin round lookin for Jenny…and told him not to bother Danny cause he was sleepin. Jenny wasn't in her cabin…so Jim ran down to the pool lookin for her. She wasn't there neither, so's Jim gave up lookin and decided to fetch his trout and get it weighed…so's our guide could get his tired ass on home. Jim come runnin back…sayin he couldn't find Jenny. He was so damned excited he couldn't spit…kept wavin his trout in the air fer ever body to see. Jim's excitement was plain catch-able (contagious)!"

When them state men (officials) weighed its dead ass (the trout)…it was two thin pubic hairs (slightly) over five pounds…one good trout turd shat (defecated) in the White River before we caught it…and there wouldna been no record in NO books! Them state wardens (officials) said we had two ounces to spare...but they don't know dick from squat (much). Jim was blowed clean away (overwhelmed)... kept sayin... "Whadaya think? Big One Huh? Ain't no bigger trout in Weston! Come on Glennys...What the HELL'S the matter with YOUR gloomy ass? Wake up Damn it! Can't you see how damned big my trout REALLY is? Take my picture...Come on Glennys...Wake up...Get with the program". Jim was always yellin that at me...and lazy pukes we both knowed... you know...always yellin...Get with the program! Wonder why?"

"Glennys wasn't showin no excitement. NONE! She just kept sayin...Yes Jim... Yes David...It's a nice trout. Yes Jim...Now come on David...Let's get back to our room. I want to go to our room...NOW! I kept thinkin...What in the Sam Hill is wrong with HER sorry ass? There Jim stood. The greatest fishin moment in his entire limp dicked (inconsequential) life! His wimpy friend Danny was sleepin...wastin HIS last day locked in a dark cabin. Glennys was actin like she didn't give a rat's ass if she bothered to breathe. And Jenny's sorry pointy ass was NO where to be found! Finally I says to Glennys... Glennys! GLENNYS! She was starin off in space like a fornicatin virgin (highly distracted). I couldn't figure it out? What the Hell WAS wrong with Glennys? I never seen her act so damned weird...not without some powerful good reason?"

"Jim finally said... "So much for my trout... my TROPHY frickin trout! I'm takin a frickin nap! I'll see yawls sorry asses at dinner!" Jim's feelins was hurt...Big Time!"

"Jim stomped off to his room. Near-about five Jim called us to see if we seen Jenny's missing ass. We told Jim... "She's not here...We don't know where she is". Next Jim called Danny. Danny acted weird...he just woke up...told Jim he didn't know where Jenny was neither? Jim went lookin fer Jenny...thought somethin bad mightta happened? Jim tried the gift shop...restaurant...office...got in the car and drove around to the puttin green...tennis court...horse shoe pits...flower beds...NO Jenny...NO where! Then he headed back to his cabin to call me and Glennys. When Jim throwed open the door... Jenny was IN their cabin! Jim says... "Where the F— YOU been?" Jimmy was pissed."

"Jenny was groggy...mumblin..."I been nappin...over by the pool...in a lounge chair...in the shade?" Drool runnin down her cheek...pillow marks on her face...she looked like caked horse shit (heterogeneous stinking matter)! Jim says...I didn't see you at the pool! Jenny says... "It was hot in the sun...So...Uh...I...Pulled my chair off the deck. Over in the shade...I was there...You just missed me...I was right there in the shade by the pool."

Jim says... "F— It! We gotta get to dinner...Wait'll ya see my trout!"

"The night before we all agreed... all of us would meet fer dinner...spend one more night...THEN drive home. We planned on meetin at six! But ever body went to the restaurant separate. In little groups...NO ONE walkin together...even though we was ALL goin to the same frickin restaurant."

"After we got our table...a naked preacher fartin Dixie (the tune) from his pulpit wouldna made things get quieter no quicker. Fact is... it was SO quiet ...the quiet was LOUD! You coulda heard a mouse pissin on cotton... except for Jim. There weren't one frickin word comin from NO body...ceptin Jim ...and his jaws was flappin like the sole onna wore out shoe (nonstop)! You woulda thought us other four was sick...CEPTIN for Jim! So there we was! Four...gloomy... sun burned faces...not sayin shit! ONE big smilin face...yakkety yakkin! Jim was so high it took him bout-a-half-hour ("???" amount of time ranging from five to forty-five minutes) to realize NO body else was sayin one freakin word! Hell! The only thing keepin Jim on the floor was a firm grip on his double martini. He was lost...tellin and re-tellin his big trout story! The Poor Dumb Bastard! He didn't notice squat...Jim was on cloud nine...maybe ten? I never seen Jim THAT happy! And. I never seen him that happy again. NEVER! Well...Not for years and years. Not THAT happy!"

"It was plain as brown shit on white paper (obvious) somethin was bad wrong. Jim told me later he thought we was all sick with bad food poisonin (universal scapegoat for the habitually uninformed)...or was tired? Jim said he didn't know what the frick was goin on? Said he thought me and Glennys was fightin bout money...which we was! Thought Danny was sad cause his wife kilt her self...which he was! And thought Jenny was pissed at Glennys...which she was! But none of them was the REAL reason we was all sittin round lookin like yearlin calfs at a slaughter house (downcast). Nope! There was a bigger...fatter...reason no body was swappin skunk oil bout nothin (chit chatting). Why NO BODY was excited about Jim's damned trout!"

"Finally...Jim said somethin to *us four down-in-the-mouths*...told us somethin BIG was *missin from our purty pitcher* (the moment)? By the end of dinner...after an hour of nobody sayin one damned word...nothin worth repeatin...after eatin and calmin down...Jim finally DID say somethin! Started askin questions like... *What the Hell IS goin on? Why the long faces? What's the deal? Why's ever body so damned quiet?*'

"But NO BODY said shit back to Jim! Ever body just stared holes in them shiny dinin room plates. No body blinked an eye. So Jim got mad...at ever body! Stood up and stomped off! Went straight back to his cabin. Leavin us four *pecker heads* (dotes) sittin there like *puffed up toads on a blacktop* (out of place). Sittin there round our cluttered table *starin at each other's weak shit* (awkward awareness). Wonderin which toad was gonna hop first? All four of us just sittin there...like lumps of cold lard. Wishin some drunk would drive by and run over our toady asses! Thirty seconds of silent starin and Danny stood up TOO...threw down a wad of cash to pay the bill...and dashed the Hell outta there...out the front door by his self...gone in thirty seconds. That left three lardy toads. Glennys! ME! And Jenny! Still squatin at our messy table! And believe me...NONE of us three toads still sittin at THAT table wanted to share *no fuzzy secrets* (intimate conversation) THAT night!"

"Ridin home...all five of us stuck in one car...was like *bein locked in the cellar with rottin taters* (suffocating). Glennys and me...we rode in the back seat...Danny rode in front on the right...Jenny rode in front...in the middle. Right between Jim and Danny! Not one word was spoke...not one...cept by Jim. He kept yakkin... mostly to his self...all the way home... about his big trout packed on ice in the trunk. He checked that damned fish ten times *tween* the Ozarks and home. And musta asked a hundred times... *What the F— is goin on?* The *poor dickhead* (unfortunate person)! He was *plumb eat up with the dumb ass* (clueless)."

"Danny and Jim stayed good friends! TOO damned good to suit *MY tired ass* (envy)! Jim did a LOT fer Danny after we buried Danny's first wife Suzy.

David and Glennys were not invited to Danny's wedding at our house... and I wondered why? (l to r) **Ex Jen-Jen**, **Bride**, **Danny** and **Jim**. (1979)

Jim took Danny ever where. Jim invited Danny to *all sorta* good parties...even invited Danny out to Game Hill huntin (envy)...no matter Shit Head (Danny) *didn't know squat* (much) about guns OR huntin! One time Jim took some really neat stuff...high dollar shit from Kansas City...over to Danny's two kids on their *frickin* birthdays! Danny eventually got his self happily remarried...in Jim and Jenny's house (see picture)! Fact is...Jim and Jenny stood up with Danny and his new bride...even hosted a fancy party in their (Jim and Jenny's) own house! *Me and Glennys wasn't even invited* (envy)."

"After Jim and Jenny got divorced...in 1981...Sweet Glennys finally up-an-told Jim zackly what it was Glennys *caught* (observed)? *Opened her pie hole* (mouth) and told Jim *the REAL shit*! We loved Jim. It woulda broke Jim's big heart to know what REALLY happened down at Gaston's...on the White River...in the Ozarks...while Jim was out there catchin his big trout! Shit Man...bout time he knowed!"

Footnote: "the REAL shit" caught (observed) by Glennys will be disclosed in another book; "Not Your Ordinary Custody Battle". DON'T miss it! Meanwhile; let's just say, "EX Jen-Jen did her level best to comfort the afflicted".

"The End"

Profile in concentration, **John James** was as excited to fish as his two brothers... if the fish were bitin! (2007)

Starting young with the right equipment... **John James** fishes the Blanco River too! (1996)

Nurse-Wife Peg's first redfish on her first wade! (2007)

Long time family friend, and mom of Captain Jason, **Karen** matches **Peg's** second big red. (2007)

Chris spent one summer in the Carolinas 'working out' with the 82nd Airborne... he and a buddy went out for catfish on a Sunday and... (2002)

Captain Jason takes off after the big ones. (2008)

About the Cover

Left to right, Long time guide **Jerry Moore**, 9 year old **John James Pepper** on his birthday, and patient teacher, author dad, **Jim Pepper** fishin for stripers on Lake Buchanan, Texas. (2000)